Young Children in China

MULTILINGUAL MATTERS

Young Children in China

Rita Liljeström
Eva Norén-Björn
Gertrud Schyl-Bjurman

Birgit Öhrn
Lars H. Gustafsson
Orvar Löfgren

Translated by
Tove Skutnabb-Kangas and Robert Phillipson

British Library Cataloguing in Publication Data

Young children in China.
  1. Children — Care and hygiene — China
  I. Liljeström, Rita   II. Kinas barn och vara.
  English
  362.7'95'0951   HQ792.C5

ISBN 0-905028-30-9
ISBN 0-905028-29-5 Pbk

Multilingual Matters Ltd,
Bank House, 8a Hill Road,
Clevedon, Avon BS21 7HH,
England.

Typeset by Wayside Graphics, Clevedon, Avon.
Printed and bound in Great Britain by
Colourways Press Ltd., Clevedon BS21 6RR.

Contents

Preface

We shared an interest in the conditions in the family and society in which small children grow up. We travelled to China to study the Chinese preschool, pre-school pedagogy, pre-school teacher training, child health care and family policy. We travelled in order to learn something about China and perhaps to learn something from China. The trip took place in April 1982 and was partly funded by Riksbankens Jubileumsfond, the Swedish Save The Children Fund and the Swedish Institute.

Our hosts in China were the All-China Women's Federation and the Chinese People's National Committee for the Defence of Children. They planned our travel programme and arranged all the study visits to the child care and child health care institutions that we wished to see. They also arranged for us to meet and have interesting discussions with the people in Peking in the Ministries of Health and Education who are responsible for day care and the pre-school, where we were also given a copy of the new syllabus for the Chinese pre-school. The official version in English is included as an appendix to this book.

Our journey took us to Peking/Beijing, Sian/Xi'an, Chengdu, Shanghai, Hangzhou and Kanton/Guangzhou. We visited about 15 day care centres and pre-schools of different kinds — ranging from the experimental preschool at the College of Education in Peking to very simple day care centres in villages — several hospitals and health centres, a home for handicapped children and two training colleges for pre-school teachers.

There are many people we want to thank for contributing in various ways to making the trip possible and such a rich and varied experience: the officials at the Embassy of the People's Republic of China in Stockholm, who put us in touch with the organizations which hosted our visit; many representatives of the All-China Women's Federation, who were extremely hospitable in their welcome both in Peking and wherever we went; all those many pre-school teachers, day care and health centre staff who so generously welcomed us in their institutions and allowed us to observe their everyday work.

We should also like to thank our excellent interpreter, head of the All-China Women's Federation's international contact department, Mrs Zhong Zhi Ming, whose patience with our inexhaustible stream of questions was impressive.

Above all we want to thank the general secretary of the Chinese People's National Committee for the Defence of Children, Mrs Zhang Shu Yi. It was a great privilege that she accompanied us on the entire trip through China. Our many long and lively discussions with her not only increased our knowledge but also helped to put what we saw into perspective. Her strong commitment to the welfare and future of the children is one of our lasting impressions of the trip.

We made the journey in order to learn something about China and China's children. Our group was assembled to cover various aspects of children's life. We found ourselves following with special interest the issues which corresponded to our professional experience — those of the sociologist, the psychologist/child observer, the pre-school teacher trainer, the drama teacher, the pediatrician and the ethnologist — and tried to let our various impressions complement one another. At the same time what we saw gave us new perspectives on our own ideas about children and child care. With this book our wish is to share some of this experience and some of the questions and points of view raised by it.

Rita Liljeström   Eva Norén-Björn
Gertrud Schyl-Bjurman   Birgit Öhrn
Lars H Gustafsson   Orvar Löfgren

Translators' Note

As translators we have had a number of cross-cultural headaches, of which we can touch on a few: problems of principle, as the translation brings together three cultures and two languages; problems of terminology, when concepts do not correspond fully (for instance, "pre-school" means different things in different countries); the problem of relative explicitness — the Swedes are at times more direct than English-speakers, as when describing bodily functions, and at other times more discreet, for instance when referring to conflicts.

The Swedish authors describe in Swedish a Chinese reality, communicated to them partly through the first-hand impressions of their visit, and partly through English, the language that the Swedes and the Chinese communicated in, mostly through an interpreter. As translators we cannot be certain how the English into which we convert the Swedish relates to the original impressions and formulations, which have been through several processes of linguistic and cultural transformation, hence inevitably of reinterpretation. This triangular cross-cultural interaction is at the same time one of the strengths of the book: the Swedes went to China to learn not only about China but about their own society, too, and readers of the English version can relate both Chinese and Swedish society to their own.

This can be exemplified at the level of individual concepts. "Nursery", "Infant" and "pre-school" refer to different age ranges and have different meanings and connotations in the various cultures of the Chinese-, Swedish- and English-speaking worlds. In Sweden the same term is used for all institutional day care for children between the ages of 2 months and 7 years, and the functions of this "pre-school" are mainly educational as opposed to child-minding. Like the Swedish authors, we have therefore, throughout the book, used "pre-school" as the general term for institutions in both China and Sweden catering for children prior to school proper, and "pre-school teacher" to refer to those who have a pedagogical training to work in pre-schools. Another strength of the book is in bringing home the fact that such everyday concepts as "aggression", "discipline", "obedience", "family" and "love" mean quite different things in different societies.

An example of differing degrees of explicitness is that Swedes, when reporting on Chinese toddlers' training in bodily functions, tend to call a shit a shit, rather than a bowel movement, or the "nuisance" that London dog-owners may be fined for. The now ubiquitous "going to the toilet" of British pre-schools does not state which of two possible purposes (neither of which is washing the child's hands) is to be accomplished. We have therefore adopted the British custom in these matters, in spite of euphemism and ambiguity.

By contrast, in other spheres of life Swedes tend to state matters in an ultra-discreet, unprovocative way. The British do not have monopoly of under-statement. Swedish culture is often described by cultural anthropologists as conflict-avoiding: constructive conflicts are a good thing, but it is a sign of bad manners to *talk* about conflicts. When a Swede writes (literally) "one can well discuss . . ." in relation to a particular social policy issue, a non-Swedish reader cannot be expected to understand that the "discussions" were fierce disputes, which is what the Swedish author is euphemistically referring to. A translation using "it is debatable . . ." comes closer to the cultural meaning of the original. Only on a very few occasions have we had to supplement our translation of the text by an explanatory footnote.

Robert Phillipson
Tove Skutnabb-Kangas

Skibby,
January 1984

1 The family in China yesterday and today

Rita Liljeström

A performance that we saw children in Chinese day nurseries enjoy putting on involves a couple of children covering their own heads with a painted head with a smiling face. The hollow head is round, as large as a pumpkin, and fits straight onto the child's shoulders. When the tiny child's body with the giant head moves, dances and sings, the effect is comical — but also strangely mysterious. The child seems simultaneously familiar and secretively distant. It struck me that the eternally smiling masks grotesquely magnified the friendly smile with which the Chinese welcome their guests. There is a teasing streak of Chineseness which makes the foreigner uncertain as to whether she has actually understood anything at all.

In the 1970s, in the wake of the official reports on child care amenities and the child's world, the position of Swedish children became a prominent topic in debates on society. At the same time impressive descriptions of Chinese children reached us. Ruth Sidel's *Freedom and Work* gave a positive picture. In the book *Childhood in China*, American researchers noted with amazement and disbelief that Chinese children seemed to be free of the symptoms of tension which are usual with Western children. None of the researchers saw any thumb-sucking, nail-biting, nervous twitches, masturbation or anything similar during their visits to day nurseries. When the psychologists asked questions about children's hyperactivity, physical restlessness and aggression, the Chinese teachers did not understand what they were talking about. The Americans were just as surprised that attitudes which we in the West regard as being difficult to reconcile were combined; for instance, intense attentiveness and calm relaxation, spontaneous joy and strict discipline, high levels of ambition without anxiety about failure. The Swedish doctor from Skå, Gustav Jonsson, on his return described his confusion when our theories encounter Chinese children as being similar to

1

trying to fit round plugs into square holes. They don't fit. Either there is something wrong with our theories or with the Chinese children.

The American researchers also stated that "the Chinese day nurseries seem to place the greatest emphasis on the interaction between grown-ups and children — and not on the children's reaction to things." The setting was cold and colourless. The material standard was then still poor. The children did not have creative materials, pedagogical aids, materials for problem solving, and toys. In my contribution to the official report on the child's world of 1975, I asked, just back from China, whether we in the West have reified upbringing so that it has become external pedagogical stimulation, while the Chinese have chosen to promote internal inducements. "They consciously give high priority to morality so as to establish human dignity in social relations." I contrasted how the grown-up's influence on children in China has the mark of being total, emotional and unequivocal, while we meet children in a spirit of atomization, facts and multiple meanings.

All the surprise and enthusiasm with regard to China's children has also given rise to scepticism. Is there anything the visitors have been blind to? Have we let ourselves be carried away? Do we travellers use China as a weapon in criticizing society at home? I feel impelled to go back to check how things really are, to find out more about what hides beneath the surface.

The opportunity came in the spring of 1982. This time the trip particularly focussed on the pre-school age group. Our team was put together to cover different professional aspects of the child's world. Perhaps our joint impressions will provide more answers to the questions which are implicit in a comparison of Sweden and China. While being obedient is almost suspect in Sweden, it is endorsed as something positive in China. The following diagram tries to illuminate the contrasting views:

| Obedience is | Implications of | |
interpreted as	Obeying	Not obeying
Subordination Resignation	1. Drill Collective discipline/ uniformity	2. Revolt, freedom Individuality Creativity
Confirmation Identification	3. Co-ordination Shared goals Solidarity	4. Deviance Egoism Disruption

While we have reacted against authoritarian leadership, the Chinese have laid emphasis on the good teacher and the force of example. Bringing up children in China is part of the education of the people, the political mobilization which has continued since the revolution. This mobilization is based on an optimistic belief that people want to develop and that it is possible to change society. It is a question of supplying the masses with arguments, of giving good reasons, of persuading and convincing. Mao's teaching constantly stressed the need to "listen to the people" and to "learn from the masses". In this respect child upbringing is completely consistent with Mao's political ideas.

Among us Swedes in the spring of 1982 I detected a tendency to be exhilarated whenever we meet noisy or slightly boisterous children, children who interrupt grown-ups or step out of line. Someone exclaims: "A healthy sign!" We applaud any deviation, every departure from the pattern. What does this say about us? What do we take for granted?

It is my lot as a sociologist to put a framework around the social scene surrounding Chinese children. In painting a background of family patterns, my point of departure is some of the mass campaigns of recent decades to educate the people. The campaigns reflect both great changes and deep internal contradictions in Chinese society. They have important implications for the family, the power of the father and women's liberation, the revolt of the young against their elders, the family's obligations towards the community. The current political campaigns are immediately visible to the visitor. They can be seen in the street and in printed matter. They form part of speeches of welcome. When the hosts of the study visits give a general introduction, they shroud their words and the local activity in the message of the campaign. The campaign is the shining wrapping which encloses all work in factories and offices, in the neighbourhood and people's councils, in schools, health clinics, organizations and committees. Even pre-school children give expression to the campaigns in their songs and dances. The goal of the campaign is repeated at one place after the other. The visitor meets the same phrases, maxims, slogans, principles from place to place, from mouth to mouth, adapted to the activities of each place.

It is as though the campaign grew to one large head which one person after the other shoulders. It provides a magnified representation of the political discussions going on in the country. The campaign, too, leaves one with a teasing streak of uncertainty.

Education of the people through campaigns

Folke Isaksson relates in his book, *At home in China*, that he mostly spoke to men of around 55 years of age. During our trip we met predominantly women, because in China, just as at home, it is women who rule over the pre-school age. It was a discussion between women. It is true that two men were included in our party; our aging hostesses treated them at times as their dear sons. We met leading women from politics and the professional world. A couple of these daughters of the revolution were past retirement age both in China and in Sweden. They were in possession of knowledge and experience from a long life. At times they gave us glimpses of the contemporary history of China, eye-witness accounts from the epoch 1930–1980. They showed openness and an awareness of the problems in our discussions. Their political commitment and human charm disarmed us. But of course we also sat through banquets along with representative "poker faces" and encountered reception committees where we never got behind the walls of the smile.

How do the campaigns influence our view of China? It is obvious that the campaigns stress the normative, in other words they say more about how things should be than about how they are. And even when our hosts mention the deep gulf between programme and reality, one is easily lulled into the impression that in spite of everything they have gone a long way. Incidentally, something similar is also true of reforms in Sweden. We like to believe that social reforms have been carried out when the parliament has come to a decision and the central authorities have dispatched instructions to local councils — not to mention what we broadcast internationally. We ignore the fact that at times they are only paper tigers. We pretend not to know that goals and intentions change character when the anchor has been raised in Stockholm.

The campaigns identify the weak spots. They show where the problems are. For instance, why should it be necessary to proclaim that "girls are just as good" if parents did not prefer boys? The campaigns follow and correct each other. They express the balance of power between the peasants of the countryside and townspeople, between a small educated minority and an uneducated majority, between the mass of poor people whom the revolution has scarcely raised above the threshold of hunger and the prosperous few, between the traditional authority of the old and the new prospects of the young, between an ancient patriarchy and the liberation of women.

The campaigns dictate what visitors notice. They provide a framework of concepts to which we relate our impressions. The campaigns place us on a school bench, and we are exposed indirectly to intensive persuasion. Then the Swedish visitor has to make an effort to shake off the shackles from the information given, but it is the campaign which has laid out the shackles which define the attempt to break loose.

It is necessary to appreciate that the mass campaigns have also committed excesses in the name of the good cause. The leaders lose control over
the forces they set in motion. The people who pass on the message are not
always disciples of the right spirit; the campaigns are exploited for personal
goals; they become misinterpreted, brutalized and bloodstained. Their victims can be counted in hundreds of thousands when the political power
balance tips towards new groups.

On the surface, the visitor meets a compact unity. We are surprised at
the strong feelings which society's progress and setbacks arouse in ordinary
people. The relationship between collective and private feelings is the
opposite of what we are used to. The Chinese are happy about the completion of new bridges or irrigation systems, about new methods of production
and about a good harvest. They seem to identify with collective achievements
as though they involved them personally. They are as joyful as the supporters
of the Gothenburg or Malmö football teams when their own side wins. Their
collective involvement can be compared with the outburst of joy which
exploded in Italy when the Italian football team became world champions —
and with the corresponding national mourning in Brazil. These feelings have
to do with socialization. While we in a Swedish day nursery celebrate a
child's birthday, Chinese day nurseries completely ignore these. What they
do celebrate is national holidays. Children are taught that 8 March is
international women's day: grandmother's, mother's and aunt's day. They
learn that 1 May is the workers' day, 1 June their day, international children's
day. 1 August is the liberation army's day, and on 1 October they celebrate
their national day.

The strong feelings of the Chinese for political efforts make the uniformity and solidarity even after rapid and complete political changes still
more bewildering for the Westerner. Yesterday's line drops like a stone
through the water. It leaves no mark behind it. The new directions are soon
assimilated.

Has this unity towards the outside world roots in feudal China? Is a long
collective tradition of loyalty to the clan, to authority, to the official line,
living on as party discipline? The party rules state that:

— the individual is subordinate to the organization;
— the minority is subordinate to the majority;
— the lower level is subordinate to the higher level; and
— all members are subordinate to the Central Committee.

I suspect that the Chinese are resigned, too, in the knowledge that we
foreigners would not understand anyway. We lack the knowledge and the

intimate cultural familiarity which are necessary for not getting it all wrong. So they choose to hide their own heads behind the smiling mask of the official line.

It is not as it used to be

Anyone who has the chance to go back to China makes comparisons with what it was like the previous time. I am comparing this tour with a study tour in the autumn of 1974, when Mao was still alive, when the cultural revolution's masses went with their red banners from the towns to the countryside in order to learn from the peasants, and when Lin Piao and his followers were blamed for all the mistakes. All this comes back in the memory during the spring of 1982. Now Mao is dead, masses of Chinese go abroad to study how they can accelerate the four modernizations — i.e. making agriculture, industry, science and defence more effective — and "the gang of four", headed by Mao's widow Chiang Ching, are now burdened with the role of the scapegoat. Truly a dramatic change of scene! The campaigns are no longer the same. Places look different now. A stay in Peking includes a walk through The Forbidden City.

In the space of a few hours the study group passes through thousands of years of history which is unfamiliar to most of us. In this old city of the emperors, we go through the three halls, the Hall of Heavenly Harmony, the Hall of Supreme Harmony, and the Hall of Preserving Harmony, to the Hall of Heavenly Purity. The city has been piously preserved, a monument to the past, untouched by what has happened outside its walls — but still not completely untouched. I recall the previous visit with all the old people, women with tiny deformed lotus feet. Here they stumbled forward supported by soldiers, like the crooked, emaciated old men accompanied by one or two soldiers.

That day the Red Army had been ordered to take care of the old and enfeebled, to take them out, show them the sights of the city, entertain them. it was simultaneously a political manifestation of respect for the elderly.

In the forecourt of the palace we observed a class of seven-year-olds. They processed through the gate, their bodies upright, a red banner at the front. They made a stop in the courtyard and went through a long, serious ritual. It ended with some of the children receiving a red scarf. They had become members of the organization "Young Red Soldiers". We had witnessed the admission ceremony. To become a member, you have to show good conduct, preferably with outstanding good deeds, in other words through being helpful. That was in 1974. Nowadays all children are members, each gets a red scarf, no special demands are made, you don't have to have deserved membership. The change could be compared to the Scouts abolishing the series of tests by which the child is encouraged to earn promotion — though in China's case it was a question of degrees of consciousness about which demands are made on the inheritors of the revolution.

In the spring of 1982 some shining new cars have been driven through the Tuan gate and placed beside the central entrance in the forecourt of the Imperial City. Beside each car there is a notice about taking photographs. I watch while a young Chinese family sits down in the car. They wind down the windows, Daddy "drives", Mummy looks out from the passenger seat, the children wave from the back seat. The photographer clicks and the family receives a photo of the kind used in our motor advertisements. You can also choose a pose by the bonnet or support yourself on the open car door. There are variations on the theme of man and his car.

Nearby there is a cardboard dummy, representing a figure in gorgeous attire. If you climb up on a stool behind it and place your head in the.neck opening, you can be photographed in this imperial outfit. But the headless dummy stands deserted, knocked out in an impossible competition. There is commotion around the cars. Many want to see themselves sitting in a modern car, show themselves off to others. Here people are initiated into new dreams. Here new aspirations are captured.

The level of consumption in the towns has risen strikingly since 1974. It is visible on the streets. There is more variety in the clothes — even if part of the diversity must be due to the time of year. The department stores offer a greater choice. There are more shoe models in new colours and styles. Small heels are on their way in. There is more vanity. Puritanism seems to be decreasing. Young people queue at the music departments for records and cassettes. Television sets and transistor radios attract buyers.

The traffic in the towns is heavier and denser, more motor-powered. Building activity is under way intensively everywhere. The low houses with internal courtyards are being pulled down to make way for high blocks of flats. The small balconies of the tower blocks are pathetically weighed down by pots, plants, baskets and tools of the kind that always used to be kept in the courtyard.

The traffic is fierce and bewitching. Teams of two or three mules pull the peasants' wagons at an easy-going tempo. Swarms of cyclists pass by, many of them heavily laden with large baskets of reed or bamboo leaves hanging on each side. Parents with children on the back wheel. Wobbly rickshaws pulled by the force of sinewy muscle — and through all this

straining, swarming and balance-seeking movement, heavy lorries force
their way down the middle of the street — the "lightweight" traffic has to
give way, they are squeezed out to the edges of the street in order to save
their skins. Tired workers and peasants lie resting on the backs of the lorries
and on the loads. All this public sleeping in the heavy traffic exudes heavy
labour and exhaustion. Now and then a hen flutters over the street. A bus
load of tourists goes past. It is as though the "modernization" had caught the
streets by surprise and the inhabitants had been unable to get away in time.
There are not yet any traffic lights at the corners, and the crossroads and
bicycles are not equipped with lamps. The traffic is a good indicator of the
balance of power between the old and the new. I could not help thinking of
Mao. Mao would not let development bolt away from the people. He
wanted to have the peasants, the elderly, the women and all children with
him.

The struggle between two lines

Mao Tse-Tung began his career as a teacher. He told interviewers that
for him the most important task was to be a teacher for the society. When
still a young teacher, he grew critical of feudal and bourgeois features of the
teaching. His later political thoughts often draw nourishment from a general
pedagogical philosophy of the liberation of people through their own activity
and participation.

During the cultural revolution this confidence in the innate capacities of
mankind was transmitted in the slogan "trust the masses". It was also called
the "mass line". Mao thought that in order to promote anyone's talents,
what had to be done was to give the individual access to appropriate
challenges, i.e. to be confronted with tasks, problems, sources of knowledge
and comrades who permit the individual to grow with the task. The mass line
rejected any notion of some people being designated as senior in advance,
any idea of "the élite's mandate from heaven" and any ideas which legitima-
ted the precedence of the ruling classes.

According to Confucius, what differentiated people and formed a
natural basis for the creation of classes was culture, morality and knowledge.
Privileges were thus built into education itself and into the manner in which
culture was transmitted. Class differences became manifest in a distinction
between those with access to knowledge and those without. And they were
also expressed in the manner in which those who possessed knowledge
treated those who had not had access to knowledge.

When the Central Committee in August 1966 announced a new phase in
the revolutionary struggle, this extended beyond the economy. It was asser-

ted that nationalizing the means of production and the party seizing power was not sufficient. New classes are formed under the cover of educational institutions, in party organizations and the immense state administration. Constant vigilance is required so that new strongholds for the creation of classes are not formed.

The cultural revolution appealed to the masses to eliminate the pre-conditions for the creation of any classes. The struggle was directed against feudal and bourgeois concepts in people's thoughts. It was necessary to remove everything that could be used to corrupt the masses or prepare for the return of old class differences in a new guise. To confront this threat it was necessary to change society's spiritual face. The directive stated that our goal is to

> "fight leading people who have taken a capitalist turn, and obstruct it, to criticize and reject the reactionary, bourgeois 'academic authorities' and the ideology which characterizes the bourgeoisie and all the exploiting classes, and also to convert teaching, literature and art and all other parts of the cultural superstructure which do not correspond to the socialist structure, and in this way to promote the consolidation and development of the socialist system."

"The mass line" dealt with the relationship between the leaders and the led, and in so doing stressed that all learning is mutual. To be able to teach his or her pupils, the teacher had to learn to understand the pupils' point of departure. Those in command had to learn from their soldiers, just as *vice versa*. Intellectuals had to learn from peasants and workers. But above all — the party had to learn to listen to the masses. Mao's *Little Red Book* sets out methods for leadership:

> "Take the ideas of the masses (scattered and unsystematic ideas) and compress them (through studies convert them to compressed and systematic ideas), then go to the masses and propagate and explain these ideas until these masses embrace them as their own, stick to them in action and try out whether these ideas are right in action. Then again compress the ideas from the masses so that they stick to the ideas and carry them out. And so on, again and again in an endless spiral through which the ideas become increasingly right, more living and richer each time." (Some questions on methods for leadership, 1943)

In this reciprocal interaction between the leaders and the led, it was important that those who had been given more, the leader, the expert, those with education, saw themselves as servants of the people. In the struggle against the corruption of the leadership was coined the slogan: serve the people. In the same spirit the cultural revolution stressed that workers and peasants are creative and knowledgeable resources for the development of the society. The watchword: learn from the people.

Part of the mass line was also belief in the decisive role of praxis. The good leader must constantly assess what the conditions are and evaluate the results of the policy carried out. It must always be possible to formulate the ideas so that they lead to action and thus become comprehensible. In order to implement a serve-the-people attitude, the leaders must themselves take part in physical work. The daily grind should open the leader's eyes to the problems of the people. Even technicians should carry out simple tasks, and workers in their turn should be educated as technicians. All this in order to counteract the creation of technical and bureaucratic power.

The criticism of the earlier view of the development of academic knowledge was severe. Intellectuals should not primarily see to their own interests but those of the people. No-one should profit from knowledge which they have acquired through the sacrifices of the people. The educated should show their gratitude by serving the people.

I recall how in 1974 we, a group of cultural workers and scientists, sat at long tables in reception rooms and warmed our November-chilled hands by clutching our steaming tea mugs while listening to the revolution committees in factories, people's councils and street committees. We sipped our tea at meetings with actors, writers and artists. We heard the message explained at hospitals, research institutions and in party committees. We absorbed the thoughts of the cultural revolution in the vintage which best corresponded to the local situation. In day nurseries children were told that they should "love and support each other". Pupils were encouraged to ask questions and to criticize their teachers. Proletarian suffering was recalled before our eyes with gripping testimony from "the old bitter times". We made a pilgrimage with the masses to the village where Mao was born in Shaoshan, and listened reverently to a description of him at the teacher training college in Changsha where he was trained from 1913 to 1918. At the museum in Shaoshan we followed his life until the time of the liberation.

The key moral-political thoughts in Mao's message moved me deeply. At times I was touched by the devotion of people that we met. The appeals to moral motive forces struck a chord in me, for I had long felt morally starved in the climate of Swedish cultural politics. Like many others at the time, I was hoping for a third way, an alternative which differed from, on the one hand the Soviet Union and the European socialist countries, and on the other the USA and the capitalist states of the west. Besides, many thought that both blocks were developing towards a similar type of state capitalism, i.e. a condition in which the state and the profit-motivated enterprises merge into a huge corporative unit with a techno-bureaucratic élite at the top. It was precisely this kind of vision of the future which the cultural revolution fought by all available means (Dahlström, 1975).

When I return in 1982 there is not much talk about Mao. The cultural revolution has been officially condemned as "lost years". It is mentioned more in passing, with a negative epithet. To my surprise I hear of the vandalism and lack of respect which prevailed in schools at that time, because the discipline was impeccable in the schools I saw. It was practically impossible for the teachers to get pupils to "criticize the teachers" — which they were insistently urged to do. But one thing is certain. If the key words in 1974 were "trust the masses" and "serve the people", the words which are repeated more than any others in the spring of 1982 are "civilization" and "beautifying". The political rhetoric has been translated into more general moral and ideological terms (Sidel & Sidel, 1982).

Since 1981 a nationwide campaign for "the five emphases" and "the four types of beautifying" has been conducted, with the goal of producing a new, well-brought-up generation with high moral standards. The goal of civilization is probably best exemplified in the emphasis on courtesy. The five emphases are on dignified and good behaviour, polite conduct, cleanliness, discipline and high moral standards.

Beautification contains four components:

— to *beautify the mind*, to refine and improve one's ideological thinking, have high moral standards, a sound character and integrity, and to defend the leadership of the party and the socialist system,
— to *beautify the language*, to use and spread polished and careful language,
— to *beautify behaviour*, to do useful things for the people, to work hard, to be concerned for the welfare of others, to be well disciplined and defend collective interests,
— to *beautify the environment*, to be particular in one's personal hygiene, and keep the home and public places clean.

Policy today favours more material rewards. The leadership is prepared to accept greater differences in earnings, and disparities between some sectors and regions and other poorer and less developed ones. It will not be possible for all to keep up with modernization at the same tempo. China is concentrating on the strong, on talent and technical expertise. Knowledge is more important than ideology. What does it matter if a cat is black or white, so long as it can catch rats.

In recent years the education system has been modified to meet the demand for rapid modernization; in other words there is a stress on a high general level of knowledge, specialization and technical skills. There has been a shift from a pedagogy which tried to develop the potential of all children to one of increased differentiation. Use is made of western intelligence tests to identify talent and stimulate it. Even in the pre-school there has been a slight shift of focus, so that more attention is paid to individual aptitude; special talents are spotted and promoted. Competition between groups and between individuals is given more scope (Sidel & Sidel, 1982).

One needs to be careful, however, not to exaggerate the differences between 1974 and 1982. Even when slogans have been changed, the content is still partly the same. Part of what is said about beautifying behaviour sounds familiar, although at an earlier date it belonged under "serve the people". Some of the changes are modifications of meaning. Children still learn five types of charity to love the mother country and the people, work, science, and to love and preserve public property. Charity remains, even if the objects change. The party and the leaders have been replaced by science and public property. As regards work, during the cultural revolution the talk was specifically about physical labour.

The gulf between manual and intellectual work has been a deep one in China. The learned mandarins with their full-length clothes and long nails despised manual labour and a rigid examination system maintained social boundaries. When "productive labour" was introduced into child upbringing, it served several purposes:

— work showed children in a concrete way how they could serve their country;
— children should learn to understand physical labour through their own direct experience;
— work was a means of teaching children and young people to respect the contributions to society of workers and peasants.

In 1980 productive labour was replaced by "civic consciousness". But school children still sweep the street, they observe cleanliness and the highway code as part of the campaign to "do a good deed". The deeds are the same, the terminology is new.

In the pre-school, people now talk less about reducing class barriers. Children are no longer urged to identify with peasants, workers and soldiers. Instead there is an increase in the significance of skills. The intellectual and the theoretical are again given pride of place. Individual interests are given more scope, even if the group has priority (Sidel & Sidel, 1982).

The sinophiles who turned the cultural revolution into their utopia easily overlook its overkill and the senselessness in its implementation. They easily become nostalgic and allow their disappointment at the moderniza- tion of China to know no bounds or nuances. The slogans of the campaigns contribute to intensifying the shades of black and white. The reality is more complex than that.

Too many mouths to feed

There are 150 million children of pre-school age in China, but the 990,000 day nurseries cover only a quarter of all pre-school children. This is roughly the same proportion as in Sweden. Otherwise it is difficult to fully grasp the implications of the Chinese population figures. China has the largest population of any country in the world — slightly more than a fifth, 22.7%, of the world's population live in China. After the revolution of 1949, mortality dropped while fertility rose. China has had a high and accelerating increase of population, as can be seen in the following figures:

Year	
1760	200 million inhabitants
1840	412 million inhabitants
1950	552 million inhabitants
1980	982.5 million inhabitants

(According to the census of 1982, the results of which were published in October 1982, the population is 1,008 million.)

As distinct from, for instance, Sweden, China has a very young population. According to calculations made in 1975:

— the age group 0–14 represented 36.8% of the population, while
— the elderly from 65 upwards accounted for only 5%.
— 65% of the population was under the age of 30.
— 5–9-year-olds were the largest age group of all.
— 10–44-year-olds were the next largest group.
By contrast, the age group 0–4 years was relatively smaller.

The Chinese are a peasant people. Eighty per cent of the population live in the country and have agriculture as their livelihood. China has as many peasants as the Soviet Union, USA, Japan, West Germany, France and Great Britain put together. The Chinese revolution was the work of peasants.

The population is unevenly distributed throughout the country. Ninety per cent live on 40% of the surface area in the densely-populated areas along the south-east coast and around the Yangtse River. A large part of China is barren mountain and desert. Extensive border regions are thinly populated by national minorities.

After the revolution there was a prevalent belief that more people led to more production, and increased production resulted in faster accumulation. This was determined by the general law of development under socialism. In addition, the reconstruction of an economy damaged by war required everyone's efforts. The propaganda assured people that the new society could guarantee a living to families with many children. The government banned sterilization and abortion.

China's first baby-boom came between 1953 and 1957. It involved an annual population increase of 2.4%, i.e. 14 million children *per annum*. It resulted in a gross increase of 58.6 million while the boom lasted. The next peak of births came in the years 1963–1972. It was larger than the previous one, with an annual population increase of 2.5%, i.e. 19 million *per annum*.

The excessively fast-growing population has meant that the standard of living *per capita* is still extremely low, although the national economy has developed enormously since 1949. The resources available for education cannot cover all young people, there is a threat of unemployment, the standard of living remains low and it is more difficult to achieve the desired accumulation of capital.

From 1970 onwards, birth control forms part of national planning. There are short- and long-term plans for 1-year and 10-year periods. Chou Enlai states that there is no point in making great economic plans if the growth of population cannot be planned:

> "We must overcome the mistake of ignoring and even denying the fact that the production of people falls within the framework of social production. An equilibrium of the essential proportions in the nation's economy depends primarily on the balance between the production of people and material production. We have to consider both."

The Chinese have tried to calculate what the ideal size of China's population should be in a hundred years' time. Several conditions for living, such as the need for labour, the need for food, and access to water are considered.

— The need for labour in a modernized economy suggests a population of 650–700 million.
— A calculation based on the need for food and the composition of the diet indicates that China can support 680 million.
— When one considers the ecological balance and access to fresh water, one ends with 630–650 million. China today has one of the lowest averages for use of water *per capita* in the world.

But if every couple produces 2.2 children today, there will be 1,300 million Chinese at the end of the century. If they can succeed in reducing the number of children progressively to 1.7 per couple by 1985, and the number of children can be kept at this level or be further reduced, the total population can be held at 1,200 million. So the policy now consists of not letting the population exceed 1,200 million by the end of the century.

So that the present level can be maintained, one-child families have to be established by 1985. But around the years 2000–2020 the overall fertility can start to be raised again to 2.16 children per couple. In 90 years, i.e. in 2070, the Chinese population should thus be stable at a level of around 700 million.

In the forthcoming decades what has to be done is to convince and persuade all fertile women that they have to be content with just one child. *There is no other way.* Even if the desired size of population can be achieved only in a hundred years' time, this has to be started at once. These harsh facts lie behind the campaign for one-child-per-family. But before going on to this, we need to take a glance at how relations in the family in China have changed. The campaign for the law of the family of 1950 provides us with essential information about this.

The campaign against arranged marriages

The Confucian ideal was that the father of the family lived surrounded by his sons, their wives and children, and his unmarried daughters. Age and sex determined the place of each and every one in the household. With time, this picture has been considerably modified. Short lives, high mortality rates, and shortage of land meant that it was in effect difficult to hold large families together. Investigations in the 1930s found that two-thirds of families consisted of three to six members. The guiding principle underlying the Chinese family was the male line, the bond which went from father to son. A man without sons was considered childless (Sidel & Sidel, 1982). Parents wanted male children. A daughter was seldom as welcome. She was regarded as a temporary guest in her parents' home. She would leave her parents early on in order to contribute to the continuation of another family's male line. For poor families a female child was a misfortune. When she had finally reached the age at which she could pay her way, it was time to marry her off. In this way the parents had no compensation for the expense of bringing her up. But when times were good, even the girls were given a share of the warmth which the Chinese lavish on children. At times of famine, sisters had to go hungry while their brothers ate. If the worst came to the worst, they were put out to die. The privileges of boys and the murder of female children were so widespread that it resulted in a conspicuous imbalance between the sexes in the first half of the 20th century.

To safeguard their children's future, parents took steps to arrange a marriage for them at an early stage. The arrangements demanded great sacrifices of both families. While it was expected that the girl should bring a dowry with her, it was customary for the man's parents to honour their son's future parents-in-law with gifts. And the right balance between the dowry and the gifts was important. If it transpired that gifts to the girls' parents were not adequate compensation for the sacrifices the parents had made to get their daughter married, this became grounds for getting rid of female children. On the other hand, if the value of the dowry did not correspond to that of the gifts to the bride's parents, the daughter was made to pay for it. A household which had incurred heavy costs for a daughter-in-law kept a watch on her, and weighed up her contribution in relation to what they had paid out for her.

In the countryside it was usual for the parents-in-law to adopt their daughter-in-law while she was still a little girl. In this way the poor could reduce the costs of the wedding, whereas in well-to-do families mothers-in-law considered it an advantage to bring up an amenable daughter-in-law themselves, and secure her loyalty to the family. In regions where the distribution of the sexes was unequal, this was far-sighted and guaranteed the son a wife for the future.

Conditions were hard for girls. Once adopted or married off, they were isolated from their own family. Visits to the childhood home took place only for special ceremonies. As there was a strict division of labour between the sexes, the person the young wife saw most of was her mother-in-law. It was the duty of the daughter-in-law to obey and serve her mother-in-law. She took over the heaviest and hardest jobs. If the mother-in-law was not satisfied with her, it was taken for granted that the son took his mother's side and blamed his wife. If things went badly, she would be physically punished by her mother-in-law and her husband. Tensions in the family, its open wounds of suppression and exclusion, took their toll in the female world, in the relationship between mother-in-law and daughter-in-law.

"It is better to have one child only". The gigantic posters are part of the huge single-child campaign.

The primary function of marriage was to ensure the male line. The bond between man and wife had procreation as its goal, and little besides. Even the slightest public indication of tenderness between the spouses was forbidden. According to traditional notions, a man needed three relationships for his emotional life: a wife for home and children, a concubine or prostitute for sexual pleasure, and a male friend with whom he could share his ideals, dreams and hopes (Winch, 1963). All of this avoided the risk of the daughter-in-law intruding on the most sacred of all family bonds, the relationship between a son and his parents.

As soon as the daughter-in-law had given birth to a male child, the worst was behind her. As the mother of one or more sons, she enjoyed respect. Over the years the relationship between the wife and the husband could develop into a kind of companionship, but as long as the mother-in-law was alive, the daughter-in-law was under her direction. Women who were fortunate enough both to give birth to sons and to live to the age of forty could experience a certain compensation for their suffering. They themselves ruled over the work of the household and they could pass on the heaviest chores to their daughter-in-law. They enjoyed the affection and respect of their sons and their grandchildren. Traditional culture permitted only one route for love between women and men, the one between mother and son, love which contributed to the strengthening of the male line.

The old family pattern first began to loosen in the towns. Women in industry contributed to the economy of the family. They could avoid having mother-in-law in the household. When freed from the rule of the elderly, the relationship between the spouses became less unequal. On the other hand, absence of the protective net of the family, and reduced social control, meant that families were split up, were stricken by destitution, unemployment, drunkenness, etc. The move from the country to the towns was accompanied by a pattern of "bigamy" among male students in the 1930s. Their parents had arranged a suitable marriage for them at home, while life in the town had taken them into a new world of education and female fellow students. One fine day they sat there with "the wife in the village" and with a "partner" in the town. Out of respect for their parents they could not bring themselves to renounce the wife whom the parents had arranged for them for their good (Davin, 1979).[1]

When the People's Republic passes the law of the family of 1950, the fundamental principles of the law are that

— each party shall marry of their own free choice,
— marriages shall be monogamous, and
— marriages build on equality between man and wife.

The minimum legal age for marriage was fixed as 20 for men and 18 for women. The law permitted divorce at the request of either.

---

1. In 1931 the Kuomintang government legislated on equality in marriage, free choice of partner, the right to divorce if both so wished, etc. Even so, the laws made the concession to tradition that after a divorce the father was usually given custody of the children. The majority of country women had never heard of this legislation. The new laws did not reach out much beyond the middle classes in the towns. During the struggle against the communists, the Kuomintang changed ideology, and old Confucian virtues were revived. Among these were the patriarchal family and the supremacy of men over women.

The extraordinary weight which the communists attached to the law of marriage, in their attempts to transform society, can be seen from the fact that the drafts of the law were written while the civil war was still raging. They knew that the implementation of the law would encounter enormous resistance.

When the new law of the family was promulgated, bringing it into force was not just the task of the courts but of the whole people. Members of the party, of the women's and youth organizations, officials at all levels, and the peasants' organizations were urged to see to it that the law was followed. The party carried out huge campaigns to publicize the law and support its implementation. Along with the land reform, the law of the family became a central theme in all propaganda for social reforms. The old system, with arranged marriages, concubines, privileges for the man, was condemned, and the new principles were propagated in newspapers, magazines, folders, cartoons, stories, posters and leaflets. To ensure that the law reached all, thousands of theatre groups were organized to put on plays and sketches in the villages. The radio passed on the law. Local reading groups and newspaper reading groups were formed to discuss the law of the family.

When the Red Army moved into villages in the 1940s, one of their first tasks was to organize the women and to encourage women to tell each other what their lives had been like. Women described the sexual suppression they had been subject to, among other things. It is reported that women at first resisted their new freedom, but once they had overcome their hesitancies it was they who formed the backbone of Chinese communism. They were among Mao's most devoted supporters (Winch, 1963).

But despite all this, the new law of the family was adhered to in an extremely half-hearted way. Investigations revealed that many marriages were still arranged by the parents. Worse still, party members occasionally intervened on the parents' side when young couples wanted to decide for themselves whom they should marry. They also sided with the husband in cases when the wife was alone in demanding a divorce.

It was disclosed that in 1950 10,000 women had died as a result of suicide or murder triggered off by discussions in the family dealing with marriage and divorce. And this applied in central and southern China alone. According to estimates in 1955, 70,000 to 80,000 women a year died, because of such "discussions". It is difficult to comment on the reliability of these statistics, but there is no doubt about the government's and the authorities' serious concern about the frequency with which women were victims of fatal violence (Davin, 1979).

The public was drenched with information about the law through all conceivable channels. The party sent directives to its members at all levels to study the law anew, to rectify their attitudes to it, and to contribute to its implementation. Tens of thousands of people, among them many of the members of the women's federation, attended courses at regional centres and then went home to the villages better trained to explain the purpose of the law and to help villagers to claim the rights given them by the law. One of the standard arguments against the law of marriage was that it was in effect a law of divorce, and that marriage by free choice would lead to total chaos. Some comrades regarded it as "a law of women to suppress men".

Since 1953 there have been less spectacular forms of support for the 1950 law of the family. Right until the 1960s books were published which stated that the content of the law was not yet fully understood. A study of 14,586 marriages in Anhui province reports in 1979 that in 15% of the marriages the partners chose each other, that the parents took the initiative in arranging 75% of the marriages, but that the young couple had been allowed to meet and approve each other. Ten per cent of the marriages were completely arranged by the parents (Sidel & Sidel, 1982). The incidence of "semi-voluntary" marriages is difficult to understand unless one is familiar with the historical background. The law has, however, strengthened the bond between husband and wife.

The question of divorce has caused more headaches than choice of marriage partner. The fact that it was predominantly women who wanted a divorce immediately after the liberation increased the suspicion of men. The land reform helped to increase their resistance. The women had been allocated their own plot of land, and they were entitled to retain it after a divorce. The authorities went to great lengths to make divorces more bearable. Appeals were made, with the help of examples of women who had been the victims of shocking brutality. The general public got as far as being prepared to accept divorce for "feudal reasons", in other words in a transitional period it should be possible to leave a marriage which one had been unable to object to. The generations which had been treated unfairly would in this way be given some compensation.

During a period at the beginning of the 1950s many divorces were granted, but the climate became harsher again in the middle of the decade. When the demand for divorces did not fall, articles started to be published with evidence of a manifest ambivalence in the official attitude to divorce. It turned out that, for instance, leaders and administrators in the communist party and its mass organizations were compelled to make long stays away from home. They experienced new things, acquired new ways of feeling and thinking. They shared less with the wife at home and met new female comrades. At the same time the party assumed that its members should set a moral example. What had to be done was to stop divorce in their own ranks. Divorces could best be defended when they were dictated by anti-feudal motives.

When our study group in 1974 asked questions about divorce, the standard answer was given that "in the years after the liberation there were many divorces, but now they are unusual, because nowadays we make our own choice".

It was not until the new law of the family in 1980 that divorce was granted on the grounds of "permanent and deep incompatibility" — or, as the Chinese call it, "total abstinence of mutual feelings". The door out of marriage is thus slightly ajar. Otherwise the law of 1980 confirms the fundamental principles of 1950. The minimum age for marrying, however, is raised to 22 for men and 20 for women. Spouses can retain their respective family names, and children can adopt either the mother's or the father's name. In addition the law stresses "the principle of family planning".

To sum up: while the land reform was the main weapon against the old pattern of power in the villages, the law of marriage has been the main tool for changing the pattern of authority in the family. It has both undermined the male line and challenged the relationships of obedience between the generations. The link between land reform and the law of the family has not pleased everyone, like the peasant who complains: "The land reform is excellent, but it's difficult when we can no longer beat our women" (Davin, 1979).

Children as a scarce resource

Giving birth to children has dropped over a number of years in industrialized countries. At present we have the lowest birth rate ever known in Sweden. A shrinking population means that in future progressively smaller age groups in their productive years have to support a large, ageing population. Politicians and demographers are anxious. Is there something wrong with a society in which so few children are born? The authorities are discussing suitable measures to encourage women to give birth to more children. How about an increased child allowance for the third and fourth child? How about a child maintenance allowance for the parents of infants who give up a job and work at home? How about shorter working hours and improved child care facilities?

Our family patterns, too, have changed. Marriage is no longer the concern of the society but of conscience. Young people not only make their own choice, they try things out by living together. They split up, get married and divorced. More and more women are gainfully employed and it is difficult to combine a job and a child. The Swedish child has become an "employment disability". In the field of housework and responsibility for children, a female line rules. I wonder whether one cannot say that the most stable bond in Swedish families is the bond between mother and child?

When Swedish women are asked why they do not produce more children, they look for causes in their own situation rather than looking for explanations in societal conditions which make it difficult to have children. They report that they lack time and energy, that they want to devote themselves to other kinds of work and other interests, they quote reasons of age and health. What Swedish men's opinion is, we do not know. They have not yet been asked, though the Central Bureau of Statistics is planning to consult fathers, too.

In China the problem is the opposite. The Fifth National People's Congress in 1978 ratified a new constitution giving the state responsibility for family planning. Earlier efforts in 1956–58 and 1962–66 had scarcely any effect outside the towns. As recently as 1970, the word was "two children are enough, three is a maximum, and four is too many". If family planning measures had not been initiated in 1970, it is calculated that a further 56 million children would have been born in the period 1970–79 (Sidel & Sidel, 1982). The campaign summed up its programme in the slogan: *late, spaced and few*. "Lateness" aimed at delaying marriage. One province tried to carry through a policy of a minimum marrying age of 25 for men and 23 for women. The 1980 law of the family was merely content with an increase of two years to 22 and 20 respectively. But lateness is not only aimed at raising the age at which people marry, but also involves recommending that young couples wait several years before they have children. It is fairly easy to calculate that if you can succeed in delaying the first child by five years, from the age of 20 to 25, this means that couples reproduce four as opposed to five new generations over the next one hundred years. The word "spaced" aims at a norm of a four-year gap between children. Until this point, the word was still: two is most, one is best.

Since the People's Congress of 1980 the message has been harsher: only one child per couple. The age structure itself, with the young people of the record years of the 1950s and 1960s reaching fertility, necessitates more radical measures so that new peaks for births do not occur in the 1980s and 1990s. The state is drawing up uniform rules in order to bring the population

The smiling mothers with their only child on the campaign posters may make one think of the Madonna and Child.

increase under control and to supply the country with the necessary economic means, scientific methods, medical personnel and equipment. The general public is being invited to discuss and re-assess the goals of national policy so that the interests of the population and the state may fit together.

Henceforth family planning is one of the fundamental civic duties. The Chinese policy is said to unite the principle of state control and the voluntary action of the masses. The state has to persuade and convince people of the necessity of one single child per couple. So the huge campaign for one-child-families has been set going. We encounter smiling mothers lifting their single child up with their outstretched arms on gigantic posters outdoors and on small wallcharts indoors. Along with the four modernizations, the campaign for a single child dominates. At times, the two campaigns are linked, as for instance when a modern woman, wearing a skirt, leads her only child over a pedestrian crossing on a huge poster, or when mother and child are shown against a background of modern technology. Television and radio are used for ideological persuasion. Meetings are organized for young couples and young people who have not yet married. Health workers pay visits to the home. Every family, every couple, every grown-up is taught about the significance of limiting themselves to one single child. Party members are expected to set a good example. From 1985 onwards no third children can be born. I almost catch myself throwing an accusing glance when I meet a family with three children in the street.

The campaign, as a method for informing the masses, dovetails with the effectively organized local control and receptivity to moral appeals. There are special prerequisites for mass campaigns in a society in which the lower units of organization are often mobilized for shared national goals. The countryside is divided into people's councils, production brigades and production teams. In the towns, street committees correspond to people's councils and neighbourhoods to brigades. It is the lower units which organize their members in connection with, for instance, campaigns and shared collective work.

The smallest units are responsible for local health care, child care, street cleaning and waste disposal. They keep an eye on the inhabitants and see to it that they are given help if needed, they organize local crafts, etc. Local initiative manages a great deal of what we have special bodies for. All this means that the central campaigns have an incredible penetrative power. There are many channels linking the centre with the periphery.

Firstborn first

Two campaign methods have shown themselves to be specially successful. One of them is the certificate. Couples who sign a contract with the local health station, in which they promise to limit themselves to one child, receive a diploma to hang on the wall at home. The nation thanks them for their sacrifice. Psychologically the certificate serves to block the wish for more children, as a breach of promise would mean that the couple lose face.

We visit a neighbourhood committee west of Peking. It forms part of a street committee of 22,000 households. Fourteen citizen's committees in the district function as links between the government and the inhabitants. There are 40 local health centres in it. We spoke to an oldish female health worker. On the wall in her clinic hung a list of all the couples of child-bearing age in the district. This showed that with two exceptions all of them had promised to restrict themselves to one child. I fear that those who hesitate to give a morally binding promise are exposed to considerable pressure. The local health worker is responsible for family planning. Once young people marry, they come to her for sex education and advice on prevention. Supplying the means of prevention to married couples — and only to them — is effective and free. The local health worker follows up her couples month by month.

The methods used in the 1970s were mainly the intra-uterine device, sterilization and abortion. Sterilization for either sex was made possible, but as with experience in other countries, the number of women who were sterilized was far greater than the number of men. The Chinese are investing a great deal in advanced research into prevention. There has been a pill for men since 1970, although the side-effects have not yet been fully researched. There is even available a "holiday pill" for couples who work in separate places and only meet during the holidays.

The other method makes use of the good example. The Chinese ascribe great importance to the force of example. Well-known people who live up to the ideal get the dividend of a good reputation in the immediate environment, fame and respect in the neighbourhood and at the place of work. It is worth a lot. But as well as such possible rewards, this time the Chinese even use economic pressure. Introducing material benefits involves departing from principles which have long been held in esteem in China. Parents who commit themselves to only one child receive a bonus on the child's birth and a monthly supplement until the child is 14 (Ching, 1982). Parents of one child can be allocated extra work points, which gives them a wage supplement while the child is growing up, in other words for 10–14 years. In the country, one-child families are given extra land for their personal use. The only child receives a double lot: instead of 60–80 square metres the family gets 120–160 square metres. A second child does not thus entail any new land. In addition the mother can be granted longer maternity leave; where possible, attempts are made to prolong the leave from 56 days up to as much as 18 months on full pay. Similarly, a family with only one child can count on being given larger living accommodation. The first child not only has priority in day nurseries, health clinics and schools, but even gets them free. Nor will single children who grow up in towns in future be ordered to work in the countryside.

Those who have two children will neither gain nor lose anything. But parents who after 1979 produce three children or more will be deprived of benefits in several respects. For example, the parents' work bonus might be withheld for a certain period. Day nursery rates can be increased by 10% for families with more than two children. There are regions where workers with more than two children do not earn promotion or an increase in wages. While the state pays the costs associated with delivery for two children, the parents themselves have to pay thereafter. The health care costs of the third child are borne by the parents, and the authorities fix a limit to the number of children from one family who have the right to higher education.

In the old Chinese family, the male line was secured through the firstborn son's exclusive right to inherit. He succeeded his father. The firstborn child's birthright has even been assured by law in many Western

The local health worker is responsible for family planning. She provides sex education and distributes the means of prevention to newly-married couples, whom she then follows up month by month. In the neighbourhood committee's health centre there is a list of all the couples of child-bearing age in the district, with an indication of those who have promised to have only one child.

countries, likewise that the sons' share of the inheritance has been bigger than daughters'. But what is radically new in the Chinese single child's privileges is that they apply irrespective of sex. If the firstborn is a girl, she is given priority in both higher education and in getting a job. She comes before little brother.

But there can't be any little brothers in one-child-families? Yes, that is the question. A study in Anhui province covering 3,396 families reports that 60% of the families hold the certificate of honour. It transpires that two-thirds of the couples who have pledged themselves to one child only have already had a son (Ching, 1982). Ten per cent of the couples who have promised to restrict themselves to one child declare that they are dubious about their decision.

Further, families which had not committed themselves were character-ized by somewhat lower education, a rather lower standard of living, and by more than half of them refusing to answer questions about the benefits proffered by the government in its one-child appeals. Some families fear that the promises for one child will not be kept. Still others believe that future governments will change the policy so that two-child families receive the same support as one-child families.

The efforts made to keep the promises to one-child families carry with them a threat of discrimination against second and third children. The parents' fear that something may happen to their only child has made it necessary to guarantee all only-children preference in hospitals. But doctors treating sick children have not been inclined to reject children from families of many children in order to give absolute priority to only children. Parents of single children are therefore demanding that hospitals reserve beds specially for single children. So far, the parents' complaints about the shortage of places in day nurseries have been louder than about the shortage of places at the university. In my opinion, the attitude of the doctors shows the difficult dilemma of preferential treatment for firstborn children.

The new policy is not yet applied universally. Bonuses and allowances for one-child families vary in size according to what the workplace and the region can afford. High productivity companies pay more than employers who lack funds for family planning. When expenses for child health care, abortions, sterilizations and food allowances are taken from general welfare funds, there is not much left for the other needs of the workers. While the government's "provisional rules" for family planning give single-child families priority in housing, 40% of the families who have committed themselves to one child in Anhui province have not yet been given the accommodation they have the right to. In another province, there is experimentation which takes the form of guaranteeing one-child families the same amount of space as a four-person family in accommodation built by the state, factories and schools. But both the shortage of housing and delays in implementing the policy mean that one-child parents are uncertain about what to expect – not to mention parents of several children.

But the campaign uses ideological persuasion most of all. It tries to convince the population of the need for lower birth rates. Three of the campaign's main ideological arguments confront familiar objections against having only one child. The first claims that *girls are just as good*. It points out that families who already have one or a couple of daughters and then try everything to get a son are caught up in a feudal way of thinking. The male line is antiquated. The recently implemented change in the law on names makes it possible for daughters to carry on their father's name. And the son can choose to use his mother's name.

It is not only concern for the male line, however, which made sons coveted. The patrilocal rule of residence meant that daughters did not count for anything. They left their parents and it was their duty to support their parents-in-law in their old age. Security for the old rested with their sons. Parents with several sons could feel confident about ageing. The sons and their wives would sustain them. As a result, the second main ideological argument asserts that there should be symmetry in the responsibility of sons and daughters for their parents, just as the wife and the husband have equivalent obligations towards each other's parents. The law of the family of 1980 decrees explicitly that it "is the duty of parents to bring up and take care of their children, just as it is the duty of children to support and help their parents". These obligations are more burdensome for children in families with only one child. If two only-children marry, they share the responsibility for two sets of parents. In addition, you have to reckon with some old people without children to look after them. The society will have to invest more in the care of old people and in economic guarantees for the old.

The principle of symmetry, equal responsibility for both sexes, strikes at the root of Chinese patriarchy, the male line and the male residence rule. The law of the family of 1950 never went as far as that.

The third argument is addressed to the peasants, and tries to convince them that the modernization and mechanization of agriculture is going to reduce the need for labour in the fields. Until now the peasants have solved the need for extra help by having numerous children.

We are visiting a rice-producing people's council in southern China. The women's organization's young chairperson, who has recently become a mother, is articulate in describing for us the work of overcoming the resistance to one-child families. Men are more difficult to convince than women. They want sons and regard a daughter as a loss to the family. Members of the party, officials and industrial workers find it easier to accept the idea of one child than do real country-people. In non-mechanized agriculture, children are used for many tasks. The chairperson is not going to have more children herself. "I am going to set a good example," she says.

The people's commune consists of 16,000 households and 76,000 inhabitants, distributed into 19 production brigades and 220 production teams. They grow rice. Down here in the south they get two harvests a year. They have orange groves, pigs and poultry. In addition there are workshops and light industry in the council. Everything I see seems to confirm the picture the chairperson gives: the council leads a stable, satisfying life. Their own labour holds out promising prospects. The inhabitants of the council can afford bicycles and clocks. The households have been able to obtain furniture, sewing-machines, radios. Some even have TV. Families get extra income by growing vegetables on private plots.

In the chairperson's opinion, the government conducts the one-child campaign in a moderate way. It is not applied, for instance, in the sparsely populated areas of the country where many minority people live. This year the rice-producing people's council has been allocated a quota of two hundred second children, to be shared out among the couples of the council.

An extra allocation of two hundred second children! That makes me inquisitive. How are 200 unborn children distributed among 76,000 inhabitants? Who gets the right to a second child? Consideration is given to the following:

— A second child is permitted to families in which the family line has been at risk on the male side over several generations.

   We look surprised. The chairperson smiles slightly apologetically and says that this is a "feudal concession". Nothing comparable applies in the towns.
— Couples who have had a handicapped child can try once more. The widespread "second child dispensation", if there is anything wrong with the first, also functions as a protection, a life insurance for handicapped children.
— Couples who have an adopted child and would like to have one of their own are allotted a second child.
— Finally, couples who remarry are allowed to have a child together, even if one of them, or even both, has children already.

It is my firm impression that the majority of second children are used for attempts to strengthen the male line. Experience tells us that roughly half of the parents will get another girl. Alas, yes.

Fewer — but better

China's leaders promise that the society will dedicate its utmost resources to children: health care, education and culture. All China's children are to be really A1. Children of the future. New people. The scientific argumentation goes along two lines; one stresses the advantages for the child's intellectual and physical development of being an only child. The other tries to throw light on the risks for personality development of growing up as an only child.

Peking University has studied 1,741 children aged 3–15. Of these, 314 (18%) were only children (Ching, 1982). Only children were judged as being superior to children from families with several children as regards imagination, linguistic competence, imitation and creative thinking. Only children achieved markedly better at school. Another research team found that a quarter of "brilliant children" are only children and that most of the other "brilliant" ones came from two-child families.

Researchers in the USA (Falbo, 1982) also concluded that only children there both have a longer education and do better in school than children in multiple-child families. The educational difference remains even when the education and socio-economic status of the parents are controlled. The Chinese investigation reports that 66.2% of the only children studied were in excellent health compared with 43.4% of children in multiple-child families. The researchers do, however, point out that as many as 37% of the parents of only children were in white collar jobs.

Chinese pre-school teachers talk of the risk of only children being spoiled. If the children neither have older siblings to emulate nor younger siblings to take care of, few demands are made on them in the home. The grown-ups are anxious for the child's favour, and the children become accustomed to getting their own way. Teachers are worried about the parents over-investing all their ambitions in the one child, who will then have to bear the burden of their great expectations alone. At the same time the number of children in each age group is great, and children and young people encounter murderous competition in which many are knocked out at every stage. The tune of the times of the cultural revolution has been replaced by a school of tough swotting and by special élite schools. A pupil at a Chinese middle school wrote the following in the autumn of 1981:

> "It is as though we are running a race on a narrow winding path. It is so narrow that most of us are going to be elbowed off at any moment. From the primary school to the middle school to the university we are running on that path every single day. The pupils compete, the teachers compete and the parents compete".
> (From *The youth of China* 22, 1981, quoted in Dagens Nyheter, 20 June 1982.)

A study of the pre-schools in Shanghai found that the proportion of only children among 4-year-olds had risen to 80%. The investigators compared 70 only children with 30 children with siblings to see which group exhibited more undesirable features. They found that, among other things, 30% of only children and 7% of children from multiple-child families fell short in their capacity to co-operate. A similar study in Peking came to the opposite conclusion, both as regards co-operativeness and disciplinary problems.

The table from the pre-school study in Shanghai illustrates the apprehensions of the nursery teachers. It indicates which undesirable features the teachers are apprehensive about and are therefore inclined to observe in the children:

Undesirable feature	Only child		Multiple-child families	
	N	%	N	%
	70	100	30	100
Bad table manners	48	69	12	40
Obstinacy	45	64	6	20
Shyness	35	50	8	27
Carelessness with property	31	44	5	17
Hostility to others	30	43	6	20
Incapacity to look after oneself	23	33	1	3
Disrespect for elders	19	27	1	3
Obsessed by dressing up	19	27	3	10

Source: Shanghai Preschool Education Study Group: "Family Education of Only Children", in *Chinese Woman* 5, 1980

As can be seen, the only child's character may be at risk. Attempts are made to prevent this through discussions with and advice to parents. The authors of the article stress that during its first years a child should not be regarded as selfish. It simply gets used to picking the largest fruit for itself, taking the most gaudy sweet, by being given the best of the batch by the parents. What is feared is that the older pre-school children will turn their earlier privileges into selfish demands on the environment.

The teachers are aware that single-child families are going to change the child's patterns of interaction. Within two or three generations, the majority of China's children will lack not only sisters and brothers but also aunts and uncles and cousins. To its parents each child will be unique. In the pre-school it will be one of many children of the same age. We may witness an increased individualization of the personality within the framework of a collective system.

The one-child family is topical in the West, too. Research into only children in the USA (Falbo, 1982) has identified four circumstances which should be considered when assessing only children:

— the prevailing cultural attitude to only children;
— whether the parents have voluntarily chosen to have one child, or have had to comply for reasons beyond their control;
— the number of grown-up members of the family; and
— the age of the child.

Where there is an expectation that the only child will be selfish, lonely and maladjusted, the grown-ups will tend to observe those features which confirm their prejudices. The grown-ups can simply provoke what they fear. Not even researchers are immune to such a propensity . . .

In rural areas, the only child is given a plot of land and an adult allocation of rice and wheat right from the start.

Where parents give priority to other values in life than having several children, a single child does not constitute a problem for them. But if the parents in reality desire more children, there is a risk of the only child being the object of over-investment.

It is common in the West for only children to live with one of the parents, generally the mother. In China, on the other hand, children as a rule have access to several grown-ups in their immediate environment. The presence of many grown-up members of the family is regarded as promoting children's intellectual development. Admittedly you need to consider the child's age when interpreting this research result. If all these factors are considered, American research does not support the cultural prejudices about the only child's personality development. It is, however, important to remember that upbringing in China and the USA stress different types of behaviour.

One further meaning of the slogan "fewer but better children" can be derived from the re-introduction of genetic counselling in China. According to a calculation by a professor at the Chinese Academy for Medical Sciences, there are over ten million Chinese with congenital defects. With better health care and a higher standard of living more and more children stay alive with handicaps which would have been fatal earlier. Expert medical opinion even holds that both environmental pollution and marriages between close relatives and between mentally retarded people increase the incidence of congenital illness.

Since 1979 genetic counselling has been given to parents-to-be. The 1980 law of marriage introduced stricter regulations for marriage between relatives. Geneticists in China recommend a law of the kind passed in Japan, which requires couples to exchange medical certificates before they marry, so that each is informed of any possible hereditary diseases. Taking into consideration eugenic aspects easily awakens associations with Europe in the 1930s, its doctrines and emphasis on the qualitative aspects of population policy. Fewer but better — how good do you have to be to have the right to be born?

When Alva Myrdal warned the Swedes about the risks in the character development of single children, it was as a matter of fact in her work for the population commission in the 1930s. At that time it was still impossible to ascertain the sex of the child in advance. This is possible in China today. One can fear that the predilection for male children will result in choosing an abortion more frequently if the foetus is a girl. In the worst case this can lead to the same imbalance between women and men as was brought about earlier by murdering baby girls (Sidel & Sidel, 1982). Technology makes intervention possible at an earlier stage. Social attitudes change slowly.

There is one large exception to the policy of population limitation. This concerns the 60 million people in China who belong to "national minorities". For them, population increase is allowed and encouraged. At the same time health workers supply those couples who want to plan their families with the means of prevention.

The narrow road

Women have benefited a great deal from the revolution, but how is the relationship between the sexes going to develop in the future? Are Western ideas on love and sexuality going to penetrate China? Will the Chinese in future be as obsessed and bewitched by the pair relationship as we are? The law of the family of 1950 described marriage as "a spiritual union of two comrades of different sexes". The goal of marriage is to strengthen and cherish the shared belief in communism, and to involve both spouses in the work of building up a new society.

For someone who has never heard of love, it is difficult to know how it feels to be in love. With no roots in romantic conceptions of love, Chinese culture has found it difficult to advise the young. What are people guided by when they marry of their "own free choice"? How does one proceed when choosing? What is it important to consider? It is certainly not easy to puzzle out the right priorities. This can be seen in Chinese films. Just when you think the communist girl and the partisan are going to get each other, they solemnly bid each other farewell. Both have more important tasks elsewhere. What counts is the good of the society, but there are of course happy endings, with personal happiness, as when father and son find each other again at the end of "Azalea Mountain".

In 1974, when we asked questions about what the Chinese attached importance to when they chose a spouse, we were generally given the answer: "We look for political suitability." We Swedes were taken aback. But when one recalls the extensive significance of politics during the cultural revolution, one realizes that the answer roughly corresponds to what we mean by "a kindred spirit" — and as such it is in accord with the law of the family of 1950.

Nowadays most marriages are still contracted through the offices of a third party. The mass organizations for youth and for women have set up a marriage service. Since the beginning of the 1980s there have been marriage bureaux in many towns — in Peking alone there are five.

The marriage bureaux look after young people who want to get married but have a problem in finding a partner. Many young people devote themselves to their studies or their work so assiduously that they have not managed to look around for someone to marry. It is also said that irregular working hours are an obstacle. Some people can be slightly peculiar in their manner and therefore need an intermediary.

The marriage services of the mass organizations have a good reputation and the trade unions support them. They get grants from the local authorities. The marriage bureaux can in full confidence obtain information about the potential spouse through the usual procedures of the mass organizations. The bureaux organize various social activities at which unmarried people can become acquainted. Until now the bureaux have been of an experimental nature, but their appearance indicates something of the difficulties entailed in the abolition of customs.

The town Hangzhou has traditions going back more than 2,000 years. It is famous for its natural beauty: lake shores edged with hanging willows; bridges linking islands together; parks, pavilions, pagodas, towers, temples, "the three ponds which reflect the moon", "The Purple Cave" and much else. Hangzhou is a popular place for honeymoons. Newlyweds flock there.

From one to three weeks in Hangzhou means holidays and free days fore-gone over a long period. And savings.

In Hangzhou China is converted to a society of twosomes. The newly-weds stroll around everywhere. Tidily dressed up and well-groomed. Neat and clean just as in the good old days. What else? The ceremony of a lifetime like this has to be borne with dignity and quivering bated breath. Am I imagining that they are not really used to being in each other's company? Are they perhaps pondering over what they should say? In China all pre-marital sexual relations are forbidden. And then suddenly you are married.

Admittedly, the strolling groups of young men, just like all the groups of girls walking together, seem to be considerably more relaxed and intimate with each other than the shy honeymoon couples. They have just been informed about the secrets of sex life by their local health worker, and at the same time been instructed about the desirability of postponing the birth of the first and only child for some years.

They pause on the narrow bridge and feed goldfish. The goldfish float, bloated from all the crumbs of bread and cake. They gobble indolently all the manna strewn over their sky. Occasional chunks of bread remain on the surface. There are rowing boats to rent if they want to be by themselves and gaze towards the domed landscapes of the shores. The rowing boats have a small built-in table so that they can be seated on the thwart for a meal. In the evening they can place a lantern on the table and watch the lights glimmer in the water.

Nothing of all this is wasted. Everything is externalized and documented with the help of the camera. The young wife poses by sculptures, floral arrangements, bridges, water towers, pavilions. In all this photographing, his interest in things technical is happily united with her self-reflecting narcissism. It does look as though part of their honeymoon happiness was due to his interest in photography and hers in the photos. Or perhaps they are only hiding from each other with the help of the camera, perhaps this is one of the hide-and-seek games of love, its indefatigable seek and find. Perhaps the camera is helping them to try out their new roles, to objectify them. They can openly bring themselves to "act out" the expectations they have to live up to. They can observe each other through the eye of the camera and by so doing work over their internal experience and their external behaviour so that they keep in step.

Then the pictures are pasted into a family album. They will document that Mummy and Daddy were once young and beautiful. The sunset's lustre over the west lake in Hangzhou, the water-lilies in the bay, and the pavilion roofs with corners ending upwards as though they were about to lift off towards the sky, everything indicates that they married of their own free choice — discounting a little help from a third party.

Foreign study groups persistently bombard the Chinese with questions about their views on sexuality. The Chinese are used to this. Our female informants kept the discussion of the topic very brief, restricing themselves to references to the distinctiveness of their culture. This implied that respect for cultural differences closed the door on further discussion. But they could also get their views across by saying "we have chosen the healthy way". In Sweden this would be called "the narrow way" of premarital chastity and marital fidelity. Many Westerners feel strongly provoked by the official Chinese repression. But I believe that it has not been only a disadvantage for China's women that they have avoided the "eroticization" and "sexualization" with which many patriarchal cultures have clipped the wings of their women.

But which way is the young generation in China going to opt for? A cultural evening in Kanton hints at this. Kanton appears as border country between the orthodox puritanism of Peking and the commercial vulgarity of Hong Kong. One senses a change of cultural climate progressively from Peking to Kanton, an infiltration from the West. Kanton is a window onto capitalism in many respects. A large trade fair is taking place.

The cultural evening at the trade centre is intended for foreign commercial delegations, study and tourist groups and the local public. The guests occupy the front rows, but the great majority of the public consists of Chinese people aged 15–30. The concert has eminent soloists. When they are presented we are told that they have won gold medals and other distinctions in music competitions with traditional Chinese instruments. We listen, fascinated. The soloists are dazzingly competent — but we are disturbed the whole time by a murmur from the Chinese public. Countless conversations seem to be taking place with no concern for what is happening on the stage. On the rows occupied by foreigners the irritation is perceptible. What deplorable audience culture!

About halfway through the programme the audience in the rear half fall silent. The ripple of noise gives way for western solos. When a large Chinese Paul Robeson sings about the Mississippi in a vibrant bass, there is a lot of applause. At the end, and finally, comes what the public has been waiting for. A young couple come on to the stage. They have an air of popular TV idols. They are dressed in Western clothes. She has a skirt and blouse and cardigan. His white shirt is casually unbuttoned over a light grey jacket. They look like sixth-formers from the 1940s or 1950s. This is what college kids were dressed in long before the time of the hippies. They look attractive and nice. They respect their parents. Their repertoire of songs is about love, the wonderful twosome love. After the first number the public burst into an ovation. Their next tune is a new duet about love's sweetness. The public is rapturous. Encouraged by the response, manifestly influenced by the exaltation of the audience, the young couple gives an encore. And then something unheard-of happens. They make some dance movements to the music. They are totally un-Chinese body movements, a quite foreign swinging of the hips and an unknown rocking going from the chest to the shoulders in the wrong order. If I really had time to grasp it properly, as it did not last long. But it was a signal which everyone understood. It provoked a riot of acclamation. Something unheard-of had taken place before the eyes of the next generation of Chinese parents. At that point I stopped looking at the stage in order to watch the public instead. It was captivated. A happy teenage girl had tears in her eyes.

In a final encore the idols try to revert to order. They sing with their backs straight, a pure look, with the voices of the faithful, as though nothing had happened. Yet all of us know that we have seen the edifice cracking and beheld the revolt of youth through the crack, the irresistible enticement of Westernization, forces which cannot be checked, a floodwave of the future as devastating and potentially fruitful as the flooding of the Yellow River in the old bitter times. But that the Chinese finally succeeded in damming. Will they also manage to divert the mudflow of Westernization into new courses?

"Girls are just as good"

In a fierce critique of the world view of Confucianism, Mao wrote in 1927 that the people in China were suppressed by three powers, those of religion, politics and the clan. For women, a fourth power was added. They were suppressed by the men, too. You can see no sign of this in the pre-school. The girls are radiatingly self-confident and outgoing. The nursery school is arranged to suit them. It fits their interests. The girls enjoy singing and dancing. One can really see how they take pleasure in mastering the most exquisite hand movements and twitches of the neck. Their competence is almost over-rehearsed. There is a twinkle in the triumph of cleverness in their eyes. They enjoy performing in costumes and make-up, reciting poems, making the place look nice, laying the table and taking part in everyday chores. They feel secure in social interaction with grown-up women, they look after the plants, they are alert and attentive.

The female pre-school teachers develop their own femininity in the educational work. They are inventive and imaginative. They sew beautiful costumes for performances. They are in command. They sing and teach the children movements. They play and nod and smile. They inform and encourage. The pre-school's female culture confirms for the girls that they are welcome in the world. The girls are not only just as good, they seem to be better than the boys, because the little boys at times seem to be a little out of place, and appear more disorderly and childish.

Generally more girls than boys take part in the performances. In one people's council, the staff locked the boys into an inside room while the performance for the guests took place. Enthusiastic and inquisitive as we were, we happened to go in there. They had been left on their own and were evidently quite bored, so they were passing the time fighting and being mischievous. They did not at all give an impression of beautifying and civilizing.

At the pre-school teachers' training college in Shanghai, it was easy for the teachers to recognize the boys' situation as we described it. They agreed that pre-school activity was less designed to meet the interests of boys. Of course they were familiar with the problem. Shortly afterwards we witnessed a dance performance with future pre-school teachers in pink tulle. They represented a coral reef, and imitated in the dance how the waves beat against the reef, sensually and almost slightly daringly. Wedding-cake figures, well-shaped and serious models for little girls.

The problem is familiar — a women's culture in childhood which boys resist, and thereafter a grown-up male climate in society in which women are easily left outside. A little girl's situation has admittedly improved since the time when she was adopted by the parents of her future spouse. But an analysis of the modern Chinese family shows that the old rules of residence, semi-arranged marriages and concealed forms of economic transaction between families live on in the country. The dominance of men still exists, without being significantly questioned.

The bourgeois epoch, which has left deep traces in the Western woman, has largely avoided China. Chinese society has moved directly from feudalism to socialism. This divides the women's experience from ours. Romantic love and the emotional expectations of marriage have not been raised so high in China. Love and passion between man and woman they have certainly been familiar with, but not as a reason for marriage, rather as a subversive social force to be brought under control. And as the interests of the society and the household have taken precedence over those of the individual, most people tried to guard themselves against the inexorable tragedy of love and the risk of being a laughing-stock. Chinese women comment on their marriages and plan the timing of their child in a professional, unsentimental manner. Their views on establishing a family are reasonable and upright. The Western obsession with the pair and women as legitimate objects for sexual advances in social life is a fairly new phenomenon even in our part of the world. In China sexuality has not been detached from marriage, nor are women fair game in the same way. Teenager sexual activity is not accepted. The eroticization of women which characterizes women in the West so strongly is scarcely noticeable in the China of today. During the cultural revolution people talked contemptuously of "emperors, generals and beauties". The beauties alluded to were women who obtained privileges and influence over men with the help of their sex and appearance. "Beauty" in this sense symbolized both the eroticization of women into a sex object and women's sexual manipulation of men.

Many foreigners have noticed the simple dignity of the behaviour of older Chinese women. They have not been deprived of their own intrinsic worth. They make no efforts to conceal their age as do Western women.

How financially independent are women in China? When the people's councils were introduced, women were granted their own wages for their work. Earlier, wages were calculated according to the needs of a household. Now it was equal pay for equal work. Admittedly the heavy work done by men gave higher work points than women's work, but the introduction of individual work points still guaranteed a woman an autonomous income. Her income was fixed without regard to the man and the household. Under the new system of responsibility which is now being tried out, the household as a unit signs a contract with the production team of the farm to cultivate a particular acreage and fill a quota. The Sidels (1982) point out the irony of the Chinese simultaneously giving the collective responsibility for cultivation to the individual households, while switching from calculating wages per individual to wages per household — in both cases within the context of the council as a collective. The production team negotiates with the head of the household, and reports from the area where this system of responsibility is being implemented indicate that the incomes now go to the household as a unit. Is this going to bring women back under the authority of their husbands? What financial choices are women confronted with if they want a divorce from their husbands?

Perhaps political participation is the most interesting aspect of the emancipation of Chinese women. Low-level units of organization like production brigades and neighbourhoods are responsible for many shared collective tasks in China. This local public activity has provided a forum for women, who have entered the politics of everyday life. They have functioned in citizen's committees, taken decisions on local matters, participated in study work and meetings. They have disseminated the campaigns and contributed to political mobilization. They have taken responsibility for many social and political tasks which are dealt with by special bodies in our country.

In the local public life of the people's councils and street committees, there are several grown-ups who keep an eye on the children, have a word with them, intervene and take time off for them. The presence of other familiar grown-ups takes the pressure off the parents. The mothers become the victims of neither idealization nor isolation, as with us. And if the women do not give birth to more than one child, there is no possibility of their identity being anchored to motherhood as the mission in life.

What a schooling in public responsibility is going to mean for the position of women in society in the long term is difficult to predict. The word today is that "girls are just as good". The promises of priority for firstborn children, even if they are girls, pave the way for equal conditions for boys and girls. But the tendencies are contradictory. Even if women are encouraged to take paid work and men are urged to take their share of child care and housework, there is evidence that the revolution has strengthened the patriarchal peasant family in a reformed version. Nor can women really trust the Western models which young people in the towns adopt fairly uncritically, as little as the Western values which follow with the four modernizations. At present it is both the peasants and the men in the towns who have strengthened their position at the expense of women.

The paternal grandmother and the future

In the old family the young woman was often treated harshly. She was either abandoned to the whim of her mother-in-law or sexually exploited by men. No other alternatives existed for women outside the family. But if and when she became a paternal grandmother, she was accorded a certain redress. By then she had fulfilled her duty to the male line and passed on the heaviest household work to the daughter-in-law. Note that the relationship between the mother-in-law and the daughter-in-law is still very important. It is still usual for them to belong to the same household. Tension between them is a frequent theme in the press and mass media. It is said that marriage counselling devotes more time to conflicts between the husband's mother and his wife than to the relationship between husband and wife. This is an indication of the emotional tumult that changes in women's lives have given rise to.

The young daughter-in-law often works outside the home. The paternal grandmother, who was once the unquestioned supervisor of the household, is nowadays mostly the daughter-in-law's helper. She cleans up in the home and looks after the child when Mummy has left for work. Some mothers-in-law have themselves chosen to go out and work, while others have simply become obstinate when times are out of joint and old values have lost their validity.

How are things going to be for grandmother in future? The new policy of symmetry in the responsibility of girls and boys for their parents and parents-in-law means that the maternal grandmother will be promoted to equality with the paternal grandmother. Bringing a female child into the world gives the same dividend as a male child.

When one describes the family from the point of view of the female members, there is focus on differential treatment by sex. The common picture emphasizes family solidarity and strong bonds between the generations. The old took care of the children and the middle-aged took care of the old. The generations were knitted together in mutual cares.

Today the state is investing in child care. A draft of a national pre-school programme has been sent out for public discussion. We encounter an ambivalent attitude to grandmother's competence to take care of grandchildren. Many parents still leave their children in the care of granny, but they do it as a concession to her. "Granny loves her grandchild so much that we do not have the heart to take the child from her." What they really mean is that the child develops more in the day nursery. They learn more.

The replies given by women we meet are tortuous. Of course the elderly have the right to demand respect for what they have achieved over a long life, but on the other hand she is stuck in her old ways. Grandmother lacks pedagogical qualifications, she does not understand modern children. She simply cannot keep up. In China, too, science is on the increase and is forcing out the laypeople-domination of the people's councils. The wise old women are in the course of being disqualified. The recipes have changed. The quality of education for child minders and pre-school teachers has to be raised. There is less and less need for grandmother.

Times change. It is becoming more and more difficult for grandparents to imagine what their children's future is going to look like. Something similar happened when care of the elderly took over with us, too; long-term medical care, blocks of service flats, and associations of pensioners try to help adjustment to the increased length of life which society has no use for.

In the West, where the generations already live separate and independent lives to a greater extent, elderly people occasionally start to feel cheated by history. They have been deprived of their role as the parents' parents without really understanding how it happened.

Could it not be the case that for people to have the energy to care about the future, for example to take responsibility for the size of the population in the year 2070, they need to have the feeling that they are placed in historical time? We need personal experience of being part of the continuation of the generations. What could teach us more about the bow of life than contact between children and those who had the care of the children's parents when they were children? Seen from the other end, the parents see how their children succeed them as parents.

Western reactions to the one-child policy in China are often superficial and negative. The efforts of the totalitarian state to control and limit birth-rates are regarded as unpardonable intrusions into the individual person's freedom. When I quote figures and arguments showing that there is no alternative, I sometimes meet the reply that "things have always worked out in one way or another earlier". The thrust of this type of "something will turn up this time too" is an implicit reference to natural catastrophes, famine, epidemics which wipe out undernourished children, wars which bleed the population.

There are certainly grounds today for gratitude, if the great powers refrain from increasing their living space through expansionist policies and from attempting to enlarge their borders, so as, instead of that, to appeal to the present generation for a great but shared sacrifice for the future. Certainly the Chinese concerns for collective welfare, the rational view of the pair, and the grown-ups' positive attitude to children are assets in the population and family policy which is to secure a reasonable standard of living for future generations.

Literature

Notes from China by 25 participants on the Swedish-Chinese Friendship Association's trip, 30 October – 8 December 1974.

CHING, C. C. 1982, *The One Child Family in China*: The Need for Psychological Research.

FALBO, TONI 1982, *The One-Child Family in the United States*: Research Issues and Results. *A Survey of One-child Families in Anhui Province, China*. The Population Research Office, Anhui University in *Studies in family planning*, Vol. 13, No. 6/7. New York.

DAHLSTRÖM, EDMUND 1975, *Den pågående kulturrevolutionära klasskampen i Kina*. Forskningsrapport vid Sociologiska institutionen, Göteborgs Universitet nr 34.

DAVIN, DELIA 1979, *Woman-Work, Women and the Party in Revolutionary China*. Oxford: Oxford University Press.

From Youth to Retirement 1982, *China Today* No. 4. Beijing Review, special feature
    series.
KORNHABER, A., & WOODWARD, K. L. 1981, *Grandparents — Grandchildren*. New
    York: Anchor Press/Doubleday.
Kvinnor och barn. 1982, Intervjuer med kvinnor om familj och arbete. Information i
    prognosfrågor 1982: 4. Sveriges officiella statistik.
LIU ZHENG, SONG JIAN et al. 1981, *China's Population: Problems and Prospects*.
    Beijing: New World Press.
Population and Other Problems, 1981, *China Today* 1. Beijing Review, special
    feature series.
SIDEL, RUTH, & SIDEL, VICTOR 1982, *The Health of China*. Current Conflicts in
    Medical and Human Services for One Billion People. Boston: Beacon Press.
SNOW, LOIS WHEELE 1974, *Kina på scen*. Askild & Kärnekull.
WINCH, ROBERT F. 1963, *The Modern Family*. New York: Holt, Reinhart and
    Winston.

2 Welcome to the pre-school

Eva Norén-Björn

What does it look like?

It was like this first time

Out in the courtyard in the warm morning sun a row of little Chinese children are hopping like rabbits. They are only three, they have cardboard ears on, and little baskets in their hands. They follow the teacher's instructions to hop one by one up to a flannelgraph, where they pick off into the baskets as many beetroot (of cardboard) as they want, and then hop, hop back again, up onto the bench and then into line and it is the next one's turn. The teacher smiles proudly. The children think it is fun. It is an enchanting sight for us northerners who have just left dirty, icy snow behind us to visit China.

Inside the large stone house, children's voices echo. Cool air meets us as we go in and I note a distinctive smell, something between tar and household soap. The people here smell of it, too, not deodorant or perfume but just clean — it must be the soap and disinfectants which are different. We talk about the question of smells on a later occasion, for several in the group noticed the same.

We are inside our first pre-school in China. It is exciting. Hordes of happy children rush past us on the stairs. They shout *ni hao anti*, hello aunts and uncles, wave and laugh. So we are welcome! The teachers we meet smile and greet us. They also seem to think that our visit is exciting!

Indoors

The children have classrooms. We go in to the 5-year-olds, who are sitting in rows roughly like our children in the first years at school. At the front of the room there are a flannelgraph and a blackboard, along the walls cupboards for materials. On the top shelf there are rows of pink rubber animals and dolls. There are various games and building sets and at the bottom masses of balls. The materials are worn and well used. Everything is either stacked in proper piles or in rows. Next to the classroom there is a washroom with rows of basins and taps low down, and WCs in doorless cubicles, too. To us the standard looks primitive, but it is clean and pleasant. All the children's towels hang on hooks. In another room the whole floor area is taken up by beds, which have high bars at the ends, and on each bed lie a pillow and a colourful folded blanket. The dormitory is pleasant and light, and has two windows with curtains that can be drawn. This one is for a five-year-old group, so there are 30–35 children. That is a lot of beds! It smells clean and of soap. But now it is time for the lesson . . .

During our three weeks in China we visit 15 different nursery schools, some only briefly and others for two days. We visit most for roughly half a day. We observe that rooms are arranged in the same way as in our first, with one room for tables and chairs and one with beds, often with colourful blankets which give the dormitory a personal touch, and a washroom. At times, instead of a washroom, there are washing facilities and potties out in the courtyard and a separate outdoor toilet with 30 little holes in rows.

The pre-schools are often housed in buildings used earlier for other purposes. The floor is often cold cement, but sometimes there is a wooden floor. During our visit to China in April it is warm out of doors but cold inside. The heating has been switched off and instead all the windows are open so that the warmth can come in. The houses are heated in winter with coal and briquettes. Northerners are not used to the difference between coldness inside and warmth outside and it is slightly unpleasant with the constant draught. By contrast the Chinese are dressed to feel good. All have at least four layers of clothes: long underpants and vests, blouse, jumper and jacket both indoors and outdoors.

The pre-schools are not overloaded with materials, pictures, mobiles, etc. The walls are painted white, or else white cardboard has been stretched to cover the walls. On the white background there are few pictures and other items, which therefore stand out all the more clearly. In a big dormitory there are, for instance, only three clear, colourful pictures. There is one of a child making its bed, another picture shows a child mopping the floor, and in the third a child is watering the flowers outdoors with a watering-can. The pictures thus confirm what is desirable behaviour. They also communicate joy and pride.

Three-year-olds hop like rabbits up to the flannelgraph, where they pick paper beetroot to put into their baskets. Every class of children has one pre-school teacher and one nursery helper.

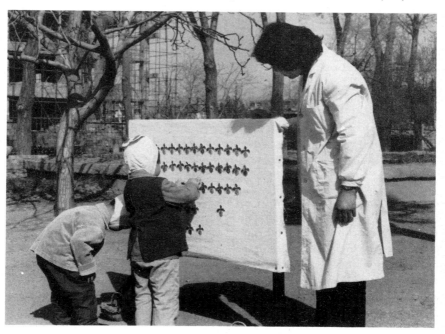

A common theme on the walls is a sparkling painting representing China's various minority peoples. They are dressed in their typical costumes, and light up and shine with joy and community spirit. Like the songs and dances, these pictures are one element in getting China's people to feel that they are *one* people.

At nearly all pre-schools there is also on the walls a picture of a beautiful tree with cherry blossom, or a big piece of squared paper with pink flowers in rows. What is this? Well, it charts an evaluation of how well the children live up to the four beautifying ideals; in other words, how well they fulfil the pre-school's demands for

- beauty of the mind
  This is usually shown in the form of a picture of the hero, Lei Feng, who represents an ideal for the children; he was the one who sacrificed himself for others without thinking of himself.
- beauty of language
- beauty of behaviour
- beauty of the environment.

(For more detail of the beautifying ideals, see the chapter on the family, p. 11.)

Sometimes it is the teacher who assesses who should receive a flower this week. But it is also common for the children themselves to decide this. At the weekly nursery in Kanton, the head's explanation for this is that "they are the ones who see each other all week. They know better than the teachers who has been good and helpful." In a nursery in Shanghai, they had cars on a racing track instead of cherry blossom. Photographs of the good children, attached to a paper car, had reached furthest towards the finishing line!

What else is there on the wall? It is usual to have some kind of weather almanack: the weather of the day is marked by a rotatable arrow, or the weather is written up day by day. The teacher's plans are also on the wall. A recurrent element in the school world is animals and plants, and in every nursery there is in one corner a shelf with each unit's own pot plants. There is also often an aquarium, a tortoise or some other animal. At the weekly nursery in Kanton they have silk worms!

Outdoors

All the places we visited had their own outdoor courtyard attached to the nursery. The courtyard is usually asphalted or has been packed down hard. Sometimes there are colourful playing facilities reminiscent of a fair:

roundabouts, slides, swings, spinning barrels, climbing frames, etc. At several places there are flowerbeds, floral bushes and trees, with fountains and beautiful flower arrangements. At the weekly nursery in Kanton there is an outdoor aquarium with fish and turtles, and a monkey has its home in a tree. The greenery mostly seems to be decorative. We did not see any outdoor cultivation by children, but at the day nursery at the Technical University in Xi'an, an untouched corner was used for picking flowers and observing insects during an outdoor lesson.

And the people

All the *grown-ups* wear at least four layers, with blue clothes outmost. Pink or turquoise edges of sweaters and blouses shine at the neck. The black hair glistens, and the white teeth sparkle when they smile and talk, talk and smile. Their brown eyes are half-closed as they tell us that you cannot have this sort of a job if you do not love children. "We are determined to give our all in this meaningful work." I note that they are far from all similar-looking. I start recognising people I know in them: the plucky one with the big guffaw; the little quiet, soft one, stubbornly strong; the maturely reflecting, purposeful one; the fat, happy, warmly generous one; and the cunning, humorously quick-witted one. We are no longer Chinese and Northerners. We speculate together about what is best for children. We give and take experience.

And the *children* are colourful. Girls are girls with bows just like those we had in the 1950s! The boys are short-cropped. The children's four layers of clothes are of all colours of the rainbow. The pullovers are sometimes home-knitted. The children often have a long flannel shirt on top, over thick wool, and they are happy, well-disciplined and rowdy all at the same time. They seem to like us, although we look funny, to put it mildly — colourless and with big noses, tall, and with strange but friendly eyes. They are happy to hug us and give us drawings, put out chairs for us, and they want us to sing and dance on and on and on! We shall never again be made so much of, I am sure. Their *sai dje*, farewell, still echoes and will always echo in my ears.

The nursery school's expansion and organization

There are roughly 150 million pre-school children in China, and only a quarter of them have a place in pre-school, or a day nursery for the youngest children. This is so despite the fact that there are 990,000 pre-schools and day nurseries. The organization, All-China Women's Federation, is work-ing on trying to establish more pre-schools of various kinds. Since the liberation of 1949, the education and upbringing of the young have had the highest priority. Six years of school for all children has been achieved. The number of pupils in compulsory schooling is just over 146 million. The care of the youngest children, up to age 3, comes under the Ministry of Health, pre-school children from 3 upwards and schoolchildren are under the Ministry of Education, while handicapped children are the responsibility of the Ministry of Home Affairs. The All-China Women's Federation and the Chinese People's National Committee for the Defence of Children are both national mass organizations whose function is to protect the legitimate interests of women and children. Their task is to seek support for and establish child care, and see to it that the activity continues in the right direction. They also have the task of maintaining good contacts with organizations and individuals in other countries in order to exchange ideas on issues to do with women and children. They also work for peace.

Child care is to a certain extent undertaken by the Education or Health Ministries themselves. There are, however, few such pre-schools, which mostly serve as teaching institutions, as models for other pre-schools. Most day nurseries in the towns are run by neighbourhood committees for children from the neighbourhood. These day nurseries are supported by the authorities as regards financing, equipment and staff education. Day nurseries are also run by factories and other institutions, schools, universities, etc. The opening hours here fit the parents' need for child-minding, for instance so that the mother can begin work again after 56 days of maternity leave. Initially the mother is allowed two half-hours off per working day to breast-feed the child. Day nurseries are not free; the parents pay a modest sum corresponding to the cost of food. Employers without their own day care service pay the neighbourhood committee to provide it. The universities which have pre-school teacher training also have pre-schools where research, experimental activity and teaching are conducted. In country districts the production brigades of the people's councils run their own day nurseries, often seasonally. In remote country districts a long way from the big towns, they may be primitive and have very little equipment and unqualified staff. At a day nursery that we visited outside Peking, only the leader was trained. She had four months' training.

Children under the age of 3 and children who have been unable to attend a pre-school are looked after by the paternal grandmother or grandfather, or else the parents take turns on different shifts. The low retirement age for women, 55 years, means that they gladly undertake a task such as looking after grandchildren. Nowadays, however, the parents often prefer to have the children at a pre-school where they get "education and learn to be together with other children".

Gymnastics for babies aims at strengthening muscles and lungs.

The pre-school fulfils a double function: to free the woman for production and, more important, to give children education and a good moral schooling which will make them responsible grown-ups who can contribute to building the country. The goals are presented in the syllabus in Appendix 1.

Grouping and the time-table

Grouping

Children in pre-schools in China are grouped by age, and the numbers of children increase with the child's age:

from 3 to 4: 20–25 children
from 4 to 5: 25–30 children
from 5 to 6: 30–35 children.

No attempt is made to give the children the chance to be with the same class-mates throughout the pre-school years: new groups are formed each year. In each group there is a teacher and a nursery helper. At several of the pre-schools we visited the nursery helper works all day in the children's group while the teacher alternates with another teacher. The teacher thus has planning and various meetings for half the day and teaching and work in the children's group for the other half of the day. In this way the teacher can always come to the lessons well-prepared.

The time-table

The day in the pre-school is carefully time-tabled and even the smallest children, aged 3, have lessons. A normal day in a day nursery begins at 7.30 a.m. and lasts until 6 p.m.

At 7.30 Mummy and/or Daddy, or some other relative, *delivers* the child. The child *is received*.

Morning tasks: the children water flowers, feed the fish or look after the pre-school's own animals. The children clean and make the place look tidy and otherwise are free to choose what they play with or look at in books. Learning to take responsibility for personal hygiene and the immediate environment is important in the pre-school. To be careful with and protect anything living, plants and animals, is part of upbringing.

Next comes *morning gymnastics outdoors*:

8.30 — 5-year-olds
8.45 — 4-year-olds
9.00 — 3-year-olds.

The teacher directs the children's physical activity outdoors. They line up in rows chalked out on the courtyard. The teacher demonstrates the movements and gives instructions. Morning gymnastics is adjusted by age so that the oldest begin first and remain active longest. These children, the 5–6-year-olds, are expected to be very disciplined. They have to move simultaneously and in straight lines. The smaller children's exercises are more like play: they are allowed to run round each other, without keeping exact distances, etc. Equipment for morning gymnastics may be dumbbells, sticks or flags.

Morning gymnastics forms one part of preventive health care. As it is cold indoors, it is important for the children to get steam up before they sit down for their lessons. In the winter it is also important to be outdoors and toughen the body against the cold. This is both part of physical training and an exercise in discipline.

In the morning, while the children are alert, there are *lessons* conducted by the teacher.

3–4-year-olds have 15 minutes
4–5-year-olds have 2 x 20–25 minutes
5–6-year-olds have 3 x 30 minutes.

The larger children have short breaks between lessons. Then they go out and play a game together, after which they go in and continue with a different subject. The time-table includes music, language, mathematics, drawing, physical training, creative play, general education (roughly what we would call social studies). The teaching is adjusted to the age of the children, and this is strongly emphasized in the syllabus because, according to the representative of the Ministry of Education whom we met, there has been a tendency to forget to adjust the manner of teaching to the children's level of development and to treat little children as though they were schoolchildren or grown-ups.

From 11.30 to 12 it is time for *lunch*, after which all the children *sleep* until 2 p.m.

At 2.30 there is *a snack*: a drink and something sweet.

In the afternoon they have various *teacher-directed activities*, such as organized play outdoors, creative play, singing, and dancing or story-reading. The oldest children have lessons in the afternoon, too.

What about the children?

Before dealing with the syllabus, with goals, subjects, lessons, etc., and other questions which come under "pedagogy" in the traditional sense, I will answer the most important question, the one which I think people want an answer to first: What about the children? How do feeding and resting, going to the toilet, dressing and undressing, care, etc. function? Is anyone concerned with the children as people? Are the childen inhibited? Don't they ever get angry? What happens if anyone cries?! In Sweden nowadays, care is an inseparable part of pedagogy, but that is not the way they look at it in China. In order to provide a description of the background, I feel it is important to report on "all these things around it", i.e. the very basis of what is called pedagogical activity first.

In order to find out more about how the children fare, I was always anxious to remain longer in a pre-school than just the time when something was being demonstrated. I wanted to know what "nothing" means in a Chinese pre-school. It was natural for our hosts to want mainly to show us their good teachers, the singing and dancing, the lessons, and children's skills. But at 4 of the 15 day nurseries we visited we also had the chance to glimpse how things were during the other daily activities.

13 April 1982. *The day nursery of the Technical University in Xi'an*
When the teacher goes off to talk to the Swedish group, I remain with the 5-year-old group whose morning lessons we attended. The nursery helper, who has a withdrawn role in the morning, now takes over the group. After playing outside, the children line up on the terrace before going in for their lunch and their afternoon sleep. There is now a clear difference in discipline. The line is more disorderly than when the teacher gives the orders. There is giggling and barging and messing around in the line. The children march in as a disorganized squad. They rush almost, and the nursery helper and I exchange a knowing glance when the little blighters chuck their balls into the ball box behind the door.

The children sit down in their rows and a well-rehearsed routine gets going. The children are almost silent and the nursery helper indicates that the children at one table at a time can go out to the washroom, relieve themselves and wash their hands. They sneak out on tiptoe, wash, and dry their hands, all on their own towels. When all from one table are ready, the nursery helper indicates that the next group can go off. The ones waiting sit quite quietly but with a mischievous glint in their eyes, whispering and giggling. They have to wait quite a long time because there are about 30 children to go out.

I try to teach them a trick when the nursery helper is not looking. I pinch my nose with my left hand and my left ear lobe with my right hand, and change hands quickly, as in the school maturity test. The children look inquisitively at me, maybe wondering how silly a white-haired one like that can really be. Then they start copying me one by one. They learn quickly! A subdued giggle erupts and spreads through the group of children. Suddenly a boy guffaws in a special way towards me. He is by the way one of those who had *few* red flags for good behaviour. With the thumbs and forefingers of both hands he climbs with parallel movements up the sides of his body like a caterpillar. When his fingers have "climbed" up to the crown of his head, he sticks up his forefingers and waves them. They look like two horns waggling! He laughs craftily and waggles the "horns" at me. So he responded by offering a small trick, and I feel honoured! I feel I am rediscovering the restrained mischievousness which I have found in some Swedish pre-schools in which clear rules are combined with warmth and making stimulating demands on the children. Although the children manage to maintain an external discipline, answer in chorus, keep their hands behind their backs, wait keeping virtually silent, they are spontaneous, eager to play, inquisitive and alert.

The procedure is that the food comes in a basket from the kitchen, and the children are allowed to go forward a few at a time to get their rice, meat and vegetables in small enamel bowls. They eat silently, with happy looks under half-closed eyelids as the only communication. Then there is another round with a flannel, lukewarm water, squeeze, wipe your mouth, and put your bowl back in the basket.

One girl, the one with the most flags, is the little assistant of the nursery helper. She deals out the flannels, goes round with the washing-up basket and supervises the washing and use of the toilet. Every now and then she goes back to the nursery helper, reports, and gets new instructions. She seems anxious that everyone should see what she is doing. She walks with her head held high and is very conscious of her position.

I wonder whether this sytem of rewards does not make children self-conscious rather than disposed to co-operate. It is, after all, an individual distinction to be given a flag or a flower, even if we are told many times that many different traits of character are taken into consideration.

While the children are going to bed and the nursery helper is pulling the curtains and the children are helping each other to pull off their long underpants and pullovers, the little female monitor is still walking round looking important and supervising. The other children's friendly giggling and helpful tugging-fights contrast with her more ingratiating attitude.

I can sense that there is perhaps a price to pay for being the favourite of the teachers, the price of not being an ordinary "giggler" among the others.

In the dormitory there is a shelf with toys, painting books and story-books, but they are not used during the afternoon sleep. A piece of cloth hangs in front of the shelf. There is no reading, the level of noise is reduced, you pull your thick, nice, colourful blanket over you and sleep soundly for two hours.

On the 15th of April, the whole group was at Chengdu number 3 for performances, among other things. I ask to be allowed to return and see how it is on an ordinary day. I can choose for myself which section to visit, and I ask to be with the 3–4-year-olds. A teacher goes and asks, and I am told that it is all right. Before the morning gymnastics there is time for a cup of tea in the staff-room. At 8.45 the older children begin their gymnastics and at 9.00 the little ones.

16 April 1982. *Chengdu number 3*

8.45. The older children (6 years) run along the white lines of a large square chalked onto the courtyard, round and round, at the command of a teacher. Then they line up on their marks and put "one foot forward" and "face to the right", "left", "right again", "march round", "change direction". The teacher calls "1, 2, 3" and the children answer "1, 2, 3, 4, 5". They now run around the square in the damp, misty morning air at a fast pace. You feel as though you have to move on this chill and damp spring morning!

A teacher arrives now with the smallest in a line after her. She is a trained pre-school teacher, but only 18 years old. Smiling, she strikes a tambourine and the children walk in step after her to their part of the courtyard. They have a smaller square with white lines and circles. They go round in time with the beats of the tambourine. The teacher now says that all the children are small rabbits who are to hop around, and at a given signal all of them are to hop in towards the middle. The children are familiar with the game and they are keen straight away. They happily hop in towards the middle into a higgledy-piggledy heap! And oops, here comes a dangerous eagle (the teacher) and frightens away all the little rabbits, who quickly save themselves out on the line again. Morning gymnastics for the tiny ones is much more fun-and-games than for the older children.

The teacher now goes off with her little troop and I wonder where. It is to the toilet, which turns out to be an outdoor one for 30 little children simultaneously. It is a priceless sight to see all the little ones in a row: the girls crouching down inside and the boys splashing against the wall outside!

On the way back to the section everyone is "flying" like aeroplanes. The teacher and the children are making droning noises and bold loops. From time to time the "teacher-plane" stops with a smile and checks that all the little planes are keeping up, and then they wing on. "Brum brum." Safely arrived, the teacher sits down at the organ and the music lesson starts (see p. 83).

After a lesson of about a quarter of an hour, all the children put back their chairs and the teacher pulls aside the curtain concealing 25 little slots with enamel mugs for all the children. The teacher now serves boiled water and the children sit down at tables and drink the water. The teacher informs me that in the morning they looked to see what the weather was like and put the weather arrow on "overcast". Then they watered the flowers and saw to the fish and the tortoise.

After drinking the water the children put the mugs back in their slots and the teacher, the nursery helper and the children go out into the court-yard which is now empty (the place has 320 children). They play mother duck and baby ducklings and the eagle, roughly as we play "come here my little chicks" or "hawk and pigeon" but the ducklings save themselves by holding onto each other in a line following the mother who defends her "tail". The ones who are caught are passed to the nursery helper and have to sit in the climbing frame. The children appear to think that this is an exciting and enjoyable game. One boy falls over and hurts himself. The teacher looks after him, hugs him and dries his runny nose and tears. The game stops for a moment while he quietens down. As it turns out that he has a nosebleed, the teacher goes in with him so that he can lie down.

10.30. Now there are more children in the courtyard. The teacher has small, red, flat plastic rings of which she throws masses out into the court-yard. The children run and fetch them. They willingly bring the rings back to the teacher, who laughs and throws them out again! A fat boy pretends that the ring is a pistol and shoots towards me. Two girls (6 years) hop around and spontaneously practise a dance and sing to it. The little boy who fell and had a nosebleed is now walking and holding the nursery helper's hand. Two gardeners (male) are planting bushes next to the playground but no-one looks at them.

Some children are up on the platform of the climbing frame and playing intensely. I ask the teachers what the children are doing but the teachers become abashed. They are playing, they reply. When I insist on knowing what the children are playing, they little by little bring themselves to ask the children what they are playing. There is great amusement among the grown-ups when the children say that they are cooking. They have gathered the fruits of a large tree as make-believe food. I get the impression that the grown-ups are not used to observing the children's spontaneous, make-believe games. They seem surprised that the children of their own accord could play what we call creative play. The two singing and dancing girls are walking arm in arm. The children are romping and running around. The teacher collects the rings and calls the children and they go in. The time is now 10.45.

10.45–11.30. Waiting for food. All the children who have been to the toilet sit down at tables. There is a cheerful and lively atmosphere. The fat boy continues to "shoot" at me. The children relieve themselves in the courtyard at the back, the girls sit on pots, and the boys stand and use a bucket. A little girl claps her hands and shouts out, "Do like me!" She "makes ears" and all copy. "Look here all of you, do like me." The clapping thunders and the girl shapes a cock's-comb. The teacher and the children copy. The children do what they want to some extent. Sometimes they get it right, sometimes they do something quite different. (Note: they are 3 years old.) The teacher asks for someone to come forward and tell a story. A boy comes out and tells a story about a sheep. The classroom is lively — as in a Swedish pre-school, I think — but the children fall silent when it becomes exciting (although there is a lot of life out in the courtyard): "the wolf came and took you", "swallow you". The closest ones listen intently. They recognize the story, for the teacher has taught them it. They are too small to think up one themselves, according to the interpreter.

After the story, all can take a little book to look at while they wait. They chat a lot to each other. The noise level is high. They have different books and exchange books with each other with a lot of talk. I note that there is a picture of Lei Feng on the wall. The teacher explains that "all the children know Lei Feng, but they are not told everything about him when they are as small as this. When they are older they will be told more. Throughout their entire time at school Lei Feng is talked about." The teacher now tells the children to go out and wash their hands. They go out to the little courtyard at the back in the warm heat haze. Along a long pipe at an appropriate height there are small holes. When the nursery helper turns on the water, 25 small jets of water are formed for the children to wash in. A large cake of soap hanging from a piece of string is guided by the teacher from one pair of hands to the next. Little fingers are soaped and rinsed, some quickly, some carefully and more as if in play. Then the hands are stretched out towards one of the 25 little towels on the towel frame which stands there and flaps in wind and sun.

In the sections for the smallest, the children are often confined to their cots, because the floor is cold. Or else they sit on potties, sometimes as here around a potty table.

When the children are sitting at their tables again, the teacher exhorts them to bend forward over the table and rest. It is almost peaceful for a moment, but then the fat boy begins elbowing and wrestling with his neighbour and it gets a bit rowdy in several places. After the rest, the children sit sideways to the table looking at the teacher. The teacher tells a story about a little rabbit. She and the children sing a song about a little rabbit. The teacher narrates with a light, involved and soft voice:

"Mummy sheep had to leave her little baby lamb. She said: 'You must take care of yourself. Lots of things happen. Don't open the door for anyone,' said Mummy. After Mummy had gone there was a knock on the door. It is the wolf, but the lamb does not open the door. The big wolf says: 'I am your Mummy.' But it isn't Mummy's voice!"

The children are now absolutely silent and scarcely dare breathe.

"The wolf says: 'Be a nice lamb and open up. I am your Mummy. I need some water.' 'No,' says the lamb. 'You are not my Mummy. I cannot open the door.' "

The children sit completely quiet. It is so exciting.

"Mummy comes and the lamb hears that it is her. *Then* the lamb opens up so that Mummy can come in."

The children, who must have heard this story many times, heave a sigh of relief. They want to hear another story. They tell each other that they have seen the story on film.

The teacher fetches a doll. "Who can tell a story about this?" Everyone wants to. A girl goes forward and holds the doll and recites a poem about the Mummy and the baby. "We have seen it performed many times." After that it is the fat boy who goes forward and holds the doll. Obviously he does not really know the poem and does not recite it awfully well. The audience recites more than he does.

11.30. The food arrives. The children get rice, bean paste and vegetables in little enamel bowls. They eat with a spoon relatively quietly. They watch amusedly while I, bent double, try to eat the same food with chopsticks. The teachers do not eat with the children. After eating, the children pile up their enamel bowls in the basket which goes out to the kitchen. Then they take a lukewarm, squeezed-out flannel and wipe their mouths and hands thoroughly. After which they go into the dormitory, take off their shoes and pullovers, and crawl down under their thick, colourful blankets. The windows are wide open, with a constant draught across the room so as to entice, if possible, the warmth of the spring air into the cool bedroom. So it is cosy to creep deep under the blanket.

2 p.m. We return when the children wake up. Some are lying silently, awake and just looking. Some crawl out and begin to fold their blankets. First twice lengthwise, then you fold up one of the short ends and then the other. It turns into an elegant parcel which is placed at the foot of the bed. It is all very relaxed. One boy goes out and uses the toilet first. One girl is helped with combing her tangled hair. One of them has a shoe missing. One cannot reach the zip at the back of a pullover. The teachers go round quietly helping first one, then another.

We talk about the business of brushing teeth. "They do that at home in the morning and evening," says the teacher. I am reminded of Swedish day nurseries' rows of toothbrushes, and the teachers confirm that the children here do in fact have a lot of fillings in their teeth. "Only five out of the 25 have perfect teeth. They are all checked once each term. They have a lot of holes and like sugar very much." The teacher laughs. For the snack, the children are given hot milk and a hard, sweet cake. My Swedish health ego is astounded.

On one occasion I see aggressive children. We are visiting a small day nursery where the children seem to be closely controlled: silent at meals and strict supervision both when drawing and when playing outside.

At first the children want to be with us and find out more about these exciting aunties. But as we wanted to see ordinary activity, they are fetched for ring games. When they go in for lunch, and are standing in a line, some boys at the end of the line grab some plastic skittles and throw them at us. We are baffled, and the teachers intervene. We ask what is done about people behaving like that. The teacher fixes a boy's arms to his sides and says: "They have to stand quietly for a time. This usually helps."

Preventing the children from moving for a time is therefore enough. Or, as our Swedish child psychology researcher, Stina Sandels, says, "Preventing children from moving is a way of tiring them out."

Why am I reporting all this? Well, I just want to say that children in day nurseries in China are rowdy, they giggle, talk, get hurt and cry, like food, clear up the table and wipe their mouths, go to the toilet and wash their hands and sleep well. They even get angry. Just like any other children! But otherwise they "sing and dance, walk in lines and are silent, with their hands behind their backs" as in one of the common images of China's pre-school children.

The adult role — adults are adults

The adults are always with the children

A clear difference between the Swedish and the Chinese pre-school is that the grown-ups in China's pre-school are with the children and guide them considerably more than Swedish pre-school staff do. This is clearest in relation to play outdoors. There are ring games with singing and dancing, guessing games, role play in concrete settings, gymnastics, ball games, the high jump, and climbing on climbing frames, and all these activities are under the direct guidance of the teachers. The teacher may, for instance, take out the high jump bar, and place it next to a slide and a climbing frame. Then the children stand in line and hop and slide in turns in a given sequence. When the children are playing buses, built of bricks and chairs, the game is guided by teachers who participate the whole time. What we call "free" play scarcely ever occurs. On the other hand, the children may of course play as they want during "creative play". But the teachers are around and circulate, encouraging the children and giving them some materials and suggestions.

When the children at a day nursery for children under the age of 3 were out playing, I was amazed that the white-clad nursery helpers were very frantically trying to activate the children the whole time. When some little ones totter up to the climbing frame, a teacher is there at once, cheering them on with "Yes, climb up then! Up, up, up! You can do better than that! Yes!", "Phew, phew, phew, phew," and applauding when the little boy with his trouser rump peeping out climbs up. At the slide, similarly, the children are cheered on so that they dare to go down. The nursery helper gives the child a ball to throw down first, to arouse the child's interest in sliding down. She claps her hands and cheers on the children one by one. The children are quiet and do not resist being placed on swings and roundabouts. Two parallel ropes have been stretched out between two trees. Two little 1–1½-year-old children are placed between the ropes. The teacher makes one little girl grip the ropes and leads her hands forward so that she understands that she is to walk and hold on. The other girl, who knows what to do, goes in front, and when the children get up speed they laugh and the teachers cheer them. When they get to the tree, the teacher turns them both around, and then they can go back in the other direction.

Grown-ups direct in the section for the smallest children

The youngest children come under the Ministry of Health, and what we are dealing with here is not primarily pedagogy but care. Our hosts saw this as a problem and consider that having staff with teacher training, even for the smallest children, is an important goal.

We visit various sections for the smallest children, and note that the children are manifestly passive. They are often confined to their cots because the floor is cold. There are scarcely any toys apart from balls, or paper flowers hanging from the ceiling, and there are many children and few staff. The children are quiet. When you are used to seeing Swedish toddlers climbing, you feel it looks a bit odd that the children stand so still that they even have to be cheered on to climb in a climbing frame, go down the slide or kick a ball.

Our experience of toddlers in China is naturally extremely limited. Even so, here follow a few examples of activities for the smallest children of all in the section for the under-threes.

14 April 1982. *Day nursery at a textiles factory in Xi'an*
The youngest: 56 days to one year.
The children are lying in their cots, drowsy after their "morning gymnastics". A tiny tot of 2–3 months lies there like a little parcel in clothes and blankets, blinking at us. The mouth extends into a little smile when we look down into the cot. There are nine light blue cots, and from the ceiling above them hang paper flowers and garlands. The children come in four shifts here, depending on their mothers' hours of work, but never more than ten children at a time. Three nursery helpers in white coats take care of them, and the mothers come here to breastfeed the children.

There are also wreaths of paper flowers above the table used for physical training, gymnastics for infants. We ask to watch this. A little girl of 4–6 months with a lot of clothes on, like a little bundle, is put on the table. She looks first at the helper, then inquisitively at us all standing around her, but she does not look frightened. The helper grasps her bundled-up clothes and vigorously stretches her arms straight out above her head and then straight down, parallel with her body. Then up, down, up, down, up, down. The girl lies there completely relaxed, allowing herself to be handled. Then the helper stretches the girl's arms out to the sides and then crosses them over her chest, out and in again, out and in, out and in. Then one arm up and one down, alternately with diagonal movements. The helper tightens and stretches the child's arms, counting at the same time: one, two, three, four. Then she says that after the arms, you follow the same procedure with the legs, following a fixed plan. She was not going to show it now as this would make the girl too tired. She has in fact already had her morning gymnastics! The gymnastics aims at strengthening muscles and lungs and improving physique and health.

Quiet!
Waiting!

All the three-year-olds are sitting in a semi-circle round a table. They have double bibs on, one of cloth and one of plastic, as they are soon going to eat.

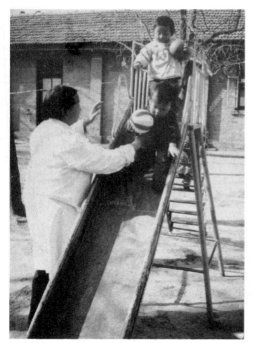

At the day nursery for the youngest children, the nursery helpers try to activate the children the whole time. At the slide they cheer the children on so that they dare to go down.

The one-year-olds are to go forward one at a time and creep through the ring. Then they test the strength of their arms by hanging from a bamboo pole which is lifted a little bit from the floor.

The one-year-olds.

In the next section the children have learned to walk. They are spread out over the whole room when we come in. There are many of us, we are tall and taking photographs, so our presence makes the children clearly subdued. The helpers make the children stand along one wall and bring out a ring (roughly 50 centimetres in diameter) threaded round with dyed raffia. The ring is secured between two chairs. The children come out one at a time and go through the ring. They bend down and step through the ring. A teacher pings with a bell each time a child gets through. The one who has just gone through goes to the back of the queue again. The children seem to think that this apparently simple game is fun. They bunch themselves up and come through with a smile of relief. Some of those waiting watch tensely how the one whose turn it is is coping, while others are shoving and squabbling a bit in the queue. One girl is standing to one side the whole time and does not want to take part. She is new. Nobody pays any attention to her, she is allowed to stand and watch.

After a while the ring is put away and the helpers take out instead a bamboo pole. Two helpers hold the pole between them and the children then come forward one at a time and hang by their arms! The children laugh and look forward to it excitedly. The exercises are one means of strengthening the breathing and lungs of the children. When they have all had a turn at hanging, the bamboo pole is put away. Next, a helper deals out little colourful baskets to all the children, and then she brings out a large basket full of walnuts! She pours these out in the middle of the floor and the children pick as many as they can and put them in their small baskets. Now the children become lively. They forget about all the onlookers and pick away to their heart's content. All the little trouser rumps peep out when the children crouch and bend for the walnuts.

The two-year-olds.

In the third section all the children are sitting around a table in a semi-circle when we come in. A flannelgraph has been put out, with carrots and beetroot made of cloth on it, and a little blue bench. One after the other, the children are given a cardboard rabbit head to put on their heads and a little basket. The helper demonstrates that the "rabbit" is to hop with its feet together up to the bench, then walk on the bench and hop with feet together the final stretch up to the flannelgraph. There the little rabbit can pick as much as it wants into its basket, and hop, walk and hop back in the same way.

The three-year-olds.

In the fourth section that we visit, the children are standing in a

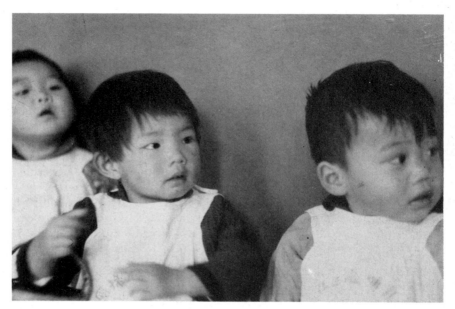

When they have overcome their first fright at the strange visitors, the two-year-olds watch us inquisitively and with interest.

semi-circle when we arrive. they have double bibs on, one of cloth and one of plastic, as they are soon going to eat. A helper sits down at the organ and plays a tune which the children recognize. They line up behind each other and hold on to the one in front, and then they sing for us: at night we sleep, but in the morning we get up and go to the day nursery. In the morning you wash your face and hands, brush your teeth, and so on. The children make the movements for the text. When they sing that they are sleeping, they rest their cheeks against their hands. One boy does this so vividly that we think he is really asleep! Then a stretching movement when you wake up, and walking on the spot, to the day nursery! With flat hands and rotating movements near your cheeks you wash your face. Then the children stretch their arms out, and the hands are symbolically "rubbed", arms held out in parallel. A finger toothbrush is pulled sideways in front of the teeth.

We can see clearly the extent to which it is the grown-ups who direct the activities. It is as though the children from the start are made to expect that everything "good" comes from the adults: being able to move, to try to hang, or to creep through a ring, and so on, all the kinds of experience that a small child in a Swedish home or in a Swedish day nursery comes by in the natural way of things, with their "own motor" — to run around, to find something to pick up and collect, to step over and creep under, to hang and cling to. Children are given the opportunity to do these things of their own free will. But here the opportunities, the stimulation are provided by the adult to the child. Could this be the reason for the discipline and the authority grown-ups have to such a dominant extent later, we wonder? Another thing which astonishes us is how these children, who have been kept so quiet in beds, on potties, bundled up in blankets and clothes, can develop such a high degree of motor skill and grace in the later pre-school years.

Distinct adult roles

There is a difference between being a teacher and being a nursery helper in Chinese pre-schools. We noticed this clear division at many day nurseries we visited. The nursery helper is a background figure and intervenes when there is a need. When a boy suddenly started having a nosebleed during a lesson which we observed, the helper discreetly took him out while the lesson continued as though nothing had happened.

Teachers and the head of the weekly nursery in Chengdu, Xi Ma Peng, explain the professional roles as follows. The nursery helper and teacher form a team. The helper has to see to it that everyday things function, that there are clean clothes, that shoes and socks are where they belong. She must know the timetable, help in keeping order, and help the teacher with the children in a variety of ways.

Could one say that the nursery helper's role is more like that of a Mummy? No! Both take care of the child and *have* to love the child!

In Sweden we try to work in working teams in which everyone has equal value. The idea of a working team is founded on a principle of equality which is good enough, but at times it leads to everyone in the team reducing themselves to the lowest common denominator. The pre-school teacher does not dare to put into application the knowledge she has acquired during her training, so as not to offend the nursery helper. According to studies of working teams conducted by Siw Boalt-Boethius, of the Department of Psychology at the University of Stockholm, it is difficult to do justice to the resources of each and every one when the roles become blurred. Nor is it possible to be either a complete beginner or to be recognized as experienced. It is naughty to depart from the average. The social pressure to be like everyone else is considerable. It is particularly older people and men who suffer from great stress in this barbarity of convergence, she claims. It is thus precisely those categories of people whom there is a wish to bring into the child's world on whom it is hardest.

How to escape this dilemma is an open question. A first step would naturally be to dare to admit that we are different and to regard this as an asset. Through allowing oneself and others to show off strengths by being good at something in a children's group it is possible to tap considerable resources.

To return to the traditional roles of nursery helper and pre-school teacher is something which is wanted by nobody who experienced earlier times, when we had clear demarcation lines between occupational categories. Then the nursery helper was regarded as having little value. The policy of the Swedish National Board of Health and Welfare is therefore, according to its development programme, to move over to a single occupational category in the pre-school in future, namely pre-school teachers. A nursery helper training is in this way the first part of the road toward a complete training.

But there might be another possible approach. I would like to claim that knowledge of how best to take care of children is not always so widespread or deeply anchored in the ranks of our young pre-school staff. Knowledge of the importance of regular fresh air, not least so as to prevent colds, is not always reflected in practice. The fact that it is good for little children to have their afternoon sleep out of doors 12 months of the year influences the routines of the pre-school only in exceptional cases. "It'll be too much trouble." Perhaps most staff know that children need to adopt habits of good hygiene, sleep at fixed times, and eat proper food, but there is still slovenliness about these basic needs. There are children who never use the toilets at the day nursery (never dare to!) or children who run around semi-clothed and with runny noses.

Nursery helpers who have followed courses specializing in nutrition, preventive health care, hygiene, child security, etc, would be able to have equivalent status, be really equal to pre-school teachers, but retain a distinctive care profile. In Sweden care and pedagogy form an entity in the pre-school, but this should not exclude clear occupational roles and knowledgeable occupational practitioners. In jobs with children, just as with all other jobs, there must be an important place for professional improvement, for recognizing the challenge that one can always become more competent and is never completely qualified!

Pre-schools, bearers of the future

"The country needs the pre-school." This was the way the head of the Xi Ma Peng weekly nursery in Chengdu described the role of the pre-school in society. Our interpreter once exclaimed, when we were chatting about the fact that China is rich in mineral resources and perhaps oil, "Yes, for this we must succeed in bringing up a responsible generation which can administer well our culture and our resources. That is why the question of a good pre-school is so important for us. We cannot have a generation which thinks only of itself. They must be brought up to think of the good of the country."

And at a banquet we are told how astonished the Chinese group which visited Sweden was at how independent Swedish children are. One of our hosts exclaims: "We want to teach our children obedience and discipline — not independence." And the Chengdu head: "We want honest children who behave well and are well-disciplined."

Ever since the liberation of 1949, education has been the highest of all priorities in China. Particularly since the implementation of the one-child family reform, the pre-school has been important. In part they want to make the most of the children they have. In part it is appreciated that it is important for only children to rub shoulders with other children so that they do not become spoiled or self-centred.

A syllabus

The syllabus for China's pre-school is included as Appendix 1. So far as I can judge, this syllabus has succeded in penetrating the whole of China. We saw the syllabus reflected in various ways, for instance through the same theme being worked on in different places, through our being frequently told the same thing in interviews and discussions. "We follow the syllabus." We saw morning gymnastics being carried out exactly "according to the rules" in several places. We were given similar answers to questions about creative play and drawing teaching in different places, which indicates that the same instructions are followed. We saw equipment for games and special arrangements suited to specific tasks in the syllabus; for instance, a string of balls hanging, just right for jumping up to and patting, or fixed heights for jumping down from. At one pre-school where I asked what kind of clay they have, the principal replied, "We have the clay which we are supposed to have according to the syllabus. The authorities provide us with everything needed to implement the syllabus."

There are naturally both advantages and disadvantages in having such strict syllabus control in the pre-school. The advantage is that there is at least a kind of minimum standard for the pre-school throughout the country. The syllabus does state in what way three-year-olds are to be treated differently from six-year-olds, and makes suggestions for what tasks are appropriate for pre-school children. The disadvantage is, of course, as always, that rigidity is the next-door neighbour to unimaginativeness. There is always a risk of the

When the water is turned on, 25 small jets of water are formed for the children to wash in. A large cake of soap hanging from a piece of string is guided by the nursery helper from one pair of hands to the next.

syllabus not being properly carried out, especially by untrained staff. In this case pure school-like conduct can take over — the precious playing time of childhood is used up by discipline and drill, by being silent at meals and just colouring with the crayon which the teacher has allowed one to take. Then the pre-school becomes a torment for the children and a squandering of society's resources. But the syllabus shows a deep knowledge about children and understanding that the way children learn is by playing:

> "The physical and psychological development of the child is characterized by the child's predilection for play, thus play constitutes the basic activity of its life. It is easiest for the child to receive teaching in the form of play, therefore play has an extremely important place in the entire pedagogical work of the pre-school."

Goals and ways of working

At Peking's number 5 day nursery, we have the chance to ask the pre-school teachers questions.

We have now been at two different pre-schools and seen that a lot of work is done with spring as a theme. They sing about the spring, draw the spring. There are flowers and birds in their games and dances. In the Swedish pre-school we also work in this way by taking up a theme in several different ways so that the children work with the theme both with their bodies and their minds in drawings and songs and so on. Is this a conscious way of working in your pre-school and what other themes do you have?

Yes, the aim is to give the children knowledge about nature. This means that we try to teach them how you can observe changes in nature, so that they can obtain a simple fundamental knowledge about nature. The aim of the teaching, like the content, follows the syllabus. The children learn step by step according to a plan. The four seasons form part of this programme. Now that it is spring we are considering some phenomena which are topical for the season, e.g. how a plant grows, insects coming to life. In the summer we go into the characteristics of that season, what changes there are and the role people have in them. We might have water as a theme, rain, steam, and ice in the winter.

In Sweden we want to teach children that things are not static. You can make things, for instance produce a cup, and there is a process which the children can follow. Another such process is cooking. Is it usual for the children to help with the cooking here?

Children can grow beans or tomatoes, and then take what they have grown to the cook and watch while she prepares the food. Unfortunately the kitchen equipment does not permit the children to do this themselves, but they can get the vegetables clean and ready and then the cook makes a vegetable casserole which tastes very good — especially with things you have grown yourself!

We wonder whether they discuss ecological relations, and that people should take care of things, that people and nature belong together, that you must not ruin the air, etc.

We also teach the children to understand what nature means for them and for the human race. Without air we cannot live. We teach them that we must take care of plants, trees, that we must not ruin things. They understand how important fresh air is for little children. But we do not talk about environmental pollution with the children.

We visited the number 3 day nursery in Chengdu and had an interesting talk with the head and teachers, and a fine performance by the children. The day nursery has a staff of 60, and 320 children. The head informs us that all the staff are qualified, and that day nursery is open for 11–12 hours a day, Monday to Saturday. The syllabus is followed and the children's development, psychological and physical, is taken into consideration. The nutritive value of the food is checked, and the children's state of health is regularly monitored. There is a careful programme of physical training, even in winter, in order to prevent colds. It is very hot in this part of the country in the summer, so that children have to be protected against the heat then. The children are weighed, blood tests taken, and so on. Because of this the children are in a good state of health.

They want to teach the children to manage everything to do with daily life, eating, sleeping, getting dressed and undressed, taking care of their own hygiene, etc., and in addition give them the opportunity to play and have lessons. They want to stimulate the children to explore their environment, develop their thinking, and give them practice in expressing themselves with the help of language. There is a constant striving after improved methods. They want to develop the children's intellect through games, and in this way lay a basis for school. They are taught about the five types of charity, loving your country, people, party, science and work. The goal is that children should be open and friendly. They co-operate with the parents and try to do their work as well as possible.

All the teachers here love the children greatly and are completely devoted to giving their all in this meaningful work!

The head radiates purposeful persistence and warmth. We do not doubt that she means every word she says.

The children have morning gymnastics outdoors. They line up in rows chalked out on the courtyard. The gymnastics is adjusted by age so that the smaller children have exercises which are more like play.

In our typically Swedish way, we then ask about the children's conflicts and aggression, and how this is tackled.

With the younger children the teachers intervene and help the children to resolve their conflicts. But the older children can try to resolve conflicts themselves. The teacher, naturally, is alert and helps if needed.

The head recognizes this Western question about conflicts and is a trifle impatient with us. She exclaims that there are very few conflicts between the children, and there is no reason why there should be that many. The children have good models to follow. They are given a lot of support and praise for being nice to each other. In this kind of atmosphere there is no need for aggressiveness and conflicts to occur. The children want to do their best. They love their class-mates and want to do their best.

The head says further that the teachers compete with each other to get the best results out of their work. The teachers have set up a research group which develops methods. They serve as good models for each other.

We wonder whether they can really collaborate if they compete?

They all share the goal of developing their work, so no envy need arise. They study together and develop their plan of work jointly.

How planning can be done

We are curious to know how planning is done in China's pre-school, and at a day nursery in Shanghai there is an opportunity for us to ask about this. It is the pre-school teacher who has been chosen by her colleagues as a model teacher who informs us.

We follow the syllabus and goals stated there. We have a rough plan for the whole term's activities, and then we meet every Friday to plan the coming week. There we make suggestions to each other. It is a kind of further training. You learn the whole time. At this pre-school all the teachers are trained. There is also an association of teachers. We meet at least once a week and talk about our work. Your can never be over-qualified when working with children . . . . The weekly plan is shown to the head. If she approves it, we follow the plan.

We ask to see a specimen plan. It turns out that at this pre-school there are two sets of plans, one for the term and one for detailed plans (general and lesson-by-lesson). Planning the term involves, among other things, fixing which lessons there will be on which days of the week. This is what the

term plan looks like for the lessons from Monday to Saturday for the oldest
children, the six-year-olds:

Monday	*Tuesday*	*Wednesday*
physical training	physical training	physical training
general education	language	mathematics
music	drawing	physical training
physical training	creative play	drawing
creative play	music	

Thursday	*Friday*	*Saturday*
physical training	physical training	physical training
general education	mathematics	language
paper-folding	music	drawing
rest, doctor's consultation	creative play	outdoor games, sport
music	intellectual play	creative play

This time-table is thus followed every week, while it is at the Friday
planning session that decisions are taken on what to cover in the following
language, drawing or mathematics lessons. The physical training varies
according to the day of the week.

We are shown examples of the goals and plans for some lessons (see
page 81). A language lesson aims at giving the children practice in being able
to tell stories from pictures and in doing so with the help of correct, precise
language. The aim is partly to expand the children's vocabulary, partly to get
them to express themselves more exactly. At the same time the idea is to
impart moral ways of thinking to the children, being responsible for your
actions and helping the aged. They also want to teach children that work is
lighter with mutual help.

Sometimes the goal may be to teach the children a song or a poem. Then
they use repetition which is varied so that the children finally know the text.
But a language lesson may also aim at stimulating the children's creative
thinking. Then the teacher would present a problem which can be solved in
different ways, or show a set of pictures, the sequence of which can be
altered so as to change the meaning or provide for different stories.

There are orders from the Ministry of Education to pay special attention to weaker children. It is difficult to give all 36 children in a group a
chance to speak. At times, therefore, some children are taken individually,
so that after the lesson they can sit with the teacher and go over the stories. It
may be easier for them then.

They can have up to four lessons on one theme. To give all the children
a chance, and not just the cleverest ones, is a big problem for the teachers,
who at this day nursery consider it very important to be aware of this.

For 5 April it says in the teacher's planning book for creative play: playing shops. She tells us that they have home-made money, with the help of which the children can learn how to count. But the children also develop morally, physically and intellectually in their games, she explains. For instance, they practise having a good attitude to the "customers", being polite and obliging. they practise criticism and usually have pencil and paper up on the wall in the shop, just as in real ones, where customers can write down any complaints they may have about either goods or their treatment in the shop.

For 7 April it says "drawing" on the time-table. On that day they are going to make something and then play with it. The task involves being persistent and actually finishing it. On this particular day they are going to make a dog and a doll. Then the children are to make up small stories about the figures and tell them to each other. The teacher also shows us a little magic paper box which is folded, cut and drawn on. You can then take it home and entertain the family with it!

We are impressed by how thoroughly they think through their work, and we ask how they find the time. It transpires that the teachers here, too, as at Chengdu number 3, work with the children for half a day, and plan for the rest of the day, when they are replaced by the class's other teachers.

Lessons in China, assembly in Sweden

We are going to follow some lessons and see what takes place:

6 April 1982, *Peking's experimental day nursery. A language lesson on the spring*

The children are five years old. About 30 children are sitting at school desks in rows. They are completely absorbed in their teacher and the picture she is showing at the front of the class. When they have greeted us they all look to the front again. The teacher is showing a drawing of a landscape in spring. She points to the blossoming trees and shows that the ice has melted in the brook. She shows and tells them that the peasant is ploughing the field and that the swallows have come. When the teacher points to the picture, the children chant in chorus the sentence the teacher has said about the picture, for instance, "in the spring the trees blossom". The children respond very loudly and at exactly the same time and all correctly. The teacher points out that you should speak softly when speaking about the arrival of the swallows but more strongly when describing the tractor. She points again, and the children respond in unison.

The aim of this lesson is to improve the children's pronunciation and teach them the right rhythm and right intonation. In Chinese a word can have up to four meanings, depending on where the stress is put and whether the word melody goes up or down (see note page 251). In addition the aim is to talk about the characteristics of the season. This theme recurs later in a drawing lesson (see page 147).

6 April 1982, *Peking's experimental day nursery. Reading lesson*
The children are four years old. They are learning the symbols for paternal grandfather and grandmother, younger sister, child, elder brother, mother, father. The teacher puts up two of the characters on the flannelgraph and one child at a time goes forward and chooses the pictures which fit with them and puts them beneath the right character. The children are deeply involved and are eager to have a turn. The teacher mixes the characters and makes the task more difficult. She puts up four characters, and the children cope splendidly. The teacher encourages the children to call out "right" when it is correct. All the children want to go forward and show that they can do it.

Now the teacher removes the pictures and characters, and takes out a character for the colour green. Alongside the character she puts a piece of green paper. The children are now to say a sentence including the word green. One child puts up a hand and says something, but the teacher does not react and instead asks another child to. In other words she did not point out that the first child's response was wrong. The second child, however, is praised for her sentence. The children say long, complicated sentences about the spring greenery, and differentiate what they say by using light green and dark green. They are very keen to be allowed to respond. They are serious and concentrate enthusiastically. One boy makes a mistake and points to a shirt which in fact is red and says that it is green. The teacher explains the difference. She then goes into the distinction between dark green and light green.

When the lesson is over and we are on our way out, the children let us go first. They are polite and say "bye bye" in English.

6 April 1982, *Peking's experimental day nursery. A dancing lesson in the Big Hall*
We assemble in the big hall with the five-year-olds who have just chanted a chorus while looking at the spring picture, and a plump, cheerful teacher (with 30 years' experience), with another teacher at the piano. 28 children sit on their chairs in a huge circle in the big hall. The sun shines in through the small-paned windows. The whole of the long wall has the form

The teacher demonstrates all the movements and the children imitate.

The teachers guide and participate in all outdoor activities themselves, too.

of a huge glass verandah with white lace curtains. The wooden floor is large and worn, and the whole hall is seething with zest for life. The teacher starts playing and the children first go round the chairs in time. Then they dance to the piano music. They clap, swing their arms, raise their arms and bend their hands beautifully above their heads. The large, plump teacher dances along with the children with elegance and joy.

The interpreter reports that at her son's day nursery they don't dance and sing nearly as much. "All parents want to have their children here," she says. "this pre-school is famous and a model for others."

They imitate a trumpet in various keys. The children are very confident in imitating the notes: ta ti ta ti taa! The children sit down on their chairs and the teacher tells of the arrival of spring and the children repeat, "The spring has come. The trees are green." Then they sing the song about the spring.

The interpreter reports that many songs have their origins in a nation-wide competition for good pre-school songs. As a child she sang quite different songs about the spring.

The next song: "The snow is melting on the roof and the drops are falling like rain-drops." "Pippi pa di da." All the children applaud. The teacher says that we are going to sing it again now with better pronunciation. Then two girls are brought out and sing the song for the others.

Now the boys stand up and sing, "A boy who was like Lei Feng, he always helped others. He did the cleaning. He tidied up things for others . . . Clean up . . . Help mother." The boys stand up to sing but several of the girls cannot resist singing with them.

Then the teacher starts playing a familiar tune and all the children stand up and sing loudly and proudly with appropriate movements: "We love our mother country."

Then it is time for a little rest. The children sit down and the teacher plays softly. The children guess what kind of music it is, what the music should represent. "A large elephant", "A little girl", they guess. "Listen to the music again." Then the teacher says that it is about the little ducklings who have to get to their Mummy but watch out for the eagle. It is a game roughly like "Come here my little chicks. We don't dare to because of the wolf. Come on." Games are the same the whole world over.

This time they are content merely to sing the song.

Then the teacher stands up and, to the music, shows the children the steps to the next dance. She does the steps, makes beautiful movements with

The children's four layers of clothes are of all colours of the rainbow. They often have a flannel shirt on top of the thick woollen pullover.

her hands, and claps. Her eyes shine with joy while she demonstrates. The children first walk to the music and then make the movements which the teacher showed two at a time. Most of them can make the movements correctly straight away, but a couple of the boys find them tricky. One of them is looking desperately at his friend who gets everything wrong, and is trying to show him how it should be done!

The dance comes from a minority in the north-west of China. When grown-ups dance it, it is more complicated, but the simplest movements are taught to the children. After the lesson they all put back their chairs against the walls of the hall.

The interpreter's boy (aged five) does not like dancing and, "He'll never get better at it", she sighs. "If he attended this pre-school, he would certainly want to. They never force the children. They are good and happy models."

19 April 1982, *A neighbourhood pre-school in Shanghai. A language lesson for the youngest group*
It is a sunny morning. We watch the morning gymnastics and then accompany the group to the lesson. There are 30 children aged three–four. They line up on the terrace outside the large hall and there they first sing a song dealing with hygiene, saying that you should always have a clean handkerchief with you in the pre-school, and then a song with car-driving movements.

All the children then file in and sit down on their chairs, which have been arranged in a large semi-circle facing the teacher and a flannelgraph. The teacher has taken out some pictures and a cover. She shows the children a sun and a picture of a child making its bed. She asks what it is and the children reply in chorus "sun". And what do you do when the sun rises? "Make your bed". Then the teacher takes the cover off the other half of the flannelgraph and shows a moon. She asks when the moon comes out. "In the evening," reply the children. What do you do then? "Sleep." The children now raise their hands and answer. And the sun rises. When is that? "In the morning." She shows the sun and conceals the moon with the cover. She removes the cover and asks "When does the moon come out?" "In the evening," the children reply. The teacher shows the sun and the bed and points and talks about making your bed in the morning. "What do you do when the sun comes up?" "Go to pre-school." The teacher places the cover over all the pictures and asks, "When the moon comes out what do you do then? When the sun comes up, what do you do then?" The children respond quickly and enthusiastically.

Then they sing again. One song is about finding a cat which has got lost, one song is about good hygiene habits, and one song has movements to it: "When the sun rises, I wash my face and hands and go to pre-school. . . ."

A language lesson with six-year-olds

There are 30 children in the classroom. They are sitting in groups but have now turned their chairs towards the teacher, who is standing by the flannelgraph. The nursery helper is right at the back of the classroom.

The teacher shows five pictures which together form a story, which she relates.

A boy and a girl are going to go out and play. When they run past a house, by mistake they knock over a pole where washing is hanging to dry. What do they do then? Well, they wash the clothes, because they know that the old lady, whose washing it is, is tired and cannot cope with it. It is such a beautiful day that the clothes dry fast. We will wash them, they say.

In the fifth picture the old lady is looking out of her window and smiling when she sees how good the children have been.

The old lady is smiling.

The teacher has now told the children the story. After this she asks one of the children, a girl, to tell the whole story to the others. She narrates:

It is a beautiful day. Some children go out. They are so cheerful. They decide to play. Then they find something on the ground. The girl asks the boy to come. She thinks they ought to wash the clothes they have found, and the boy agrees. The old lady is not too healthy. We can do something for other people. We do not have to play just now and the old lady will be so happy and she will say you are nice children.

There is a burst of loud applause. The girl is praised by the teacher for her articulate story. The interpreter points out that the girl is very good at expressing herself. The teacher asks whether anyone else wants to tell the story, and all do. She lets another girl tell the story. All listen closely and she is applauded.

In the discussion afterwards, I ask the teacher whether it is difficult to teach language to such a large group. I wonder whether it is in fact the best ones who do the talking. She admits this. She consciously asked who wants to tell the story, knowing that it is the most able ones who will. She then lets them talk, appreciating that this is additional repetition for the weaker pupils. In the following lesson the same story is covered again. Then she tries

to choose children who did not have a chance to say anything the first time.
She is aware that there is a great risk of the able children dominating and she
tries to reach those who find things more difficult.

6 April 1982. *Peking's experimental day nursery. A singing lesson*
   The children are three years old. There are 24 children present in the
group. they are sitting in a circle on their chairs, with the teacher in the
middle. The teacher leads the singing. One at a time they come out and sing
solo. The whole group then answers. The other teacher accompanies. The
teacher's introductory story and the songs deal with various animals. The
teacher talks about a Mummy-bird protecting her little birds against a
danger. The little ones promise their Mummy to be careful and so on. All the
children have a cardboard bird-picture fastened to their foreheads. The
birds are pink or pale green, but no distinction between boys and girls is
made when giving out the colours. There is a good deal of chattering, and the
children make faces at us visitors. While they are singing the song, they stand
up and then they walk round in time and clap their hands. Some of the
children are quite oblivious of their audience, while others make funny faces
at us.

   I am irresistibly charmed by these happy, well-disciplined but still
strongly personal children who sing for us in such a clear and spirited way.

16 April 1982. *Chengdu number 3. A music lesson with three-year-olds, 15
minutes*
   When the children come in from morning gymnastics, their little chairs
are in a circle in front of the organ. The teacher sits down and begins to play
and the children walk round the circle of chairs to the music. They are
chicks. Then the music becomes more rolling. The children become flying
birds. They hover around! Then the teacher asks them to sit down on their
chairs while she plays. The children clap their hands in time. Then the
teacher changes the tune. She plays rather softly and asks "What kind of a
song is this?" All the children reply in chorus, "The little children cannot
speak." All of them like this song. You can hear this in their delighted
shouts. They sing the song with gestures, "The little ones cannot speak. The
little ones cannot work. They do not cry." The children cover their faces
with their hands. They point with their forefingers and end the song softly
with a gesture extending their hands.

   Then the teacher plays a new tune, "Chin chini", which is about an able
girl who is a little shy. They all sing it together and then the teacher asks who
would like to come out. Most of the children put up their hands and the

teacher selects five children who go out and sing "Chin chini" again, about a shy girl who reads books and is so able.

Then the teacher plays some notes from a tune about "the train". She asks who would like to be "the engine". The children put up their hands and two are allowed to go out. In time to the music they go round the circle. They tiptoe with their hands at their sides and pick up a "carriage" each. "Hoo, hoo", says the train. Each gets five carriages.

Then the teacher plays "I am looking for a friend" and the children jump up and dance and sing. They stand two by two. Clapping. Take your friend by the hand, clap, tap your friend on the shoulder, and in between, the graceful movement of raising the hand which is so typical of Chinese dance.

Then the teacher asks the children to put their chairs back. The children at one table at a time can now go and fetch their mugs from a cupboard, and then they are given some boiled water to drink before playing outdoors.

This was a selection from some of the lessons we saw. More examples are given in the chapters that follow. A regular feature of the lessons is that they have been well prepared by the teacher and that the children seem to enjoy them. The lessons we saw have been well suited to the age of the children as regards music, singing and moving (and stories about animals for the tinies and more abstract themes for the older children). So far as discipline goes, considerable demands are made during the lessons. The children are expected to sit with their hands behind their backs and answer in chorus, or reply when they have put up their hands and been singled out by the teacher. The duration of the lessons is adapted to the age of the children, as indicated earlier, and the teachers demonstrate that they are able to vary the lessons so that there is alteration between lively, active phases and quieter ones. The teacher lets one or two of the children tell a story, sing or dance, and alternate this with whole group activity. In this way a rhythm is created which means that the expectations that the children should be well-disciplined do not need to weigh so heavily on them.

In Sweden there are, of course, no lessons as such in the pre-school. The nearest equivalent is assembly. For some years, there have been doubts about assembly as a form of learning and community life, but its use is now more widespread again. The pre-school has rediscovered the value of coming together each day, all who belong to the same group, and in this way strengthening a sense of belonging together. For many to assemble and play or sing provides rich experience which the small group cannot give in the same way. The doubts about assembly have led to group size and age composition being more adapted to what one intends to do, which is certainly what is best of all.

Cultural clashes

We are so Swedish

When we ask questions about the pre-school, we often notice that the questions are very Swedish or at least Western. It is typical of us to ask questions about aggression and conflicts and questions about sex roles, we realize that. We focus on the individual and nurture the thought of the importance of personality development and individual realization. We are not used to thinking about what is good for others and which role each and every one has for the whole. "Everyone for himself" probably applies more in Sweden than an expression like "everyone for the people". "The servant of money" or "the servant of the people", that is the question. Although we have goals for the pre-school agreed on by parliament, judgements of what a good person is and of the goals of upbringing vary enormously among different groups in Swedish society. That, of course, is what we label living in a pluralist society. We are therefore not used to being in a country in which the ideology is more uniform and where it means so much more in everyday life.

The five charities, beauty and goodness

In 1981 there was a campaign to select families which were especially good models for other families. There were five criteria:

- The members of the family are well educated and participate actively in further education.
- They are careful about health and hygiene.
- Their budget is planned and they make wise purchases.
- They form a unit and help each other. They help others and have good relations with the mother-in-law.
- The children are given a good education.

With the inspiration of the campaigns of the Chinese for the five charities and the families with the five good qualities, we could try to find their counterparts in Sweden, "The five catastrophes" or "The five unfreedoms". We do tend to look at socialist countries through stereotypes. We believe that *we* live in the free world and they in the unfree world. But it does not always feel quite so obvious that freedom is something that exists

The three-year-olds wait for their turn to cycle round a track on the day nursery's tricycle.

Four−five-year-olds should, according to the syllabus, be able to "jump over two parallel lines at least 40 centimetres apart".

only here and that there is only lack of freedom there. The five unfreedoms in our society, in relation to China, could be formulated thus:

- The unfreedom of constantly being exposed to the pressures of *commercialism*, conformity, and artifical needs due to so-called fashion trends.
- The unfreedom of being exposed to the transmission of culture through the *mass media*, rather than actively contributing to the development and expression of one's own culture.
- The unfreedom of being *ahistorical* and without pride in one's own country.
- The unfreedom of *children being a private matter* and of the generations living separate lives, children on their own, "the productive" on their own, and retired people on their own.
- The unfreedom of having *ever-expanding private* transport rather than well-developed public transport.

Strangely enough, it seems to be easier to think of unfreedoms and catastrophes (the atomic bomb, energy, environmental pollution, narcotics and unemployment) in relation to Sweden than anything to do with the beautiful, the good or charity, as in China's campaigns. We may well have something to learn here, to provide positive ideals for children and young people as a counterweight to destructiveness and inertia!

Ask a question and I know who you are!

We often realize that our questions and comments reflect the fact that we come from a society which is quite different. I ask, for instance, whether they have clay to work with. No, we have modelling clay as prescribed in the syllabus, is the reply. When we are out in a country district where the housing is primitive and they live by growing rice, we see for the first time a child playing with clay. He is sitting on the edge of a field and rolling the clayey earth into a sausage. It strikes us that it may not precisely be clay one needs or wants to have, to give children the education one is so proud of, when one has just shaken the clay off one's feet.

For a long time there have been discussions in Sweden about the importance of children participating in everyday life. Our children live so far from working adults in their daily lives that they believe that food comes from food trolleys and that floors clean themselves. We want to reintroduce work into the everyday life of children in order to create a sensible balance. Without work, play is not suitably nourished. The balance between play and work, which is so important for the child to become a good member of

Five – six-year-olds in a marching run around the courtyard and stretching diagonally with hands angled outwards at the wrists.

society, will not materialize if we do not let children participate more, bake, clean, sort out things, run errands and help with a variety of tasks. I therefore ask whether the children participate in the cleaning, when I hear it is the time for cleaning the day nursery. The interpreter looks uncomprehending. "No, they do not need to. I don't think that's anything for children. Sweeping floors you will have enough of anyway. They can play instead. That is much better for them." Then I recall that her hands feel very coarse, and I note that they look red and swollen. Which reminds me of my grandmother, who stood boiling the washing in a cauldron over a wood fire in an outhouse, and who used to say, "You children play while you can, the time will come . . ." And I understood how contemporary-Swedish my thoughts are.

Our Swedish view of creative activities, sticking on things which are semi-ready indiscriminately and throwing out what is left over, is also foreign to a country where everything is made good use of and no one can afford to waste anything. We have a lot to learn about how cardboard boxes and other potentially exploitable things are used, for instance as material for role-play (see the section on play in the syllabus, p. 260).

There are many such cultural clashes because China has so many people and such limited resources. We are, of course, merely eight million! For instance, we described our excellent system of age-integrated groups. They smiled and said they were familiar with it, but that a great deal of organization is needed if the children in the various age groups are to get appropriate stimulation. And in Chinese pre-schools there are generally about 400 children! Swedish pre-schools have from 40 to 60 children.

Our hosts understood that we thought that gymnastics for the babies was a weird idea. Swedish babies and toddlers actually move of their own accord and exercise themselves quite naturally and train different capacities quite spontaneously through playing freely on the floor, climbing on wallbars and over hills, rolling on grassy slopes and trudging through snow. In China they do not have warm, light rooms, with good wooden floors and carpets, as we do. They may have to resort to housing a pre-school in a building with a stone floor (we visited one which had been a stable), where the cots are the only healthy place for a small child. Resources and traditions therefore mean that it is not so simple as just altering methods and letting the little ones "loose".

When we speak of the importance of there being men in the pre-school, they merely state soberly that they know this is important in Sweden, as so many children have divorced parents. But here we have almost only complete families. The children have both a mother and a father, and now that people have a single child, the fathers take a considerable interest in the child and its upbringing.

Play in the pre-school and in the street

Doing it yourself and playing grown-ups — make-believe games and playing materials in the pre-school

The most important form of play for children between three and seven years is make-believe games and role-play. In these games the children re-create and work over their knowledge of life around them. They get a taste of the grown-up world, but not as mere observers, as active participants. That is how we regard play in Sweden, but how do the Chinese look at play? After a day of intensive lessons in language, singing and dancing, drawing and play outdoors, we see the following:

4 April 1982. *Peking's experimental day nursery*
The large open floor space has been set up for various groups, and intensive make-believe games and role-play are taking place. In the middle of the floor the children have built up the shape of a boat with wooden boxes: large light-blue building bricks consisting of boxes with sawn-out holes for the hands. In the boat a group of six-year-old boys are playing. They are wearing pirates' hats. One boy is looking through a telescope made of a long cardboard tube. They are deeply involved in their journey over the seas. They signal and wave with little red flags. The room hums with life. There are 30 children playing here in the same room.

Over in the light by the window which resembles a glass verandah, the corner has been divided off with the help of tables. There are two "reception hatches" made of large white blocks. It turns out to be a "doctor's clinic" with a "pharmacy". At the hatch you have to state why you want to consult the doctor, and then you can go in and be examined. Both the reception nurse and the doctor have white coats and white doctor's caps on. The doctor bandages broken arms. Checks the patient's throat. Listens to the heart. Some patients have to lie down for a moment on a bed of chairs put together. The doctor has various instruments in a little oblong dish on the table. She also has a little paper notepad on which she writes prescriptions. These patients who are allowed to leave after being examined take their prescription with them to the pharmacy hatch. Here you are given one of the little boxes of various kinds which the pharmacist has lined up beside her.

In the dolls' corner two girls are playing. The equipment is little furniture, dolls and other things. In the doll's bed lies a cardboard doll with black hair and black eyes. Another doll is lying in a bed of two chairs put together. The doll's crockery is made of painted cardboard, and on the shelf there is a toy clock and a toy TV. The "Mummies" are settling their little ones, taking them up and rocking them.

At the hairdressers on the opposite side, there are mirrors and chairs arranged in a little row. The customers are supplied with a cover and then they are combed and have their hair cut carefully. The comb runs easily through the short-cropped hair of the boy customers!

Beside the hairdresser two children sit playing a simple form of Mah-Jong. Alongside there is a large table on which the children are building a landscape with small bricks, animals, paper and play objects. The teacher is standing making make-believe food and sweets from modelling clay. She makes whirls and twist-biscuits, good to look at. The children will use them in the shop later.

The noise level is so high that you can scarcely hear each other talk, but this does not seem to worry anyone.

So here we can see that make-believe games have a definite place in the Chinese pre-school, but they too are served up and "dealt out" by the adults. The adults participate the whole time, they go round smiling at the children, talking to them and giving them ideas, suggestions and materials. Above all they show, through praise and support, that playing is important. Their smile says, "Exactly, I know what fun it is," and there is a twinkle in their eyes.

In a discussion with the head of the experimental day nursery and two teachers of psychology and pedagogy at the pre-school teacher training college, I refer to *Childhood in China* by a group of American psychologists and educators who visited China in 1973. They say "that they seldom observed any drama — here there were no Wendy houses or doctor's surgeries, which are so common in the pre-school context elsewhere in the world" (p. 109).

"Oh, gosh!", a sigh and an exclamation. The teachers' reaction is strong and lively, and they all talk at the same time. One of them talks in a melancholy way, and points to the friendly little head, who dismisses what she says with a smile:

> "There have been many lost years. Over a ten-year period so much was destroyed. The importance of play was not recog-

nized. There was so much else. You were not allowed to have
dolls and such unnecessary things. But now we are working to
rebuild everything that we had before. Our head here has put in a
lot of work trying to reinstate what was good in the old days. It
will take many years to build up what was ruined, but she has
done a fantastic job."

The head's gestures indicate modest dismissal of this. You don't sing
your own praises in China. But we can see that she is a warm and inspiring
person, and that her day nursery is a model for other day nurseries.

Swedish pre-schools have much to learn from how make-believe games
are organized here. This is really the case. Above all we can learn from the
wealth of imagination used in making simple playing materials out of
"nothing". The materials are closely linked, moreover, to the reality surrounding the children.

In the dolls games at Chengdu number 3, the children had real little
mops made of a stick with shredded rags as the mop, plus wash-tubs with
wash-boards and a beautiful wash-bowl for washing in. They were just like
the real thing.

We are going to see some more make-believe games, called creative
play here.

8 April 1982. *Peking. Day nursery number 5*

In one room different settings for make-believe games have been
organized. On a large table a kind of fairground has been built up with
bricks. The trees are twigs decorated with wads of paper, a tiny mount of
paper flowers, and so on. In two sandpits the children have built bridges
between mounds of sand with the help of plastic building-sets. There is also
an arch of wooden blocks and plastic toys. These children are thus playing
with miniatures in their make-believe games, but most of the children in the
room are role-playing and acting.

In the middle of the room there is a high, old fashioned camera with a
tripod and a cover for the photographer to creep under. The camera is made
of cardboard painted black. We are invited to sit on the chair and be
photographed.

In one corner there is a doctor's clinic. The doctor takes blood pressures, gives injections and writes out prescriptions.

In another corner, dolls are being played with. There is a row of dolls'
beds and the little mother walks around carrying a little doll baby. She later

The teacher shows four-year-olds how to
bounce a ball, precisely following the syllabus.

gets started on the washing. She washes dolls' clothes in a little wash-tub with water, wrings them out and hangs up the clothes on a line in the dolls' corner.

In the next corner, two proud girls stand behind a counter with large trays and baskets of made-up sweets, pastries, bonbons and fruit, everything carefully wrapped in pretty paper or in tiny moulds! They are dressed in white. They are particular about hygiene in their shop.

In front of a large mirror the hairdresser is working with a comb and a home-made hair drier. The customer is wrapped up in a white cover and the hairdresser has a white coat on. He combs and clips frenziedly.

At day nursery number 5 there is the opportunity for a long, interesting talk with the principal and teachers.

We have seen that the children perform the most fantastic role-plays. Do the children themselves make the arrangements for free play or is it the teacher who builds up and structures the play?

The children think them up themselves. The teacher goes with them to the shop, the hairdresser, the doctor, etc., so that they see what happens there. Then the children get ideas. Afterwards the teacher asks them what they would like to play. It may be a restaurant or a shop or a hospital, and then they build up the settings together and make the equipment. Simple things such as make-believe bonbons can be made by the children themselves, but they may not be able to cope with everything. So the teacher does it instead when she has a moment. As you appreciate, there is a lack of materials for playing with, which is why the teachers make things themselves.

During our tour we see many examples of this. A section of a pre-school in Shanghai was equipped in this way. Most of the materials were made by the teacher, at times with the help of the children. They have made little human figures to play with out of small bottles, about 5 centimetres high, plus some cloth and colouring. For the hairdressers', the teacher has made a drier out of cardboard, a shower and a hose, and the children have access to a mirror and comb. For the shop there are gold coins of various values and banknotes of cloth with figures on, and cards representing, for instance, cakes which you can buy in the shop. There are even home-made books, and their prize object is the little clothes-rack for the dolls' clothes. The clothes have been sewn by hand, and the clothes-hangers are made of twisted steel wire. This rack is kept at the front of the classroom, high up on a shelf, and next to the piano the section's dolls sit in a row together with the section's books.

On the resources shelf there are also boxes of crayons, puzzles, slabs of clay and modelling clay, ping-pong bats and badminton balls, coloured paper for folding, little saws and pieces of wood. In a cloth bag there are toys made from pipe-cleaners, dolls and animals. There are small handbags for playing shops, frames for embroidery and patterns for paper-clipping, various cardboard shapes: circle, triangle, square, etc. in various colours, little cardboard houses and trees and several different boxes of blocks, some big wooden white ones, cards with numbers and matching pictures. There are also picture-books. On the shelf there are some pot plants and in a jar there are some snails creeping.

I wonder about some small discs with nails in. The nursery helper shows how one can stretch rubber bands round the nails and make patterns or shapes. The boys like making cars with them, she says.

Outside in the courtyard in the morning sun it is humming with life and play. Several groups have "creative play" on the time-table, and there are scenes from the health centre, the hairdresser, the shop, etc. being played. In one corner a few children are sitting watching their home-made TV. On large tables, landscapes of bricks, trees and the like take shape. There is no mistaking the joy of playing.

Did they have so many splendid, home-made toys and lively make-believe games at all pre-schools? No, we visited pre-schools in country districts and on the coast in fishing districts where there was in fact nothing to play with. But they could dance and sing!

"Creative" play is fairly closely directed in China's pre-school. It is therefore particularly interesting to study how children in China play on their own, without grown-up supervision. Perhaps play in the street can tell us how Chinese children play spontaneously.

Play in the street

There are double obstacles to play. In the first place, there is nothing to hand which the children can change or do anything with. When there are no detachable objects to do something with, nor any "junk", there is nothing to be sold in the make-believe shop, no planks or ropes to build up a keep-off-the-ground track with, using your own imagination. Playgrounds have over-programmed play. Furthermore, many children live in environments where there are few grown-ups, and, moreover, few elderly people and few men. The adults' workplaces are distant and the children have little input as models for their play. Reality provides nourishment for play, but what happens when play is running idly, when inspiration comes only from TV and comics, and none from job and play together with and near adults in productive work, adults interacting with other adults to form a meaningful community?

No, this was not about China. It is about Sweden, and comes from a description of the conclusions of an investigation of play in playgrounds in the autumn of 1974 and 1975 by the Council for Children's Play.

In China children are strikingly often in the presence of grown-ups, the elderly, people working and playing. Life is clearer and easier for children to grasp. People live to a great extent out on the street. You see everything that happens.

In Chengdu I went for a walk in the evening down a little twisting street. This is what I saw:

17 April 1982. *Evening in Chengdu*
I walked down a long street. Outside most houses there is somebody, young or old, sitting. The houses are low and small, presumably with just one room to live in. A hen pecks at the gutter where there is nothing, moves on to a wickerwork dustpan and scratches out the rubbish. An elderly man

has turned his bicycle-cart upside down and is frenziedly scraping and chipping to get off the thick layer of mud which has accumulated there in the course of the day's work. Another man is doing carpentry and there are drifts of shavings screwing themselves out of his open door. A bunch of boys stand chatting. A little girl aged about five has drawn a line and a circle on the street. Beyond the line she has marked two crosses and she is shoving an iron lid from the line to the circle. There are some grown-ups sitting outside their houses casually watching the children playing. A bit further on some boys (about eight to ten years old) are playing a kind of hop-scotch. They have white clumps of paper which are thrown in a special way into a pattern of squares drawn on the street. Some are sitting watching the people go by. The tall, blond, single Swede wearing "just a vest" is probably the sensation of the day. A woman is threading her washing onto a long wooden pole which she secures to the tree outside her house. A man is going home from a shop with raw meat in a bowl.

A mother and a little girl are sitting on the ground in front of their house eating spaghetti from bowls, while a young and an elderly man (father and grandfather?) are playing a kind of chess with round flat counters. A man is crouching down changing the earth in his flowerpots. Two little girls, about six years old, are walking together, giggling arm in arm. An old woman sits looking straight ahead. What does she see? Her memories, perhaps.

A young mother comes briskly down the street with her little baby bundled up and with a towel over the baby's head. She goes quickly to a friend of the same age, and, chatting happily, they lift the towel and talk proudly and cheerfully about the baby (I guess it is a girl.) She seems to have woken up. They speak to her gently. A father and mother and their one-year-old child sit outside a house nearby. The father frolics up the child until she gurgles and laughs with her whole body. A woman on the other side of the street is putting bricks in a square to make a fire. She uses the stones which form a border round her little garden.

Very many eyes follow me with cheerful interest. Little children wave. Men smile. A woman laughs in a friendly way. Another woman stares and turns around for a long time.

In the refuse there are no wrappings or tins, but the feathers of a plucked hen crown the pile! On the way back, the little one-year-old laughs with even more gusto. Back again on the large wide street by our hotel, I see a father with his little five-year-old boy (standing on the baggage-holder of the back wheel, with a strap around his back) work their way out of the sea of cyclists and he lifts the boy down to the pavement. The boy relieves himself and then they ride on in the crowd.

In China, *production* and *reproduction*, i.e. the producing and manufacturing of goods and the restoring of strength and the upbringing of children, are not yet so fully separated as in Sweden. Society is more visible for children. They have input for their play and the opportunity to take part in work where they live.

On a "free" afternoon, on Liu Ling Chang street in Peking I catch sight of a group of boys (10–12 years old) playing on a mound of sand from which construction workers fetch sand for the buildings which are going up in a nearby residential zone. Seeing them reminds me of the words of Bernt Klyvare in the film "The Sweet Years" about grown-ups not understanding that a good place for playing is one which "is not so bloody permitted", "so thought-out and educational that there is nothing to work out for oneself". "A heap of sand which is suddenly just there one day, not because one is supposed to play in it, and then it has gone again the next time you come. That is something to get going on. In the grown-up world there are many closed doors and many locks. Locks which we had a feeling we had to pick, as though we understood that we should somehow have a use for them for life." (Freely from my recollection of Bernt Klyvare's film.) These words run through my head as I watch the boys, and I feel I have to stay to see whether China's children still have something which our children have perhaps lost.

10 April 1982. *Peking, Liu Ling Chang*
    1.30 p.m. The boys, some with satchels, are playing a kind of "king-of-the-castle" game at the top of the sand mound. They divide into teams, two groups, and try to get up and get shoved down by the ones on top of the mound. Some workmen are loading the trailers of two little tractors. The boys are playing at the top of the sand mound. The ones at the top start rolling large clods of sand down on the ones below. They try to aim at each other. They tease and hunt each other.

    1.35. The boys have now gone down to the workmen and some of them are allowed to help with loading sand and stones onto the trailer. It becomes a popular activity and in the end the boys have taken over all the spades and the workmen sit down in the sun and have a rest. They smile and chat and shout to each other. The men loll back in the sunshine and relax. The boys shovel enthusiastically. One of the trailers is half-full in a flash! One boy is allowed to sit beside the driver in the driver's cabin.

    1.40–1.50. I retreat to a shop, as it would be too obvious otherwise that I am watching them.

1.50. Now the workmen have taken over the loading again and go off with the tractors. The boys are on the far side of the sand mound. They stand in a ring and confer. They look as though they are planning a game and may be having a discussion. They talk and gesticulate.

2.00–4.45. I was observing other things.

4.45. Some of the boys are still up on the sand mound.

But there are more interesting games further down the little street.

In Liu Ling Chang, which is towards the centre of Peking, they are demolishing an old part of the town consisting of small stone houses with grey tiles on top, densely packed, dense with narrow alleys and small courtyards between. In their place they are building large rows of tower blocks, whose tiles shine frivolously orange against the old grey houses. In the name of "modernization".

You must not come now. Come in a few years' time when everything is new here, an old man says to me in a shop.

About a third of the area has already been demolished, and here I sit down to watch children play. Fortunately the sun is shining so I can pretend I am sunning myself. I sit on one of the large marble blocks scattered over a stony, messy area. Beyond this there are ancient Peking houses in which people still live.

2.00–3.30. Two boys and a girl of about seven are playing before me on the street. They draw a line on the street with a stone from a demolished house. The girl has a small cloth bag filled with sand between her feet. The idea of the game is to hop with both feet together and simultaneously project the cloth bag so that it lands on the other side of the line. If you don't get the bag over the line, it is the next person's turn. But it does not matter if you happen to land with your feet on the line. The children enjoy the game. They laugh and play enthusiastically. The girl is best at it. She has presumably practised a lot! The ones not hop-projecting watch with interest.

All the time while the children are playing, there are adults and children going past on the street, and many walk and cycle and pull carts or drive cars straight through their playing area. One moment there is a huge cartload of white noodles wrapped in lilac rolls of paper, the next someone comes dragging a heavy load of briquettes, bundles of paper, or tiles.

The paternal grandfather with his little grandchild in its splendid pram walks past. Some elderly women, one with a stick and a pipe, come out of the houses behind me. But this whole flood of people does not worry the

"Now, everyone, turn round and shut your eyes!" The teacher selects one of the children, who hides under a sheet. "Now you can turn round and look! Who is hiding under the sheet?"

children. They play on with concentration, move to one side if necessary, and then continue the game without being disturbed and without irritation. A girl of about nine joins the three children who are playing and takes the bag at once and projects it higher and more cleverly than the others. The ones waiting for their turn are sitting on a large, two-wheeled cart alongside.

But now something new happens. Three boys aged about ten run up. The boys gather together some half-bricks and place them across the middle of a rectangular sheet of marble which is lying in the middle of the rubble. One of them fishes out a ping-pong ball from his pocket. One boy uses a piece of strong cardboard as a racket, but the others use the surface of their hands and at once the ping-pong starts!

Something happens on the large cart now, too. Some boys, also about ten years old, come and sit down on the cart and watch the "bag game", which is still in progress. At one point there are eight boys, but some rush off. The ones left behind begin bit by bit to climb higher and higher up the shafts of the cart, knowing all the time that at some point the two-wheeled cart is going to tip up. They climb carefully higher and higher and notice that it is "hotting up". The rear of the cart begins to rise. They reorganize themselves quickly so that they are sitting in pairs at precisely the same spot. Two are sitting up above and two are hanging below the front part of the cart and then . . . the cart tips over. A delighted shout comes from them when the entire large cart rebounds so powerfully that they bounce back and then, in a flash, it is back in place again!

An old man with a pram walks past. He shouts and yells reproaches at them, but they still carry on. A man of about 40 also shouts at them severely as he cycles past. Finally, another man comes walking past and shouts that they should stop playing on the cart, and then they trickle off. The bag game and the ping-pong continue throughout. Some of the "cart boys" organize their own ping-pong table, so now two ping-pong matches are taking place, one with two participants and one with three. But the boys who jumped off the cart, where did they get to?

At one point there were eight children on the cart, but some dash off with howls of joy to a large heap of what used to be inner walls of wood and masonry, which lie piled up. The pile is three–four metres high. The boys join a lot of other children who are running up the heap. Once at the top they jump off onto a strong, black cable which is hanging down from a pole. I really hope there is no current in it. I think of the Swedish security norms. They swing like Tarzan in the liana.

4.45. There are now no children in the street but on the pile of rubble and the "liana" it is full steam ahead!

I leave the demolished street in among the narrow alleys between the houses, where I do not think any foreigners go. Just where the narrow alley broadens into a little triangular square, I again see children playing. One boy is balancing a stick on his nose just like a real acrobat.

After having seen children in China play so imaginatively and with such zest, I can only state that there is every hope for China's future. Children who are able to play will certainly become real people!

What can we learn from China's pre-school?

In China, as in Sweden, much can be improved. The expansion of the child care service is incomplete, education has not been extended to all, and so on. But there are some things in particular that I recall and that I would like to "bring back home".

- "Everyone working in the pre-school should love children." This should go without saying. But even so, one is taken aback when anyone claims this as a *requirement*. There should be a "love test" in the entrance examination for pre-school teacher training. And a further requirement that one should have a sense of humour.
  Personality + Temperament
- The pre-school teachers know and teach many poems, songs, dances and games. The children acquire a rich repertoire, and can revel in vanity and colourfulness, and gladden others with their performances. The efforts of each and every one are reinforced by being part of an entity.
  Music + Rhythm
- The teachers know *what* they should go into and work on in the pre-school and also *how* they should do this with children of different ages. This applies as much to content as to morality and value judgements. The clarity of the syllabus definitely contributes to teachers giving an impression of confidence and lucidity when they direct games, have lessons, or sing and dance with the children. They are well prepared and can devote their energy to doing their job well, observing the children's feedback and reactions, and refining their methods.
  Guidelines
- The children are made to work over what they learn in many different ways: in dance, songs, poems, creativity with colours and shapes, through stories, pictures and games, in addition to regular lessons. In this way a balance is achieved between action and feelings and intel-
  reinforcement

lectual processing. This is how the Swedish pre-school, too, works when it is at its best.

- Planning covers play as well. ("Creative play" = role-play.) Excursions to the market-place or a visit to the doctor are worked on through play, and most of the materials for this play are produced on the spot.

- The grown-ups are always with the children. They are constantly with their group of children, doing something with them, both indoors and out of doors. This is in striking contrast to Swedish pre-schools, a contrast which invites us to discuss our ways of working in Sweden. Which is right? What is best? Should children play alone? Should grown-ups lead the games more? There is already discussion in Sweden about the culture of children's play. Let us rethink it once more. Are we inhibiting children's play by playing with them?

- The introductory learning of the written language, the Chinese characters, is included as a natural part of the pre-school and is conducted in a playful way.

- The pre-school has a well-balanced rhythm, with alternation between activity and rest, games with movement and concentrated lessons, food, sleep and exercise. Taking care of flowers and animals, making your bed, washing your hands before a meal, clearing the table, and so on, are included in the activities. You learn to respect living things and to look after yourself.

It is up to us adults — we can never escape from this. This is what I wrote in my conclusion when, with Märit Norenlind, I made a study of Swedish pre-schools.[1] And it is what I write again, with double underlining, after studying the pre-school in China. It is the goals, the methods and the ardour of the adults that it depends on. Ardour in the belief that a good pre-school is a privilege and the chance of a life-time for the children who can be there. China is investing to improve its pre-school. Let us do the same!

---

1. The Council for Children's Play, now the Council for Children's Environment, carried out an investigation of the function of teaching materials in the pre-school, at the request of ULÄ (Investigation of the market for teaching materials), and published in Norén-Björn, Eva: *Förskolepedagogik i praktiken (Pre-school pedagogy in practice)*, Liber, Lund, 1980.

3 The pre-school teacher in China

Gertrud Schyl-Bjurman

The force of the good example

Long before our Western time calendars, there lived in China a famous philosopher called Mencius. It is said that as a child he preferred to play rather than study industriously. Once when Mencius's mother yet again saw her son stop reading his books in order to play, she cut over the warp of the cloth she was weaving. The mother wanted to show Mencius tangibly that it was only through persistent and patient work that one can reach a goal and achieve anything. The cut-off cloth was to symbolize the interrupted studies.

Another Chinese story tells of the author, Kong Rong, who lived right at the beginning of our time. Kong Rong was four years old when the family sat together one day eating pears. After the adults had had their fruit, there were two pears left. Kong Rong took the smaller one and left the larger one for his brother.

These two little moral tales, Sunday school stories we might say, are examples of anecdotes which have been told and are still told to children in China, generation after generation, in order to instil in them, by the force of example, exemplary behaviour with respect to industry, bold courage and also humility and generosity towards others.

Upbringing with the help of the force of the good example was advocated by the ancient Chinese philosophers, but it is also present in Mao's thought. Mao appealed to party members to serve the people and put the needs of others before their own, to work with all their energy, and patiently and humbly train their capacity to learn from others. Moral and social education is important in China and deeply rooted in old traditions.

KEY.

In China today you meet a multitude of well-brought-up children, children who not only behave well but also appear to be infectiously happy, open, confident and spontaneous. You cannot avoid comparing them with Swedish children, who do not always look as happy. Swedish children have great freedom, but they all too often show all sorts of signs of insecurity. Where can one try to find the causes of this obvious disparity? It is difficult to get to grips with this. I can merely speculate, but one of the causes may be this very tradition of morality.

There are in China simple, clear rules for everyday behaviour and for human interaction, and the message can probably be transmitted so that even small children can understand what it is all about. Children learn by imitating the behaviour of others, through identifying with other people. The fact that adults attempt to function as models for children is bound to result in education which marks clear boundaries for behaviour, but also marks out what is to be developed in relation to the environment. It is possible that Swedish children are exposed to far too little boundary-marking. They are given freedom to develop, but not supervision or rather guidance as to what they as future adults should be developing towards. In this way we also leave them in uncertainty.

There is a second tradition in China to which we have no counterpart — formulating vital messages in short slogans. As a Westerner one is first taken aback, perhaps laughs, but finally one starts inclining to a feeling that it may be pedagogic brilliance. For instance, Mao has formulated the five types of charity which the people should embrace, namely to love the mother country (that is what they say in China), to love the people, to love work, to love science, and to love and protect public property. Take the last type of charity, loving and protecting public property: you look after what you love. Mao does not say that it is forbidden to ruin and vandalize. He sets a good example.

The five types of charity are included in the official pre-school syllabus for initial and basic moral and ideological education. Even three-year-olds are educated to love and guard public property, in accordance with the following instruction:

> "To love and guard toys, books and necessities, to treat them carefully, not throw them around, not damage or break them. To love and guard trees, flowers and plants, not pick or break indiscriminately."

This is firmly formulated education to ensure carefulness about every-thing there is in the immediate vicinity of the child. Care for toys and

The children sit in a semi-circle on little green chairs facing the teacher. Then they trot round while a teacher plays the organ.

story-books is easy to understand, care for trees and plants perhaps a little more difficult. There is, however, a shortage of trees in China. All the Chinese have been exhorted to plant three trees during their life and in addition to take care of and guard their trees. I could scarcely believe my eyes when I saw, in a city street, ordinary people, adults and children together, out loosening the earth around the trees in the street, building up the earth in a high circle around the trees so that the water would not run off, and then lime-washing the trunks. It is only when our park trees run the risk of being felled that we Swedes discover that they are our public trees and then keep a watch over them, quite literally.[1]

In China, the education of three-year-olds to care for trees and plants begins in the pre-school. The pre-school syllabus states that "the physical setting of the pre-school must be emphasized. A plan must be followed for planting trees in the courtyard and ensuring that the children can live in an environment which is clean and neat and aesthetically appealing." Seeing that grown-ups care for "their" trees, in public places too, makes this education even clearer for the children and imprints it on their minds.

You do not have to be very long in China, studying pre-school children's care and upbringing, before you understand that these concerns are important and vital for the society, and taken deeply seriously. Of course, the care of little children is considered an investment for the future, a guarantee of the continuation of the new China and development into a communist welfare state, but I believe that there is also a conviction that children are important in themselves, that they are worth all the care and love that one is capable of giving them.

Old wisdom about children's upbringing has not been lost, but has been combined with components, primarily with political content, which serve the interests of the new China. Political education starts in the pre-school, but not until the intermediate class for four–five-year-olds. They are to learn to love their home district, love the toiling masses and learn from their good traits of character, and respect the Chinese flag. Six-year-olds in the highest class are to learn from the good traits of character of the veterans, heroes and model figures of the revolution, and respect and love them — in other words education through the force of the good example.

Translators Note
1. This is a reference to one of the first extra-parliamentary environmentalist actions in Sweden. The city authorites were going to fell all the elms in Kungsträdgård, a park in Stockholm. These were centuries old and were to be replaced. The decision was met by massive demonstrations: for several weeks people kept watch around the elms day and night and this physical blockade prevented the municipal gardeners from felling the trees.

As I write these lines about the political schooling of Chinese pre-school children, my thoughts get mischievously going and I ask myself: do we ever try in our country to explain to pre-school children that we live in a democracy, and what we mean by this? Naturally, the words which pay homage to democracy are woven into the overall stated goals for the pre-school, but how do we demonstrate for the children what the words mean? Do we tell them that both a democratic constitution and democracy between people are important for us, for the continuation and further development of our society?

Pre-school staff work in more or less well-functioning teams, the parents have more and more say in the pre-school, and the children take part in planning activities. These are indeed good examples of a democratic way of working, which our children are growing up with and can learn from indirectly, but is this enough? Are children given help to understand and to work over the fact that these are examples of democracy? When working teams in the pre-school cannot agree, when conflicts between adults cannot be solved, and children experience that the grown-ups cannot reach agreement, how much then is the message of the democratic way of working worth?

This may sound a little smug, and perhaps moralizing to many, nevertheless there are reasons for reflecting on it. In China the messages dealing with upbringing are not just words which are pronounced and then disappear into thin air. Words lead to practical action. And this was exactly where I found creativity among the pre-school teachers I met, in their way of putting into practical effect what is laid down in the official pre-school syllabus. Their work was not uniform or standardized, but full of variation and often of imagination.

Constantly active with the children

My special topic of study in China was pre-school teachers. I am myself a pre-school teacher and teacher trainer. What were the pre-school teachers capable of, what kinds of methods did they use in their work, and what kind of professional aura did they have?

We visited roughy 15 day nurseries during our trip. The selection of pre-school teachers we met was, of course, pitiably small when seen in relation to such an overwhelmingly large country as China. It is therefore difficult to say anything general. So my impressions are explicitly subjective, and what I noticed and was heartened by was quite definitely influenced by what I wanted to see; in other words, things which I believe are good for small children in their contact with adults.

What was most striking was how the pre-school teachers radiated joy and warmth when together with the children. They had fun themselves, often laughed, and could become completely immersed in games or, for instance, in dances. Their whole person was engaged, here and now, in what they were taking part in. In Sweden you at times hear pre-school staff say that they are *not emotionally involved* in anything. Our experience in China was that the staff were really *emotionally involved* in what they were doing. Obviously they were presenting themselves and their group to foreigners, and wanted to do their best to give us a positive picture, but the spontaneous joy and warmth when together with the children was unmistakable.

A group of four-year-olds in Shanghai was having a lesson indoors. For once I had no interpreter beside me, I had slipped off alone to this group at a large day nursery so as to be able to concentrate entirely on the interaction between teacher and children without the comments of the interpreter. I was fascinated by the teacher's warm radiance and by the children's frank and happy response.

The lesson soon ended and it was time for free play outside. The children chose what they wanted to play, and collected materials for playing outside. One group of six–seven children wanted to play kitchens, which mostly consisted of slicing vegetables finely, just as prescribed in Chinese cookery. The kitchens game clearly required them to wash their hands and put on an apron. One by one the children went up to the teacher for help with tying the apron. The teacher was sitting on a low stool, knees wide apart. She tied the knot, not by spinning the child round so that she had the child's back to her. No, she took each one in her arms, gave it a discreet hug and simultaneously tied the knot with her arms around the child's waist. A few words were said to each child, who then leaped off to the courtyard as children do when they feel happy and gay. This little scene showed real mothering. That it stuck in my mind is possibly connected with the fact that we never saw grown-ups and children cuddling or fondling each other in the pre-schools we visited. The children never sat on the knees of a grown-up, yet the atmosphere radiated motherliness, sincerity and loving interest.

There was also respect, or rather deference, in the teacher's attitude to the children. And it does say quite clearly in the syllabus that "teachers and other staff must love and respect the children and show this in word and deed." The teachers' clearly considerate attitude to the children was matched by a trusting attitude to the teachers on the part of the children. There was a "well-brought-upness" on both sides such as does not exist in

Lesson on the spring. The picture of spring on the board functions as a prompt for both the discussion and the singing.

Reading lesson for four-year-olds. They learn the characters for paternal grandfather, paternal grandmother, father, mother, elder brother and younger sister.

Sweden and which we for several reasons have learned to be suspicious of. What does such well-brought-upness lead to in the long term? Are they people who cannot give expression to what they really feel and think? Disciplined people who can be manipulated? By contrast, what is the end product of upbringing, be it ever so free and supposedly democratic, if it lacks elements of respect for others, expressed in, among other things, courtesy and a feeling for the integrity of others? I can merely state that in relation to little children in China, this mutual respect in education is counterbalanced by joy, warmth and spontaneity.

In our discussions with pre-school teachers, they made the point that they set an example for the children. In Sweden we talk at times about the same issue, but our way of expressing it is that the children identify with the teacher. In the Chinese pre-schools that we visited, my feeling was that the adults really were adult in relation to the children. It was clearly shown that adults do not behave in a childish and immature way, which does not exclude recognizing the child in oneself when it is a question of joy and, for instance, curiosity. The strange thing was to experience an absence of neurotic mechanisms, of tensions between adult and child. On the rare occasions when the children had a clash with each other, the teacher amiably talked the child/children into being sensible, or isolated a child from the group for a moment. This took place without the teacher being upset, as though she felt it was obvious that this child at this particular moment in the interests of harmony needed to be given support in the form of reasoning and amiability.

The absence of tensions between adult and child and the few instances of conflict between children that we saw made me inquisitive. I asked a few times how pre-school teachers regarded conflicts and whether the staff disagreed among themselves at times. Either my questions were not understood or else I was provocative and made my point too bluntly, when I tried to explain the Western belief that conflicts can have a positive function and that resolving conflicts can imply development. Their response at any rate was that the staff should set an example for the children, meaning that conflicts should be avoided. Nor is there a single word in the pre-school syllabus about conflicts or the resolution of conflicts. It speaks instead of serving your friends and the community, of being friendly to people, of being able to take criticism from others and, if one has done wrong oneself, knowing how one can remedy this.

What we saw in the Chinese pre-school was a soft, peaceful atmosphere which probably resulted from a number of compromise solutions. This may not sound terribly exciting, perhaps a little dull, some may feel. No, it was refreshing. It is possible that we have a blind faith in the positive effects of confrontation between people and of the potential for development from conflicts? How often do we solve our conflicts, and how harmful for ourselves and our children are tensions and struggles for power?

The methodological competence and confidence of the pre-school teachers was striking. This was true both of the way of planning and managing lessons and of the way of dealing with groups of children and individual children. The teachers' confidence, like the clear and unambiguous message in relation to desired behaviour, must represent significant pillars of security for the children.

Activities for children organized by the teacher have pride of place in the Chinese pre-school. The children should develop their capacities and skills gradually. Meal-times, getting dressed and undressed, the management of going to the toilet, etc., are largely taken care of by nursery helpers. I do not think that these functions are considered educationally interesting except for the smallest children. Routine situations count in the pre-school syllabus as training for independence, but they form only a small part of the syllabus. It might occur to one that we in Sweden over-emphasize those aspects of upbringing which deal with self-evident everyday realities, with the result that other activities which are essential for the children have been overshadowed. The main focus in the Chinese pre-school is on what the children can only be given in the pre-school, namely group activities, play and training under guidance, and stimulation to seek an intellectual way of solving problems.

The pre-school teachers in China were constantly active with the children. During the lessons — 10–15 minutes for the smallest children six–eight times a week, for the six-year-olds half an hour twice a day — it was natural for the teacher to actively teach. The teacher demonstrated something, asked questions, delegated tasks more or less as in a school lesson. Of greater interest, however, was their active participation in the free play, regardless of whether it was a question of the wide range of role-plays, building with bricks or sandpit games. The teacher was always to hand, found out what the game consisted of, and if necessary prompted with questions or suggestions, perhaps by providing a supplement of new materials. The games outdoors involving movements were always led by the teacher, ranging from regular gymnastics to running and jumping games, catching or ball games. The involvement of the teachers in the free play probably means that the children become more absorbed in the game. I never saw any children jump from one activity to another; what I did see was a small group of children completing a game together and then getting started on a quite different activity.

Mathematics lesson. The teacher cuts up a piece of paper into a variety of pieces, splits an apple, breaks a cake into four pieces. Behind her are the rows of flags for the chldren's good behaviour. The children listen attentively, their hands behind their backs.

There is an ancient tradition of teachers in China always being honoured and respected, and there is no doubt that the pre-school teacher is regarded as a real teacher. The pre-school is the responsibility of the Ministry of Education, which also decides on the content of teaching. The pre-school thus forms part of the entire educational system and is seen as an important and basic part of this. The teaching of reading, writing and mathematics starts at the pre-school level and leads naturally into school teaching. Proper lessons are to lead to basic knowledge and skills.

In Sweden the pre-school is the concern of the Ministry of Health and Social Affairs, and at the local level of the Social Welfare Board. The pre-school is a social policy institution with an educational content. In this way the pre-school comes within the ambit of the social services law. There is a great risk of the pre-school becoming a sort of social reserve granny, inasmuch as the Ministry of Health and Social Affairs largely lack educational management competence and are in any case geared to social goals. In addition the day nursery's function as a minding-institution suited to the needs of the parents has been emphasized at the expense of the needs of children for pedagogic guidance in groups. These differences in where the ultimate responsibility lies in the Chinese and Swedish systems mean that the role of the teacher in China is much more distinct.

The professional pride of Chinese pre-school teachers was palpable. They were the living image of purposeful, well-qualified professionals. The discussions in Sweden a few years back about whether it was reasonable that child upbringing could be gainful employment, these seem, well, distant and artificial when meeting these enthusiastic pre-school teachers.

Group size, streaming by age and staff/child ratio

The Chinese pre-school is for children of between three and seven. Each age group operated strictly independently. The three-year-olds may be 20–25 in a group. As the children's age rises, the groups become larger. There may be 35–40 six-year-olds in the same group. Normally each group has only one room at their disposal. All the pre-schools we visited had, however, a large outdoor playground, and all the games which could be conducted out of doors were arranged there. Any necessary furniture was simply moved out. Even organs were dragged out for singing and dancing games. Attendance rates are very high, compared with ours, because in China they seem to have gone a long way towards controlling nose and throat infections. The institutions are large, at least in the towns. The institutions we visited had as a rule 300–400 children. This necessitates, naturally, good organization of the space, inside and outside, co-operation among the staff, and good discipline on the part of the children.

The staff/child ratio presumably varies, but a usual model seemed to be with two pre-school teachers and two nursery helpers sharing the responsibility for a group of children in two shifts. The pre-school teacher plans the work and is responsible for teaching in the widest sense. She never leaves the group. The nursery helper assists the teacher, taking responsibility for meals, visits to the toilet, and the afternoon rest. The division of labour between the teacher and the nursery helper is very clear-cut.

The working hours for everyone in China are 48 a week. One day a week is free, and there are no holidays, only extra time off for national days. Pre-school staff work for six–seven hours a day with the children. The rest of the time is used for planning and preparing activities, making clothes for performances, and preparing materials for games. For financial reasons it is necessary to make use of "useless" materials and set one's imagination free. We saw how flattened sweetpapers were used for paper-folding, worn-out rubber balls had been trimmed into little baskets or bowls for playing kitchens, cameras for photography games had been produced from cardboard boxes, and so on endlessly.

This is what the pre-school syllabus says explicitly: "natural objects, refuse and materials which are not poisonous or harmful should be fully exploited". It is also stated that teaching materials can partly be selected from the Ministry of Education's range of teaching materials, and otherwise should be *made* (my emphasis) or selected so as to suit local conditions, in order to enrich the content of teaching constantly.

It is also stated in the pre-school syllabus that the educational tasks, content and demands are brought about through all kinds of activities, games, physical activities, lessons, observing (by the children), work, entertainment, everyday activities, etc. Nothing should be neglected, to the benefit of anything else. This demands a good measure of planning. The daily work of the pre-school is planned and prepared thoroughly by the teachers. They first make a rough plan.

In Shanghai some of us were able to take part in this planning work with a group of pre-school teachers. At this pre-school, each class had a planning book for each subject; for instance, language training, painting and modelling, nature studies, character-building and moral education. In the books they wrote down the goal and purpose of the teaching according to the pre-school syllabus, and exercises and games of increasing complexity over a period of time. Observations on completed points in the programme were noted down, along with comments on the children's progress. It said, for example, that in the coming week a picture book would be shown to the children, for them to tell stories to build up their language, by training particular items of vocabulary and the meaning of certain concepts.

In this pre-school the weekly plan was to be ready each Friday, then to be passed to the principal to read it through, comment and approve, so that the programme could take effect in the following week.

Play, games and lessons

"Play represents a very effective method in the implementation of the entire pedagogy of development affecting body, intellect, morality and sense of beauty", it says in the Chinese pre-school syllabus. In principle it is the same attitude to which we give expression. The role of the teacher in children's play is formulated as follows:

> "The teacher who is a good leader allows free rein to the children's enthusiasm, initiative and creativity when playing, and allows the children to choose all kinds of games and activities in freedom and with joy. This is done to promote the development of their intelligence and personality."

This refers to the art of leading, and means, as far as I can understand, that the teacher should be able to provide the framework within which the children are free to act. We could see also that pre-school teachers in general had in fact developed this ability to lead.

How then can the children's freedom to choose games be reconciled with, for instance, formal lessons? Well, the time-table for each day includes what we call free play, one or more short lessons, gymnastics, exercises in observing, work such as planting or protecting plants, taking care of animals, helping with various tasks, and in addition entertainment, which may be TV, puppet theatre, slides or performances.

Lessons and the other activities have to contain elements of play or be based completely on play, as children learn by playing and because it is natural for children to play. Free play is subdivided into creative play, consisting mainly of role-play and games of construction (see page 156), and intellectual games. It was my impression that role-play dominated in the free play. I have studied pre-schools in many parts of the world, but I have never seen such well developed role-play and such variety in these games as in China.

In Sweden we also consider that role-play is important. It is in this kind of game that children can enter into the roles and functions of the adult world, and work over impressions of different kinds, both the ones which are fascinating and good and also those which are frightening and hurtful. Grown-up observers can at times see in Mummy–Daddy–child games how unaltered the sex roles can be, and hear the atmosphere of the interaction at home, which the children have snapped up. We leave it completely up to the children to find impulses for role-play, apart from providing basic materials to get started with as a rule. The children are thus left to their own devices as long as they are not being a nuisance.

Role play

In China they are systematic. Children go on a study visit and observe reality. They are supposed to learn about their immediate surroundings and know about what is involved in various types of work and occupations. This forms part of general education in the pre-school syllabus. Safely back at the pre-school, the teacher and children think over together what could be needed so as to play what they have experienced. It is worth pointing out, now that I am going to give examples of common role-plays, that I did not see anywhere the type of playing families which is most common in Sweden. On the other hand there were individual children playing with a doll, dressing and undressing it and putting it to bed.

due to... Regular health visits

Examples of role-play were the hospital, the hairdresser, the photographer, the telephonist, a warship, a shop, cooking, and washing clothes. Playing doctors was the most frequent. Several children played together, in different roles. One child was the receptionist checking patients in, most often one child with a doll, the sick child. The receptionist registered the patient, who was then shown in to the doctor, who examined the patient. The doctor made a diagnosis and wrote out a prescription, which was then left at the pharmacist's hatch, where the medicine was supplied as well. A general feature of the role-play was that every imaginable element or step was there, so that the children undoubtedly learned enough to get an overall conception of the scope of one area of work.

Role-play thus often emphasized the social interplay between people as a precondition for the game. A bus game in Peking can serve as a further example.

A bus had been built up with big bricks. In the bus were the driver, the conductor with ticket equipment, and passengers who got on and off. On the "street" stood police controlling the traffic, signalling with flags when the bus could drive or should stop. The three principal actors were the ones who naturally enough persisted in the game longest, but they had to recognize finally that the passengers had got tired of their more passive roles. The teacher did not change the main actors at this point, but allowed the game to fade away of its own accord. For a time I watched some movement games and when I returned to the "bus" after a while, a completely new bus crew was beginning to form. The teacher was close by throughout, supporting the game, in particular the traffic police whose task was to let the traffic move forward and stop it at regular intervals, but she let the game die out, perhaps to show that if there are no passengers, the bus is not needed.

I was curious about the lessons, because teaching of little children in this way is something that we in Sweden have decided against. I shall describe two such lessons, which in their different ways gave me a great deal to think over.

We were in Xi'an, the ancient Imperial City right in the interior of China. Twenty-eight four-year-olds were going to be taught about the concept "glass". The pre-school syllabus states that the children should become familiar with a number of everyday manufactured products, know what they are made of, their special features and their uses.

The children were sitting on low benches and the teacher at a table in front of the children. All the children had their hands behind their backs. They put their hands up when they wanted to say anything, and stood up when they spoke. The teacher had a collection of glass objects on the table. There were a pair of spectacles, an electric light bulb, a glass of water, a bottle, a vase, an aquarium, a thermos flask, a glass fish, a syringe and fragments from a smashed window-pane. She talked about glass and its uses and the characteristics of glass. Some children were invited to go forward and touch the objects and, facing the other children, describe what they saw and experienced. "You can cut yourself on the bit of glass, it is sharp." "Glass is transparent", and so on. The teacher showed how the syringe works, and said how easy it is to keep it clean and that you have to have really clean things in hospitals. Finally she put some of the objects into the aquarium and two children at a time were allowed to go out with these in order to practise being careful, because glass is fragile and cannot sustain knocks.

The second lesson really took me aback, and turned upside down what I had thought was possible for children to do. It was with a group of five–six-year-olds who were to fold a paper basket.

The teacher had prepared the lesson by laying out for each child on their desks a square piece of paper, four smaller squares and one oblong piece of paper. She showed the children a specimen of the basket they were to fold. It was really very complicated, but I asked to be given a pile of paper so that I could try to follow. The teacher started demonstrating. After four steps I thought that she would make a pause and let the children begin folding, but she continued and folded until the basket was completely ready, before the children were allowed to start. The demonstration took about 15 minutes. I tried folding but could not manage more than a few steps. The children were supremely competent, they worked intently, at times watched each other and discussed quietly the sequence of steps. Only one child needed help, while the others succeeded in folding the basket themselves, even if different children needed different amounts of time. One of the children gave me her basket when she saw how clumsy I had been. It sits now on my desk, as a reminder that one should never be too certain, and that children have potential that we may not suspect.

paper folding
↓
very involved
in sequence
of steps!

This entire lesson took about 40 minutes, during which the children sat still and concentrated. I followed them out, and saw how the boys began wrestling with each other and the girls started dancing spontaneously, and I thought, this at any rate applies to both Sweden and China, that children have to relax by vigorous movement when they have been concentrating deeply and are tired, in order to restore balance.

OK, paper-folding is an old tradition in China, probably in the pre-school, too. Of course, these children had folded paper many times, and had done so with increasing complexity. They were undoubtedly fully familiar with a basic pattern and could add new variations to it. But they had never before folded this basket. In several other pre-schools we saw children fold paper quite spontaneously and with great skill and speed. In the Swedish pre-school there was once paper-folding too. One wonders why it disappeared completely. There is a great deal one can do with a square piece of paper, and similarly a great deal a child can practise to turn paper into something.

The weekly nursery

There are two kinds of pre-school in China, one corresponding to our day nursery, the other a weekly nursery. There is no equivalent to nurseries attended part-time, like those we have. In the countryside there are also seasonal nurseries, which take care of children over brief periods at harvest-time, as was done in Sweden not all that long ago. There has been a fierce debate in Sweden about "night nurseries": that children should sleep at home in their own beds is a right which people have wanted to protect. Children can have a rough time in all sorts of ways without us getting very worked up, but if they are to sleep some nights a week at their own night nursery, then we think things are going really wrong.

In China, apparently no one questions whether the weekly nursery is a good thing or not, yet it is a fact that the weekly nursery children barely have a chance to get to know their own parents. For six days and nights a week the children live at the weekly nursery, which is used not only by parents working shifts but also by party people, officials and others whose work involves travel and a good deal of absence from home. At times one almost got the impression that weekly nursery children are considered specially privileged. And the children, well, they were as happy and spry as the children in day nurseries. In the dormitories the beds were arranged close to each other, certainly creating a sense of belonging together among the children. There was no sign of personal toys or other comforting treasures, just a place for their own personal clothes.

The youngest children

The pre-school proper does not begin until the children are three, and, as indicated, it is part of the educational system. What do they then do for the youngest children until the age of three? Maternity leave is for less than two full months, 56 days to be precise. Day nurseries at factories have a room for breastfeeding the youngest of all. The children lie well tucked-up in cots, and are taken up for changing and feeding. The slightly larger infants, the ones who can walk, are cared for in special toddlers' sections. The care of the youngest children is the concern of the Ministry of Health's Office for Maternal and Child Care. It is not really considered an educational form of care, meaning that health care and questions of diet are primary concerns. It is therefore logical that pre-school teachers are not involved at all with these groups of children.

The day nurseries we visited generally had cement floors which were cold at this time of the year, and the children did not move freely around in the rooms. They sat on benches along the walls or round a table. They often sat on ungainly potty-chairs. Obviously the standard of care varied, depending on the physical conditions and also on the expertise of the staff. Two sections for the youngest children in particular have remained in my memory, both at factory day nurseries.

In one of them the atmosphere felt cheerful and good. The children sat lined up on benches, but the nursry helpers were active and arranged various exercises which, even if simple, were fun and good for children. More can be read about this in the chapter "Welcome to the pre-school", p. 65.

Singing lesson. First the boys sing about Lei Feng, the one who always thought of others first. Then it is the girls' turn.

The other toddlers' group had a dark little room with completely bare cement walls and cement floor. The children did not have their own beds here, but along two of the walls there were long, broad benches on which they were wrapped up in blankets and placed crosswise next to each other, more or less as you pack stuffed cabbage leaves in an oblong dish.

During our visit, most of the children were stuck up against the wall on a low bench. In the middle of the floor there was a clockwork toy, a lion which limped around. When it stopped, it was replaced by a little aeroplane, which whirled round. None of the children got up or tried to take hold of the toys, and there was no sign of toys which the children could play with themselves. The children's faces were reserved and serious-looking, and in glaring contrast to the happy and welcoming children we saw in pre-schools. I tried to make contact with them, smile, play around a little and clown, but met only large, serious eyes. It is obvious that they might experience us as frightening, quite different in appearance and clothing from what they were used to, but I do not think that that was the whole story.

Being a child in a Chinese pre-school is probably good for both body and soul, as an individual and as a member of a group. In a group for the youngest children you are more of an object, which certainly has all its bodily needs well attended to, but where the chance of discovering things yourself, touching, tasting, twisting and turning or manipulating things in other ways does not exist.

Here again there is a conflict between our Western notions, what we believe is important for very small children, and Chinese ones. We believe that all sorts of stimuli are important straight away for the tiny baby. We hang up mobiles for children to watch, ensure that they have plenty of opportunity to touch things, we talk to them and sing for them and activate them by all possible means so that nothing is missed out in an important and fundamental process of development. We could find very little of all this with groups of the smallest children in China. The three-year-olds who had just started in the pre-school, however, did not appear deprived or under-stimulated. They were cheerful and spry, inquisitive about the world. When looking at the six-year-olds — but this is naturally a superficial observation — they seemed in many fields to have come further in their development than can be observed in a corresponding Swedish group.

The question is, what would happen if one let the pre-school teachers loose on the groups of the smallest children, and educational concerns were given pride of place?

The division in the pre-school into care and education used to exist in Sweden, too. The threshold for educational guidance was put at four, only then were children considered to be mature enough to function in a group. Children below the age of four were the domain of the nursery helper. It was at the end of the 1930s that care came to be regarded as education, and pre-school teachers little by little began to work in day nurseries and make the claim that children's care could be conducted in an educationally stimulating way. However, many years passed before the pre-school teachers took over responsibility for work proper with children in the sections for babies and the very youngest, too.

The majority of children under the age of three in China are cared for inside the family, most often by a paternal grandmother, because right up until our times the woman has left her own family on marrying and become a member of the husband's family. They are trying to alter this pattern, and in the future a young family is supposed to be able to choose between living on their own or moving to the husband's *or* the wife's family. At all events, the paternal grandmother is still a key figure when it comes to caring for the youngest generation, and we often saw elderly women outdoors carrying or tending little grandchildren.

The training of pre-school teachers

The pre-school is a recent institution in China. It is only since the revolution of 1949 that a pre-school system proper has been built up and the training of teachers started. There were pre-schools earlier, but there were few of them and they were generally attached to mission schools. There is a great shortage of pre-school teachers today. In the towns some 40% of the need is met. In the country there are probaby infinitesimally few qualified teachers. The shortage of pre-school teachers is covered for the time being by emergency trained staff. There is also a clear shortage of classroom methods teacher trainers, a factor which limits the training capacity.

It is interesting that they not only have training for ordinary pre-school teachers but there is training in parallel for administrators, principals, classroom methods teacher trainers, and researchers in the pre-school field. This type of higher education is attached to universities and is found at five places. The training takes four years and follows completion of the upper secondary school. It seems to be a brilliant ploy to educate these groups together. They follow the same courses for three years and only in the final year is there an occupational specialization. The actual pre-school teacher training is included and constitutes the essential core of the higher degree.

There are various options during the first three years as well, in the form of specialist courses. There is some scientific training for all three groups, not just for the future researchers. As far as I could understand, this is for the present focused on a further development of the state pre-school syllabus.

At the Teacher Training College in Peking, I was able to watch two research students in action. They were testing a number of children in an experiment inspired by Piaget. I noticed that for each task they noted down only whether the children responded correctly or incorrectly for their age level, or whether a child was particularly clever for its age. They did not listen to what the children actually said or how they reasoned in dealing with the problem. My interpreter, who had a child in a pre-school herself, was clearly interested in what was happening, and I asked her to translate as literally as possible what the children said and how they explained problems verbally and solved them. After the tests, I asked the students why they did not listen to what the children said, and I explained that for me this is the royal road to understanding how a child thinks and is therefore of educational interest.

They did not understand me. To record the children's achievements was what was really important, so that one could more appropriately adjust the pre-school syllabus to the potential prerequisites for the development of children at each age. It is not that long ago since we in Sweden also believed in testing as the big educational aid.

There is a professor of psychology attached to higher pre-school teacher training in Peking, and some of us had a talk to her. I told her about the students I had seen in the testing situation described above, and I asked how it could be that the students were not at all interested in the qualitative answers of the children. The professor's response was that what was most important in the students' task was research methodology, the statistical analysis of the children's achievement. This was a case of important knowledge which was to be used for the further development of the overall pre-school syllabus. On the basis of a large corpus they wanted to find out what children are really capable of doing at different ages, so that pre-school teachers should have a sound basis for working out appropriate exercises.

The ordinary pre-school teacher training lasts two or four years, depending on previous experience, in other words on the amount of basic education. The two-year variant builds on a completed upper secondary schooling, and the four-year one complements an incomplete secondary education, what they call middle school, and therefore covers a good deal of usual school subjects.

To graduate with a degree you have to pass a series of examinations. Thereafter students can continue their university studies for three years and get a doctorate.

Some pre-school teacher training colleges, like the one in Shanghai, are independent, but others are attached to other teacher training colleges. There are 28 independent colleges of the same kind as the one in Shanghai and 60 attached to other colleges. This may seem a lot, but these training resources need to be seen in relation to China's 150 million children of pre-school age and 990,000 pre-schools, including institutions for babies, plus the fact that these institutions cover only one-quarter of all pre-school children. The figures are dizzying and become unreal, and one wonders whether they can ever win the race to train enough pre-school teachers. But there is great optimism, and a strong belief in the future in this as in other areas.

Let us have a closer look at the college in Shanghai, which dates back to 1952. We attended several different lectures there, and had an interesting discussion with the principal and a group of teachers. The students are divided into 17 different groups, making 670 regular students in all. There are also courses of advanced training for, for instance, pre-school heads, and specialized courses for ordinary pre-school teachers who want further training in specific subjects.

Two educational principles were emphasized: in the first place that teachers in training should have a thorough basic knowledge of mathematics, physics, chemistry, social sciences, literature, etc. — in general, have a broad educational grounding. Secondly, the students should in the course of their education become competent above all in teaching methods, but also at playing an instrument, dancing, singing, and so on. The students are offered extra courses to improve their skills in drama, recitation, puppetry and probably also in other subjects. In each subject there is a special methods course so that the students learn how the subject can be handled with children, and this was the essential component of the subject.

It was clear that teaching methods is incontestably the central subject in pre-school teacher training, and that it is a subject with a clear profile. The students learn and practise how to prepare lessons in various subjects, how suitable play materials can be produced for particular purposes, and how the lesson is then conducted. The students also learn how free play can be developed in a creative way, so that it results in a thorough working-over of the children's impressions of their surroundings. Training in teaching methods therefore contains thorough exercises in planning in detail both shorter and longer periods of time, following the intentions of the pre-school syllabus, so that the future teachers develop an in-built habit of thinking up games, exercises and materials for a particular purpose themselves.

Teaching practice is also important. It is divided into three steps. It starts with an observation period in which the student is passive in relation to the children. After that the student is allowed to take part in the actual work with the children and to try to take responsibility for minor parts. The responsibility is gradually increased to cover planning, preparation and independently carrying out increasingly larger portions of a day's time-table. The training as a whole is completed with 6 weeks of practice with a full teaching load.

Pre-school teacher trainees were taught in the old school way. They stood up when the teacher came in and greeted loudly and politely. The teacher spoke, and the students answered questions. There were hardly any group discussions. We saw one lesson in which one of the students had prepared a maths lesson and produced some materials. She used her fellow-students as a group of children. Afterwards the others were allowed to criticize her teaching and materials, and then there was a lively and critical discussion.

Musical competence is important for pre-school teachers. No students graduate unless they can play an instrument. There was plenty of space for music practice and pupils even sat outdoors practising playing the accordion. In all the pre-schools we visited, live music was there as something natural, accompanying songs, dancing and rhythmical exercises. If they could not afford a piano, there was an organ and/or an accordion available.

I asked the people in charge of the college about the role of psychology in the teaching, and I was told that the college did not have regular teaching in the theory of child psychology and pedagogical applications. As far as all the independent colleges in the country are concerned, the college in Shanghai is probably representative, so we can just conclude that pre-school teacher education in China does not include psychology teaching as we understand it, as a basis for the design of education for young children. They were, however, taught in the subject "education" about the characteristics of the different age groups, what kind of achievements can be expected, and what sort of upbringing is appropriate if children are to develop as well as possible.

Our visit to Shanghai came towards the end of our trip. We had seen competent, capable and well-functioning pre-school teachers in all the pre-schools we visited. It is possible that the state pre-school syllabus can provide us with a clue as to how it could be explained by their training.

The syllabus begins with "the teaching task and age-specific traits". There is a description in physiological terms of children's development between the ages of three and six, of their increasing weight, the skeleton's rate of ossification, the characteristics of muscles and joints, the skin, the heart, the lungs, the digestive system, the brain, etc. It indicates at the same time, why, for instance, caries develop, what can disturb the normal functions of the digestion, why outdoor activities are important, why children should not be exposed to monotonous and long-drawn-out activities, etc., all excellent reminders against a background of knowledge of physiological development.

The syllabus also goes into children's perception, attention, memory, imagination, cognition, language and emotions. Their development is described, and related to what teachers should think of in their guidance and upbringing of children. The information is presented concisely and comprehensively, and somehow manages to grasp the totality, body and mind in relation to each other in an educational perspective.

After the description of the characteristics and educational implications of the developmental process, there follows a specification of what the pre-school ought to do, and there the whole care picture is included, everything from food, hygiene and health to psychologically developing activities, moral education, the imparting of cultivated behaviour, and instruction in music, dance, art and literature, and so on.

From a training point of view, this document, with its orientation towards physiology and phenomena in developmental psychology, is undoubtedly the very backbone of pre-school teacher training. Presumably the syllabus's concise points are studied in detail and pursued in depth during training, and this is no bad starting-point for future pre-school teachers. The message of what the pre-school teacher should do in the guidance and upbringing of children comes to the fore throughout. For instance, they do not talk about the development of fine and gross motor skills, nor of when a child can hold a spoon or a piece of chalk correctly. They say instead that painting and modelling train harmony and flexibility in the movements of the muscles of the hands. Explanations are given for why children have to move a great deal, preferably out of doors, but it is pointed out that stretching and bending exercises should be avoided because the joints are shallow and the linking sinews are relatively limp.

One can comment in the same way on what is said about children's cognitive development. There is a brief description of the essentials of the development of the child's way of thinking, from the three-year-old's concrete thinking up to the six–seven-year-old's first attempts at abstract logical

For the "creative play", role play, there is a good supply of home-made props. The photographer has a camera (of cardboard) on a stand and a black cover to creep under. Afterwards he draws "the photograph".

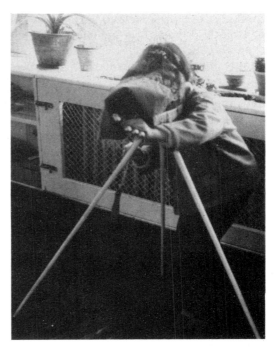

thinking, but presented in such a way and with words so chosen as to constantly provide firm points of reference for educational supervision. I can only conclude that the whole syllabus is underpinned by solid knowledge about children's development and that it is skilfully presented.

One more observation can be made. Swedish pre-school teacher training unfortunately does not provide students with the same physiological knowledge. It focuses primarily on child psychology as a basis. In that field there is a breadth of knowledge which is presumably absent in the Chinese syllabus and training. The question is which is best for functioning professionally, a selection from the fields of knowledge which are absolutely necessary in order to guide children, and going into these deeply, or a broad wealth of knowledge which easily remains superficial and where the students cannot always sift out what the essential points are and enter deeply into these to acquire real insight and thus educational readiness?

If we go on to compare pre-school teacher training in China and in Sweden, it is clear that Chinese training seems in many senses old-fashioned. Teaching styles are authoritarian, and actually I do not really understand how the training can produce the kinds of pre-school teacher whom we met on the job, who were so exceptionally competent professionally. I can merely try some guesses as explanations. At the college in Shanghai there was a will to tread new ground, to change the training, to grow further, and also an ongoing pedagogical debate about topical and vital problems in the pre-school. The students can hardly avoid becoming committed to this college's attitude and becoming aware of the importance of it in relation to their future work. The cause, i.e. the pre-school, is what they work for.

Another essential element lies, I suspect, in the practical side of the training. The students are given firm guidance, they are prodded methodically and successively into more and more demanding responsibility, and they identify with the pre-school teachers that they meet on teaching practice. In this way, personal commitment to both the children and to methodological expertise is propagated. The pre-school teacher profession is still so new in China, perhaps there is still a pioneer spirit, a feeling of clearing new ground. The pre-school teacher profession has not yet had time to become routine and everyday.

Can we learn something from China?

One gets a strong feeling that children are important in China. They are very proud to show their pre-school children to you. There is probably not a single study delegation, whatever the purpose of their visit, nor a group of tourists, for whom there has not been at least one visit to a pre-school. Children are essential for the future of the country, to continue the young People's Republic's work of building a welfare state along Chinese lines in which people have high morals for the sake of the community and know how to share out the beginnings of prosperity.

Studying and reflecting over the Chinese pre-school syllabus's section on ideological and moral upbringing, one is forced to conclude that in Sweden we do not have any corresponding conscious upbringing. We can also see the results — young people who are completely without respect for public property, scribble graffiti and vandalize. The visit to China has made me unsure. What is it that is good in our child upbringing, and what is it that is not good in our democratic society? As far as the pre-school is concerned, is it the case that we agree upon and give expression to formulations of nice democratic and social goals in the syllabus for the pre-school, but that we then do not manage to see or to get going on how they should be applied in general and in detail in actual day-to-day life? Are we aware that the behaviour and attitudes of teachers and other staff must accord with the goals and intentions of the upbringing, if the message is to be clear for the children? The same is, of course, true of parents. Does this make demands on adults which they do not have the energy for, or which they do not wish to be fully committed to? It is a question of the adult example as a strong force in children's upbringing.

I incline to the view that this is one of the secrets of the adults in the Chinese pre-school. Their personal attitudes, their actions, are in accordance with the message of upbringing which they are to communicate to the children. The adults are also able, I believe, to give a positive picture of what it means to be adult, a picture which does not create anxieties but is reassuring and expresses hope for the future. This is the only way I can explain my impressions of happy and open children in the pre-school in relation to guidance from the grown-ups which certainly made demands on them.

We may think that the Chinese pre-school syllabus is full of demands. It does not merely talk about development, it also expects children to know something, and, as far as I can judge, to know useful things by the time they leave the pre-school. We can think that children should be allowed to be just children, have access to a lot of free play, and not be pushed constantly forward to new achievements, to increased competence. The Chinese syllabus should undoubtedly be seen in the light of a multitude of circumstances. Among these are naturally China's need to make use of talent and help it on. China is still a developing country, and building up China into an industrialized country naturally requires the sifting and application of talent. But it seems that they are equally keen to find and make use of artistic talent. Another factor is that the Chinese pre-school has limited resources of premises, play materials and staff. A strict and relatively highly regulated syllabus partly solves this problem.

I am personally a little ambivalent in my attitude to the Chinese pre-school syllabus. Some of it is very good, parts I am uncertain about, some I am quite negative towards. I have already partly reported on my positive reactions, but I would like to make the further point that the equivalent of what we in Sweden refer to as societal orientation is worked out in an exemplary way, with a plan of work to follow. It is not a question of a single inflated visit to, for instance, the fire brigade or to some randomly chosen place of work, but of fairly systematically guiding the children so that they become familiar with and knowledgeable about their immediate environment. What confidence and security this programme must provide, quite apart from laying a real foundation for knowledge.

What also impresses one is the concern of the Chinese to find a balance in the plan for the children's day, so that play, lessons, work and entertainment form a good whole. The process of finding this balance contains in itself a kind of upbringing and preparation for adult life, which I think implies taking childhood seriously. Children are not just to be occupied while waiting to become adults, at which point they are expected to show adultness and responsibility. They are instead to be guided, via good habits, in slow process of maturation through the routines they develop.

My criticism of the Chinese syllabus has mostly to do with the strict streaming by age of the children, and with the way in which at various points things are laid out in such meticulous detail, as can be seen above all in the physical training. It has elements which are close to drill, and the pedagogy can become rigid and insensitive to the real needs of little children.

If I now contrast this with Swedish conditions, where absence of a clear pedagogic programme is striking, I have to ask myself: do we over-stimulate our children by swamping them with all sorts of play materials, do we permit so much free play that children merely jump from one thing to the next without being able to become deeply involved in what they are playing and without processing all their impressions? Perhaps we also underestimate children's need for knowledge during the pre-school years, for really learning something with the help of adults, so that they feel step by step that they master and understand progressively more about life. The affluent society with its wealth of superfluous goods perhaps competes with the involvement and insightful guidance of the adults.

Swedish children live in a consumer society. Compared with the Chinese, everyone in our country has a lot of leisure, leisure which at times it is difficult to occupy with sensible content. Primarily through television, Swedish children encounter at much too tender an age a flood of information which they cannot understand but which frightens and creates insecurity. In Sweden we think it is harmful for children to be at a day nursery for too long each day. In China it is just the opposite. There are no superfluous goods. There is minimal leisure. The flood of information to ordinary people is very limited and certainly controlled. They consider that children attending both day nurseries and weekly nurseries are in a desirable situation, despite the limited contact with their parents, and this is the case in a country where the family is something important.

When you travel to a country with one thousand million inhabitants and with a communist regime, it is easy to imagine that the individual is not given much scope and that the collective is what has been implemented throughout. I expected to see the big difference between the Swedish and the Chinese pre-school in precisely this regard. But I believe that there is also room for the individual person in China.

I believe that in the Chinese pre-school, when it is at its best, there is a good balance between focus on the individual child and on the group. However, teachers single out individual children in a different way from our practice. They aim at training children to be able to behave in a confident, sure and bold way, as a distinct individual, without being shielded by or hiding in the group, a kind of training for personal fearlessness and independence. The training is combined with being brought up to know that you belong to a collective group and that you must show consideration for the interests of both the small and large collective.

4 Patterns and models in child culture

Birgit Öhrn

If I were a four-year-old in China and had a place in a day nursery, I would be happy and glad, because that is what I learn to be. I would have many friends of the same age — perhaps 30–40 — and I would have teachers and nursery helpers to look up to, obey and learn from.

My environment — in both space and time — would form a natural pattern, where everything had its place and I myself would adjust to the place indicated as mine calmly and consciously.

After living for three years somewhat like a chrysalis, I would have a clear perspective of time backwards and forwards. The buildings and rooms of the pre-school and the children of all the other sections would remind me each day that I am *a person in growth*, a child who with each school year — as a five-year-old, six-year-old, etc. — will step by step acquire the skills and knowledge, the qualifications of understanding and feeling, which Chinese society, through its institutions, its teachers and my parents, clearly expects of me.

I would probably not want to be in a hurry, because in China one certainly feels privileged as a child. The demands made on Chinese pre-school children are gentle, and generally expressed as encouragement and positive faith. Physical and mental development are allowed to run in parallel and presuppose each other. The pre-school teachers make use of well-tried methods and procedures in order to adapt the learning to the preconditions of the children's development.

How they study and research into children's development, and how people in the teaching profession step by step work out thorough programmes for what children should learn — this my fellow travellers describe from the point of view of their specific area of competence.

132

I travelled to China to study child culture, because my work as a teacher of drama in pre-school teacher training presents me with substantial problems in just this area. I wanted to relate these to everything I had read and heard about Chinese child upbringing and culture.

The problem I meet in my work could, if one follows a popular Chinese model, be listed more or less as follows:

Lack of training, meaning that future pre-school teachers during their studies generally only manage to get a rough familiarity with the area of child culture and become conscious of the fact that the pre-school is a cultural environment, but they do not have time to collect enough knowledge about how this should be cultivated.

Confusion about goals, which in our so-called pluralist society means that cultural work in the pre-school may be "optional", that value judgements are accepted without validation, and that pre-school staff are given the freedom (or they are indifferently left alone) to work out the cultural upbringing that the children get.

Commercialism, which in a sophisticated system of influence surrounds children and parents in all situations, in all phases of life. What a commercial culture which is as integrated as ours means for a Swedish pre-school teacher, I can only describe as a blind battle to clear a way, to create a protected space in a tangle of creepers.

Poverty, which masks as virtue the authorities' lack of interest in child culture policy, and which is allowed to make more profound the injustices in the environments in which children grow up, inequalities between rich and poor councils, residential areas, day nurseries and staffing.

This is not a total picture of Swedish pre-school culture, but a personal map of obstacles which I believe many experience as I do. I wanted to compare cultural work in the pre-school in China in order to see and learn, fully aware that the problems are different and the solutions radically divergent.

I have very clear examples of how an exchange of experience can put the familiar in a new light. During the three weeks in Chinese pre-schools, I thought a lot about Swedish day nursery children: about their unrestrained freedom, their uncontrollable activity, the way they take it for granted that each one can burst into violent emotional shifts, and their considerable capacity to question, to fight back — but also to make alliances, make friendly and loving contact.

Back home and freshly at work again, I thought a lot about Chinese pre-school teachers and their scarce resources, simple rooms and equipment; their seemingly natural authority, their professional soundness and *ideological order*, which gives them calmness and confidence in their work; their competent supervision of large groups of children, supported by firmly planned procedures, and added to this their involvement and at times almost explosive energy, as in physically demanding activities outdoors.

Collecting my thoughts around what I experienced takes the form of a continuously changing sequence of pictures, as when the slides in a projector push each other on, and at times are projected on top of each other. One way of imposing order on the flow of pictures is, as a pre-school child does, to sort out, find sequences, and read off patterns which can be labelled and evaluated. Even if the concept "child culture" may seem limited, it covers so many areas that it will be necessary to simplify and account for some tendencies at the cost of others.

My pictures will primarily shed light on impressions around the following themes: how the pre-school in its own environment forms a cultural pattern, how the pre-school teacher functions as a cultural mediator, how the children receive and create in the wake of their models, and how child culture opens up the road to adult culture.

None of these parts can give any comprehensive picture of a Chinese reality which is certainly more diverse and contradictory than we could read off on one visit. However, our three weeks of travelling cover visits to very different child environments, from a day nursery in the smallest neighbourhood unit of a metropolis to an extraordinarily simple day nursery housed in a stable in a rice-growing people's council. We were able to make the visits relatively lengthy, which allowed those who wanted to follow activities from start to finish, outside and in addition to the more scheduled performances which are always bestowed on foreign guests.

The pre-school as a cultural environment

Does it make any difference what a pre-school looks like? Does this say anything over and above what it says about the institution as a place of work, and rational and pedagogical considerations?

To an outside visitor, naturally — yes! Go into a day nursery and look around you: you get practical arrangements and details of the interior design pointed out to you, but irrational details are certainly decisive for your impressions to just as great an extent. Are there table-cloths or not, are they made of cloth or plastic? How are materials placed and stored, what taste do the curtains, pictures, flowers and mobiles show? You read off the degree of cosiness of a Swedish pre-school from the supply of pillows and cushions, old stripped furniture, little rooms with decorated walls, huts, rope-ladders and other unexpected additions to the interior design. These are welcomed by the staff and the children as potential for exploitation, for doing something positive with.

It is easy to recognize a Swedish day nursery. It can often be used as a point of reference in the immediate environment — a detached, clearly visible low building with "cheerful" windows, and a playground which is scantily fenced in but still clearly exposed. Even the day nursery slotted into a block of flats signals its presence by decorations on windows and the entrance, and the place for play outdoors is open for the neighbours to see. Swedish day nurseries have names: the Blue Anemone, the Capercaille, the Soprano, etc., with links to the family names in the adjoining blocks. When compared to the Chinese day nurseries I have seen, the Swedish ones are really open for examination and communication between the sections and the world outside. The inside regions can, however, be difficult to see one's way around — at least at the beginning it takes time for visitors and staff to literally "come in" to the institution.

A Chinese day nursery is not so easy to find from the outisde. With a number rather than a name, it turns its back on the rush of the street, just like the traditional family residences in cities such as Peking, Shanghai, Chengdu or Kanton. Even in recently-built blocks where the tenants of the high-rise flats send messages from the balconies with their flower pots, washing-lines and diverse household goods — the day nursery will still lie in the background and be secluded. It would be tempting to conclude that in a vibrant environment teeming with people, by tradition the need for marking limits is important; that a courtyard of one's own, be it ever so small, has symbolized a certain standard; and the higher the status, the larger the number and size of courtyards.

For the day nursery, being screened off means calmness and security; no dangerous running out into the traffic, no uncontrolled intrusions from the outside world.

Around the courtyard — or courtyards — in larger day nurseries — the children's rooms lie in long rows, linked by corridors with double rows of windows. One row is at grown-up height looking into the children's rooms; the outer one looks onto the courtyard and at times has no window-panes and then resembles galleries. So once one has succeeded in finding the pre-school it is easy and quick to get an overall picture of how it is organized.

It is equally simple to grasp the overall structure of each and every group-room for the children. This is how the day nursery at a large textiles factory in Chengdu was arranged (478 children of 7,000 employees, 18 groups with a staff of 86).

From out in the corridor you can see in through three windows into a large, spaciously furnished room. Against the wall with the corridor windows and door there are four low tables with room for five–six children. The three corridor windows have opposite them as many similar windows looking onto a strip of an outside courtyard with trees. The "lower" of the shorter walls has its central section decorated: a stylized tree drawn with clear contours and completely covered with pastel shades. Otherwise the wall is painted a light colour like the others, with no other decorations. In the corner of the corridor wall, the children's little chairs have been piled up, and in the corner of the outer long wall there are a blackboard and a towel-stand. In the corner at the front by the short wall there is a shelf inside the door with a cloth cover hanging in front of where the teaching materials are stored. Alongside, there is a lower shelf where the children's food bowls are piled up, and an open cupboard higher up, where today's snack stands waiting. In the further corner of the outer long wall stands the organ, facing a semi-circle of three–four-year-olds on their little chairs. Near the organ between the windows, the teacher's "grown-up" chair faces the children.

Right now a music lesson is taking place, about 15–30 minutes alternating with dancing exercises. The children have their afternoon rest in a different room, further down the corridor, and this room will also be used by other groups, for instance when this group is outdoors.

For curious children's eyes this environment offers no particular surprises, and, as far as I understand, that is not the idea either. Curiosity, the ability to observe, and the joy of discovery are directed by the teacher towards the material she presents. Interruptions in this routine are the planned study visits, or the visits by delegations, which both the staff and the children are very much used to receiving.

Chinese children do not run around among different activity stations, and cannot pick and choose from toys, games or materials. Nor do they form any spontaneous groups around activities they have hit upon themselves, but they are taken and put in and out of rooms earmarked for particular parts of the time-table.

A glimpse of the environment, as presented here, naturally says a good deal about the special educational features of the Chinese pre-school. The external and internal order in all the exemplarily executed details can

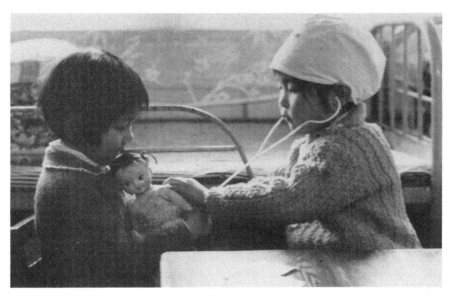

The doctor listening to the child has a white doctor's cap with a red cross on it and a fine stethoscope.

At the hairdresser's, the customer's shoulders are covered with a cape. The home-made hair-drier is of cardboard.

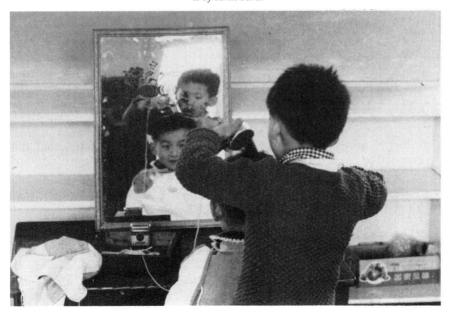

contribute to explaining the discipline shown by the little children which Westerners are so astounded by. But I suspect that this discipline would easily shatter if it were not founded in a *cultural* upbringing which permits the children to experience their own behaviour as something important — perhaps the most important thing of all. (Conduct is, by the way, judged and evaluated every week using a points system and the results are explained publicly to the whole group.)

For behaviour, many models are given in texts, pictures, ballads and stories. This is what I imbibe as a child and *nothing else*, and my environment facilitates and guides my learning of basic attitudes such as patience, attention, concentration and self-control.

If this is not experienced as monotonous drudgery, it is due, I think, to the *aesthetics* running through the environment and the materials. The frugality which first strikes the visitor gradually comes over as discernment, a calm and neutral background to the equally scarce materials which they are allowed to handle. Sparse but colourful — this must have a strong impact on the children, arouse their interest and joy, tune them in to harmony.

If, as a child, I can experience myself as a highly-coloured flower, not least because my clothes are so strikingly resplendent against the adults' uniform background colours, then I must surely feel that the colours of the pictures belong with me, hence their message too.

If I am consistently treated as a loved and cherished plant in the large children's nursery, then I must surely identify with the colourful little boys and girls, rabbits, ducklings and other enchanting beings who in dances, games, songs and stories constantly *learn* good things and overcome little vexing shortcomings which are a completely innocent carry-over from the stage of egoistic imprudence.

There is nothing controversial in the teaching materials presented, no irreconcilable contradictions, no intractable problems. There is often *one* solution, *one* conclusion which is so logical that not even a Swedish drama teacher with a predilection for creative chaos can see a reason for making a problem out of it.

The trusting harmony of the message corresponds to the sharp contours of the shape, the pleasant curvature of the line, the dance movements' combination of balance and pliancy, to the singing style's strong striking of the note and extremely clear diction, to the melody's unison major key resonance and the rhythm's regular — never at any point excited — pulse.

Together these stylistic features express an aesthetic ideal which presumably has deep roots in the classical Chinese cultural tradition, and which the ignorant visitor can merely have an inkling of, or recognize in the cultural historical sights — the temples, sepulchres, palaces — and which recurs in contemporary art, in popular music, in stage productions, yes, even in the official advertising.

Let me attempt to sum up this ideal in words such as *lightness, clarity and gathering* and contrast them with heaviness, multiple meanings and chaos, perhaps not words to which tribute is paid in Sweden, or even in European culture, but nonetheless fairly well known in our artistic life.

I see lightness striven for in Chinese architecture, for example, palaces and temples which despite monumental size and splendour seem to lift up their own weight through the effect of perspective in the totality and a series of details which raise and lighten the mass of the buildings. This includes staircases and plateaux which lead the eye forward and upward, roof angles and the curved-up corners which lead one's thoughts to the dancers' upward-angled hands and feet. It includes the pagodas, the strange tower buildings where every floor carries a new one up in a swaying balancing-act which resembles cycle acrobats on the stage. The lightness and clarity I also find in Chinese visual art, which favours brushwork for elegant drawing and light, airy colouring (they have no Rembrandt or Evert Lundquist in China). The lightness and clarity are also a feature of the traditional dances and the popular juggling acts, and a spectrum of pastel shades dominates all the decorative things in everyday life, children's clothes, toys, combs, washbowls, etc.

Gathering is to be my word for bringing together, the tendency to figuratively tie together ornamental lines and movements to a single *gestalt*, a kind of emblem which the eye can grasp at a glance. Thus, for instance, the most far-flung dragon loops in a relief are gathered into a coherent archetypal picture, thus the porcelain pattern catches its own tail, thus a performer on the stage comes to a standstill in a given posture, a group of gymnasts in a figure, a dance in a still configuration, and — most clear of all — every distinct scene on the stage in the classical Peking opera.

It is in my view not a question of something exclusive in isolated high culture, but on the contrary the most general features of the cultural picture which meets the masses and which as a result children experience too, and cultivate contact with in the pre-school.

To me it seems natural to trace this ideal in body language, the way every person, irrespective of artistic talent, uses and shapes what she or he

When playing kitchens, they slice and chop vegetables in the Chinese way with the right kind of semi-circular knives.

Building with wooden bricks of different shapes and colours. There are sets of instructions to follow.

wants to be. The pre-school brings up its children according to this ideal from the very earliest years.

It seems to start so early that it appears miraculous that children learn to stretch. In the course of three weeks I did not see any children crawl, none totter around, none hang on in the way we have come to regard as natural in the motor development of babies.

For reasons of time I must refrain from closer studies of institutions for children under the age of three. These have a different superior (the Ministry of Health) and apparently a different, more limited goal which focuses on the child's physical care. My superficial impression is that here the children are trained in a gentle, anticipatory way — some teachers employ a "passive training system" to stretch arms and legs, use the children's strength by, for instance, letting them hang by their arms from a bamboo pole, or sit up straight with straight arms and legs. The really small day nursery children lie packaged up and made me think of chrysalises. I understand why they are not encouraged to crawl. The cement floors are often bare and unsuitable for that. But it seems to me as though the Chinese chrysalis-children have some built-in bell which signals, "Now I can stand on my own and begin to walk!" No thick bulky nappy hinders the movements after that. Potty training and the conveniently open trousers seem to be an excellent solution to that problem.

When the three-year-old has grown out of split-bottom trousers and moved over to the day-nursery (or kindergarten as all pre-school forms for three–seven-year-olds are usually called), the style ideal encountered is *the stretched-out body*. For this, our familiar "headpipe" would be an appropriate symbol. It is quite strange that I did not see this obligatory self-portrait in any children's drawings. Not that the children's arms and legs move from the head without joints, but in children's awareness of their bodies this seems to be the case. The central parts of the body, trunk, pelvis, bottom and stomach, which play such a large part in our children's conceptions of their bodies and movements (and which are stressed through imported Afro–American styles of movement in early games with hula hoops, shake and rock dances), these appear to be completely absent from Chinese movement training. The trunk is only a knot between arms and legs, and the children are trained in the pattern of peripheral movement which dominates in Chinese gymnastics and dance and which we can feel akin to in classical European ballet, where the body embraces and conquers space, everything from the statically stretched-out arabesque to all the jumps and lifts with which the apparently winged dancers defy the law of gravity.

However, Chinese children are not drilled in any positions or stretching movements which are at odds with natural anatomy. What they do learn early on is to perfect the stretched-out, preferably diagonal body-line, with feet and hands angled outwards, to use the flexibility of the shoulder joints and the neck so as to lift up and turn the head and its smiling front side.

This is how we see the children in the pre-school's obligatory performance for visitors. When my travelling companions provocatively wonder whether Swedish children are less talented than Chinese, or whether they might be prevented from learning such enchanting acts by misguided pedagogy, one would like to think that this is a show put on by the élite, with some specialities which are popular with foreigners.

I believe, however, that what we see is a result of the entire culture of the pre-school, uniting and branching out *upbringing* and *the ideal* in all the situations of the day. The skilful show is just a part of a pedagogy which gives prominence to exercises and delight and makes good use of the joy of learning and knowing things.

The pre-school teacher as a cultural mediator — the children as recipients

A Chinese pre-school teacher is always a woman. Our colleagues in China were completely convinced that this is best. Women are better at coping with children, are more loving and patient, and understand children better — this is how our questions were answered. Better? Than men, implicitly, who have other qualities. Whatever your attitude to sex roles and equality — and we discussd this on a good many occasions — their attitude seems for the present to be unshakeable and says something important about the human model that the pre-school teacher (and the nursery helper) have to be. She thus displays a selection of desirable personal qualities and lacks or suppresses others; for instance, excitability, impatience, aggression, the fighting spirit, the desire to experiment. You do not see many of these attributes among the children either.

A Chinese pre-school teacher appears confident. She combines pride and humility in her view of the work, she is involved but never anxious. In the first place she relies on the general principles of the pre-school and on the plan which has been prepared, and approved by the principal. There is also her training — which can vary a good deal — and which she wishes to supplement. But she knows what she has learnt and she knows that she can apply it.

At the large table on which they play with sand, a landscape emerges amid lively discussion.

It is reasonable, in contrast, to describe a Swedish pre-school teacher as self-critical, insightful, and torn between conflicting ambitions, committed, and constantly anxious about personal inadequacy. There are lots of things which are "hard" in the pre-school, and children often share this opinion.

A Swedish pre-school teacher is "supposed to" be displeased with her or his training. "Too much theory and too little reality" is a common judgement. "Reality" also makes such big demands that pre-school teachers more often see themselves as social workers than as cultural mediators.

Swedish pre-school teachers do not play a musical instrument or sing so naturally and undauntedly with the children and in the presence of visiting adults. They do not lead ring-games and folk dances with such instructive pre-eminence as the Chinese, and they prefer to resort to the tape-recorder, books, puppets, or the like, rather than using their own capacity for dramatic expressions to tell stories or animate situations. "I'm no good at that," people say, and thereby communicate to the children the pattern of under-estimating yourself as a virtue, and the children learn this all too quickly.

Dancing lesson. They learn complicated steps and moves, at first in pairs. Arms are stretched out in a diagonal movement, hands angled outwards.

This is an unjust comparison, which leaves out much of what Swedish pre-school teachers do in their work, and do well. For example, listening to children, encouraging independence and creativity, delegating responsibility to the children, helping them to sort out conflicts. A Chinese pre-school teacher does not share our view that all this is necessary, and does not need to fight with the problems which such a way of working entails.

But with respect to the limited aspect of the pre-school teacher role which I am addressing here, namely that of the cultural mediator, the comparison provides food for thought.

When we illegitimize ourselves as the bearers of our culture, we, as a staff team, suppress each other. We also absolve ourselves from the responsibility for the children becoming familiar with a cultural tradition which to some extent can provide a counterweight to the commercial rubbish culture. We can partly ease our guilty consciences by involving ourselves at a more structural level, by demanding a greater cultural provision for children, by organizing petitions and demonstrations.

Now I emphatically do not think that we should refrain from demanding resources from society for cultural work. On the contrary, Swedish pre-school teachers should be furiously enraged about a cultural policy which haggles over a few pence for children's theatre, libraries, music and exhibitions for children. But if these same pre-school teachers were able to indicate proudly how they are personally responsible and do their work so that the children do not become neglected cultural consumers but actively take part in a culture society — gosh, what politician would then dare not to take them seriously?

Chinese pre-school teachers are not in conflict with society, their loyalty is not open to discussion. Of course they have wishes and hopes for increased resources. But scarcity is no hindrance to their *teaching the children what they know themselves,* and this is very impressive. No shyness or embarrassment trips them up, no competition or envy between them poisons *the joy of being a teacher.* This is what the grown-up role in the pre-school really is, so one cannot describe how the pre-school teacher communicates cultural patterns without at the same time stressing how important the children's role as *recipients* is. Perhaps it is precisely this interaction itself which is the fundmental culture of the pre-school.

That this pattern of learning is happy, friendly — yes, loving — will, I hope, be apparent in some examples.

Some lessons in loving

Our study group came to Peking at the very beginning of April, and were met by the first tender greenery of spring. Next to the teacher training college's beautiful pre-school, the spring was also bursting out, in the trees of the park, in the songs the children sang and the pictures they drew.

"Spring is here, spring is here!" is the sound of the chorus in a song which starts the first lesson of the day for a group of six-year-olds. They are going to start school in the autumn, so they have at least two lessons a day, not including morning gymnastics.

A lesson lasts for 20–25 minutes. After the morning gymnastics, a health check, and a moment of free play, they are now sitting at their places in their classroom: four rows of desks on each side of the central passage, four children at each set of desks makes 32 pupils. Bright-eyed, brushed shiny — the girls with a voluminous rosette on the crowns of their heads — all sitting up straight and with their hands resting behind the backs of their chairs. The nursery helper adjusts some feet or hands, but discreetly and from behind, so that the children's attention is not disturbed.

The pre-school teacher stands in front of her class. She is wearing the impersonal suit of adults and over it a white coat, as all pre-school staff with the possible exception of principals do. She looks cheerful and speaks in a lively way and gesticulates while she puts up a spring picture on a stand. With gentle hand movements she follows the picture's contours, a mountain with terrace cultivation, some trees in the foreground and a couple of birds high up in the clouds. The picture is called "Beautiful spring", and now the pre-school teacher sings through the spring song, on her own at first, and then with the children. I think the children are fairly familiar with the words, they sing along loudly. But the teacher wants them to be precise with the melody.

Is it a beautiful song?

Yes, yes, the children reply emphatically.

Let us sing it beautifully, says the teacher, now with the aid of a pointer. She lets it trace the lines of the terrace cultivation from the bottom upwards to the top of the mountain, just as the melody climbs up the scale. Then she rhythmically picks out the two birds and in so doing marks the two notes which conclude every verse before the refrain "Spring is here". The apparently unartistic colour drawing, pinned onto the stand, functions brilliantly as both text and picture score.

Then the teacher asks what they themselves have noticed on the arrival of spring, whether they have seen anything change outdoors. The children put up their hands and say something one at a time. The teacher sums up and now sets the children the task of drawing a picture of this. The nursery helper has distributed pencil-boxes and A4-sized pieces of paper and the children are now told to open their pencil-boxes. Before they begin drawing, the teacher stresses that the children should think of their own impressions and that each of them should do his or her own picture.

It is fascinating to see how the children really pause for a moment and gather their thoughts before they get going with the crayons, and how they become completely absorbed in the work without peeping at their class-mates or letting themselves be disturbed by the fairly unconstrained visitors, who stride around and peer over shoulders with their snap-ready cameras. A few times a child puts up a hand to call for help from an adult with a rubber — everything breathes calm industry. I do not have the heart to disturb them any longer but pop into an adjoining room where a group of four-year-olds are also having a picture lesson.

They are sitting at a lot of little tables, six tables with four children at each. The teacher hands out the drawings done by the children a few days earlier with pencils out in the school park. All the children could choose their "own" tree and try to draw a picture of it. Now the teacher goes round with new crayons, and each table is given a limited assortment.

The children's sketches vary a great deal, but present in each is some-thing of the tree's basic shape, its trunk and branches. That it is really a case of different types of tree is apparent from the children's work. One girl shows real picture-creating joy and makes the branches "spurt" from the trunk of the tree. One boy puts large green leaves on a couple of branches. The adults "serve" materials silently, pick up any paper or crayons which have managed to land on the floor. From time to time there are small interruptions: a boy turns his head to look at a class-mate's drawing opposite him, a girl fidgets with her hair rosette. Some children watch the visitor going round and exchange a surreptitious comment. The grown-ups inter-vene only to adjust the children's posture. They seem to be very particular about the children sitting and holding their hands in the right way. The left hand should lie stretched out in the top left-hand corner of the paper to keep the paper from moving. This is to avoid straining their eyes, they explain.

There are many varieties of tree in the park and I rediscover their characteristics bit by bit in the children's pictures. The slender poplar, the softly branching willow, the fruit trees with blossom on bare twigs. . . . Now the teacher is standing behind a boy who has looked worried for some time.

All he has managed is four green leaves on a twig directly adjoining a thick trunk. The teacher takes his hand in hers and colours in his drawing with the crayon, reinforcing what he has done. Then she continues to guide his hand in drawing movements without leaving any trace on the paper, out from the trunk, branches and twigs.

You have to see this silent scene in order not to be appalled at what looks like authoritarian interference in chldren's free creation. In the first place, here we are not dealing with free creation but with studies. These four-year-olds have thus followed the signs of spring in the trees, and they are working on the elaboration of their pictures in 15-minute units. Loving your work and studies has turned into much more than a slogan for me, because it is natural for the children to return to their pictures and complete them step by step. And what love there is in the teacher's discreet way of *reinforcing and intimating what the child can do!*

The class of six-year-olds have finished their morning lesson and I chat for a moment to the teacher and some children.

— Are they all right-handed, I ask.

— In this class, yes, but children are of course allowed to use their best hand. The teacher considers drawing with pencil and crayon very important so that the children have developed a basic skill when they move on after some time to Chinese characters. They have in any case started with reading training, so their competence is built up in good time.

— Is spring a good theme to work with? I ask, having often heard criticism of the tedium of the seasons recurring as a theme in the Swedish pre-school.

— But for the children the spring is new each year, the pre-school teacher feels. And the children agree when asked.

I try to tell them something about how wintry it was when we left Stockholm and how we are enjoying the sun and everything green. So I am given a pile of the class's drawings, "because everyone loves the spring".

A conversation like this one and many others at different pre-schools is a singular experience. The children and teacher adopt the same friendly and measured attitude: no interruptions of turns, no contorted moves or shy evasion. Of course they are influenced by there being an interpreter and the special situation with foreign visitors, but here, too, there is a pattern which underlies the variations of the moment. The children are fearless and mature enough for the tasks given them by the teacher; for instance, showing guests the way, presenting the numbers in a programme.

That shyness is a weakness which can be overcome is exemplified in a little role-play. Follow me to the large, beautiful hall of the day nursery of the teacher's college, in which all the institution's classes have their dance and theatre teaching.

The hall, on the upper floor of the old main buiding, is a big room (I measure out 11×11 metres) with high windows on three sides, and the fourth is a half-wall with a row of little windows at the top of it and separating the hall from the stairway. The room has a very nice, dark wood floor and all the windows have decorative white folkweave curtains and pot plants. Round the walls there are benches and chairs, and there is also the usual organ.

An imposing, plump, elderly teacher has just finished a lesson with a class of five-year-olds. This woman is a phenomenon I shall never forget. In her dull suit, with her straight, short-cropped hair, and with solid walking-shoes on her feet, she evolves a unique grace and suppleness, she literally radiates vitality, and carries the children along in quite intricate combinations of steps.

The five-year-olds pack up and carry out the little decorations they have used, and a new class, consisting of four-year-olds, help to put out a trellis with artificial flowers and to build up a gateway with a Chinese "moon window" with blue bricks of different shapes. The teacher takes from a basket the headgear which is such common equipment in the pre-school — a headband of cloth or cardboard, with a colourful figure on it, generally the head of an animal. Here the children are turned into birds and hares. There are also gossamer butterfly wings of tulle to fasten at the neck and wrists.

A girl has the main part in a play which the children have evidently rehearsed a little.

"Spring is coming," she declaims and points with exaggerated gestures at imaginary trees and birds. "I am so happy — come and play with me!" Then the hares come in a line, hopping to their places with their feet together, and the birds fly in to theirs. They each chant their own short rhyme, with expressive gestures: "Let us play a game!"

The idea of the game is for one at a time, with eyes shut, to recognize a friend. The girl feels a bird.

— I know who you are, you have long legs and are good at dancing.

— Yes, that's me, replies the bird proudly. Now it's my turn. The bird shuts its eyes, all change places, and the bird captures the girl.

— Who's that?

— We know she sings nicely, say all the animals in chorus. But she's so shy!

Everyone laughs and disappears and the girl begins to cry. Her mother, played by the teacher, comes and asks why the girl is crying.

— Have they hit you?

— No, but they are laughing at me because I don't dare to sing.

— You would find the courage if you asked a teacher to help you, says the mother, who suggets a bird.

The girl goes to the bird and asks to be taught how she can become brave.

— I will teach you, says the bird, if you sing a song first!

The girl sings one verse with a feeble voice and her head hung low. The bird says that she is very good at singing, but that she must overcome her shyness.

— Here are your teachers, says the bird and points to a group of hares. The hares promise to teach her to be brave if she sings a song first!

— We can look away, they say, and round they hop.

The girl sings, this time a little louder and with her head up.

— You are very good at singing, you just need an even better teacher, say the hares and take her off to the butterflies.

— Let us sing together, they suggest, and inspired by the gestures of the butterflies, the girl sings with more expression now. But the butterflies take her off to an owl, who shuts her eyes and asks:

— Who are you?

All the animals shout in chorus:

— Say who you are!

— I am a girl who is good at singing, but I'm too frightened to sing for so many. I'm not brave. But you are wise. Perhaps you can teach me?

— Yes, the owl promises. And the animals chip in with:

— If you sing a song first!

The skilful performance is just one part of a pedagogy which makes good use of the joy of learning and knowing things.

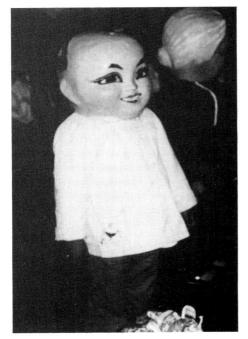

In a performance that the children enjoy putting on they place a giant head, made of papier maché and with a smiling face painted on it, over their own heads.

And then the girl sings more and more fearlessly, and the mother comes and witnesses the joy of this, and the play finishes with song and dance.

Perhaps an older reader will, as I did, recognize features of the old end-of-term play, with children clad in crêpe paper in tableaux, laboriously rehearsed and put on with the actors tense and anxious about the fatal *faux pas* of having a "blackout". And certainly there are parallels between the short singing play and teableaux that Chinese children rehearse and the synopses in popular children's books.

There is no free, improvized drama at all in the Chinese pre-school. Even theatre of this more conventional kind is quite rare. One understands that the teachers at the Teacher's College in Peking are pioneers and exceptionally competent, that they work at an admirable, well-equipped institution.

But the pattern, the ambitions and the pedagogical line are easy to recognize at every pre-school we visit. The staff are also familiar with the latest guidelines in the syllabus and everywhere they emphasize the importance of singing, dance and handicraft as steps in the children's personal development and in building up a moral mentality and a cultivated style of life.

So there are high ideals and ambitious goals, but my experience is that there may be a considerable gap between intention and implementation. I therefore concentrated my attention on the question of how they realize their goals. My notes are full of lessons, each more competent and more consistent than the last. Perhaps a few more examples will illuminate the role of teaching methodology.

Take gymnastics and outdoor play as an example. The children's physical development is studied in detail in order to find the most effective methods for prompting it. It is obvious that the pre-school children need a great deal of intensive body movement, particularly as they do in fact work hard when sitting still and concentrating for large parts of the day. But the children are let off for unstructured play for very short periods of time, perhaps ten minutes. At all other times the teachers guide and participate and follow up education for order, purpose and — not least — patience!

A line of three-year-olds, queueing up to cycle round a particular track on the day nursery's tricycle is a common sight. Or they squat in straight lines waiting for the teacher to put a headband with a role symbol on each child. It may be the very widespread hares or rabbits which the children represent when training to hop with their feet together on two low benches placed parallel, two lines, two children at a time. First they make a few hops on the ground, then up on the bench and steady their hops on this, then on the ground towards a flannelgraph with beetroot or radishes. Each animal takes some and then hops back, to the back of the queue.

In gymnastics, chairs are used for training the muscles of the back and the stomach: you sit right out on the edge, support yourself on your hands and lift your body like a sloping plank. The opposite movement is, of course, bending forwards and touching your toes. They signal with flags in their hands and co-ordinate with stretching their legs, diagonally with both flags to the right and your left foot stretched out, etc. They also use small but surprisingly heavy dumb-bells to stretch the arms, while at other times they shake wreaths with flowers, jingling bells or ribbons above their heads when running on the spot. The gymnastics programmes are very varied and well thought-out, so as to train every possible movement, and the movements can be directly carried over into dances. Naturally the pre-school teacher carries out the programme simultaneously in front of the children, and if necessary the nursery helper rectifies any minor individual deviations. Marching in and out is in orderly file, the time beaten out by a little bell, triangle or tambourine. They are prepared to go to the lengths of moving out an organ for the dancing games, or else they may play the accordion.

Here is a sample lesson in a class of little children between the ages of two and three:

In from the morning gymnastics in a careful march. When told to, the children sit down on their miniature chairs in a horseshoe. A one-minute song together, clapping in time. Then the children stand up, sing a short song involving putting one hand on your side and bowing your head. Then a tune sung sitting, with one hand on a kneecap, the forefinger of the other hand beating the time. The tune reminds me of "*ja må han leva!*" The teacher plays on the accordion a melodic call, meaning "Stand up", and the opposite set of notes for "Sit down". An additional musical signal, a tremolo chord, gives the children a starting point and a time-limit for moving to a given place, in this case the children from one row of chairs move out to the floor. They perform a song, with clenched hands winding round their outstretched arms, also lasting a minute.

The tremolo chord again, the children from a different row of chairs move out, and their chairs are taken by the ones who have just sung. The teacher puts the new children into a ring and we see a repeat of a meeting-departing dance which we have seen many versions of everywhere. One inner circle, one outer. The children in the inner circle pause opposite one child, tap three times on each shoulder, then grip each other's hands, swing round once and the friend then goes into the inner ring, on the final "*zai jian"* (Goodbye). By the end of this 10–12 minute long programme, the whole class have sung and danced together so many times that all the children have had a turn in the inner circle and have "asked" a friend to dance.

This is how early the basis is laid for musical and motor concepts, and with such simple but consistently applied names. The music signals seem to follow the children over the years, they functioned everywhere. The singing game, too, with more difficult turns such as polka steps and side swings added.

A precondition for the few staff to be able to cope with the work is, of course, that the children learn to be in a large group so early on and to alternate between doing things oneself and learning from what others are doing. Children are brought up directly and indirectly in a collective spirit and it was difficult to trace any sign of egocentricity or obstructiveness. Collectiveness means co-operation, palpably illustrated, for instance, in a charming "rabbit dance" which the children in Chengdu demonstrated. Each rabbit has a cube, half a metre high, with parts of a pattern on all the sides. During the turns of the dance, they try to combine the cubes in various ways, but they cannot get the whole pattern to match up. They try out many variants before putting their heads together to form a joint plan and manage to build up the large joint picture of a splendid beetroot.

But collectiveness does not equal uniformity; it can vary, and different groups can co-exist side by side, as can be seen in this little role-play:

They are five-year-olds practising. After volunteering by putting up a hand, five children get headbands with animal symbols: a duck, a fish, a turtle, a goose and a frog. The other children get green headbands without a symbol. They are to be tadpoles and other "children" of the five animals. The role-play begins with the tadpoles waking up and beginning to move. One child at a time is the narrator, and the children act out and speak their lines in dialogue.

"In the spring, when there is a breeze and sunshine, the water hops with tadpoles. They are searching for their frog Mummy. The Mummy Duck arrives with her baby ducklings, who are copying her. The tadpoles try to, too, because they think that the duck is their Mummy. No, says Mummy Duck, your Mummy has two big eyes and a big mouth. Go and look.

"The tadpoles search on and meet a fish with her baby fish, they imitate her but are told that their Mummy has four legs too. Go and look! The tadpoles search on and meet a turtle with her little ones. She has four legs and they try to copy her behaviour. But no, says the turtle, your Mummy is fat and has a white tummy, go and look!

"They meet the goose with her goslings and think the description fits. But they have trouble in imitating the goose's ways, and she says: your Mummy has green clothes, she sings Croak-Croak. Go and look and listen, good luck!

"Now they finally find their Mummy, but — the tadpoles complain — why aren't we like you? Why don't we have four legs, and why can't we sing? When the day is over, you will have four legs and then you will be able to sing, comforts the Mummy Frog, and jumps in the water with her children, and the play is over."

The children have done a rehearsal of the role-play right the way through without interruption and been careful to get their entrances and exits right. The teacher asks via the interpreter whether I understood, and I show that I grasped the various animals and their distinctive ways of moving. The children chuckle delightedly when I repeat the "choreography", but when I praise their concentration and capacity to remember the long story, the teacher objects. She queries whether the children correctly understood all the situations, says that the children speak much too softly and that they do not act convincingly.

— Was that story fun?

— Yes, say the children.

— So, the teacher says, when you get home today you should tell your Mummies the story. Then you will notice that you are speaking and acting better.

Children as creators of culture

One is bound to wonder whether the Chinese pre-school's way of occupying the children intensively leaves them any space to develop spontaneously their own creativity, whether they are given the chance to learn from each other and learn by experimenting in the way that we want our Swedish pre-school children to do. An important point of departure for our pre-school pedagogy is that children do have an innate creative drive which finds its own means of expression. We believe that the pre-school should provide stimulation and the conditions in which children can find each other spontaneously and link up their ideas and impulses. We try to encourage the children to use their imagination and their capacity for vicarious experience independently, and in their own genuine way to express themselves in pictures and form, movement, sound and music, in play with words and roles. Admittedly there are great shortcomings in our training, and staff are to a large extent forced to fumble their own way into a scheme of guiding which works, but I think that most are aware how important it is for children to be allowed to take initiative themselves and be creative.

I did not find any corresponding view among Chinese pre-school teachers. The concept creativity was connected with activities like "arts and crafts" and "creative play". In practice this mostly meant that the children at given times and in an orderly way were occupied with a kind of lego construction or with cutting or folding paper. The shape construction was carried out at the little tables which the children sat around on four–six chairs. They used wooden bricks of different colours and shapes, and they had little sets of instructions to follow. The children worked individually side by side and seldom interfered in what the others were doing. They all had their own pile of bricks, their own instructions and their own construction, and there was never the slightest dispute on their territorial borders, but no mutual profit either. I actually saw at one pre-school some boys co-operating on balancing things high up (and in my thoughts sent a greeting to Homburger-Ericson who generally claims that boys build phallically and girls uterinely, i.e. towers and rooms respectively).

There was also another type of material, a series of plastic pieces in the beloved pastel shades, and with curved, ornamental shapes. This was mostly used by the children for two-dimensional compositions. Although it was possible to place the pieces upright, they were mostly lying-down pictures of very "Chinese" character. I am not sure whether there were prototypes for this kind of material, or whether there is a tradition equivalent to paper-folding. Instructions were given for it, at any rate for the very complicated operations which some of the figures required. This activity, too, was impeccably organized round the work-tables and the children worked silently and with concentration, being handed "new" little sheets of paper when one figure was ready. Everything from newspaper to brightly coloured glazed paper was used, evidently time and time again, as there were old folding lines on the bits of paper — something that the children were not disturbed by!

These were two activities which usually took place everywhere and, as I have said, were carried out in a disciplined manner. The teachers remained ready to be helpful, but did not take part. The children's products were not saved either, but the bricks and paper were generally sorted out and put away when the work was finished. On the other hand, here and there you

A group of teacher trainees in their observation period watching as five—six-year-olds at the large day nursery of a textile factory practise before a performance. The children are dancing with large red paper flowers in their hands.

could see the children's drawings with their names on pinned or pegged up. Experimental play with clay, sand or water scarcely ever took place, nor did I ever see an example of textile creation. But I did see role-play, which deserves a more thorough description.

The world of work in miniature

Role-play, or creative play, as they call it, is written into the staff planning book several afternoons a week. It is said to be preceded by study visits out in society and it is arranged with the help of materials in the pre-school's largest room (which, however, need not be larger than an ordinary classroom) or, even better, outdoors. Close to each other, different settings are built up, and the children keep to their own setting in little groups, and play, soberly and with strikingly earnest joy.

Here you can find the doctor's surgery, the photographer's studio, shops, the hairdresser's, the ship, the restaurant, and domestic scenes with children and dolls. Here there is also a kind of model-game with construction models which the children stage on a few little tables put together. It may be a zoological garden with animals in their enclosures, or a town scene with houses, trees and buses, or a country setting with horses, buffaloes, bamboo shoots and buildings.

The children display great activity in building up their scenes and remain in their roles a long time, often until the time is up. There is a certain amount of contact between the groups, often prompted by the adults, so that the professionals have clients and visitors.

Although there is usually a dearth of play materials to a greater or lesser extent and the children are trained to take turns over the right of access to a toy, there is paradoxically an abundance of things for role-play, which, of course, does not really require more than imagination and entering into the spirit of the thing. The photographer has a camera on a stand (of cardboard) and a black cover to creep under. The doctor's clinic has supplies of white coats, a stethoscope, syringes, test-tubes, cotton, small bowls and bandaging materials. The shop displays naturalistic fruit and vegetables of plastic or modelling wax, and there are price-tags on everything and even small change. At the hairdresser's, the customer's shoulders are covered with a cape and they use a comb, scissors, rollers and even a hair-drier (most of them in cardboard) and on a cardboard mirror a head has been drawn. Family life continues in the same old way around the dining table and the dolls' beds, there may be a cardboard TV set with different pictures on the screen. The parents are very busy with their dolls, and both Mummy and

Daddy are intensively occupied with the weekly wash, which is rubbed with minute bars of soap and is rinsed with many changes of water in a hand-basin and hung up on a washing line with pegs — or strung along bamboo poles, the typical local way in Shanghai.

In the restaurant kitchen, the cooks are busy with the chopping and arranging of Chinese cookery. They have little semi-circular chopping knives, and clever fingers are dealing with real lettuce leaves, beansprouts and onion stems. All the tiny little food is served on miniature dishes together with beautifully shaped clay bread and chopsticks the size of matches. On the ship, built of large bricks, the boys are on duty in uniform caps. The mate is at the helm, the crew look after the anchor and flags, the signaller flags when ordered, they use a speaking tube and a telescope, and sometimes the ship is armed with cannons. Any study visits they may have made do not seem to have provided desperately fundamental knowledge, because the boys seem to be more interested in showing off than in acting out their roles. Besides, no form of war game or military exercise ever occurs, according to the staff. (They disappeared along with the rest in the Cultural Revolution.) No role-play at all has fighting or hunting themes, nor is there any aggression or other undesired behaviour.

I was particularly interested in trying to take part in role-plays using dramatic means of expression. After a few moments' surprise, the children welcomed us with delight, especially the male members of our group. We had a shampoo and hair-cut following all the rules of the art and a girl promised me a modern and lasting curly hair-do. (Perms and "curly tails" were popular at the time in China.) I asked how she liked her job, and she told me through the interpreter that she had had several years of training and loved her work.

At the photographer's I was carefully positioned and turned for the right camera angle. When I wanted some children in the picture, too, this was arranged in a symmetrical group, and several pictures had to be taken "because you don't sit still". I paid and was given a receipt and went on to the doctor's clinic. After a while I was examined, a diagnosis was made, and I was given an injection, very professionaly administered. I was then elegantly bandaged by the nurse, and given a prescription for the pharmacy. From their store of bottles and bags, my medicine was selected, and as I was leaving I was met by a messenger from the photographer's, and was handed "the photograph", a drawing of a tall person with blonde curls with exactly my stripy cardigan, and two children drawn in less detail.

Taking part in all the role-plays, however, was not completely un-complicated. For instance, at the doctor's, if I showed signs of anxiety at being operated on, the playing stopped in confusion for a brief moment. The children did not seem to be prepared for unexpected developments, but they accepted, somewhat puzzled, that I wanted to hold somebody's hand when in trouble. And in the shop, where I tasted my way forward and reacted to what was sweet or strong, dropped money or hummed and ha'ed when choosing, a similar vacuum occurred. The role-play stopped and the children become observers instead of participants. When I was extremely politely invited to dinner with a family and borrowed a doll child in order to feed it, a certain amused confusion arose too, especially if my doll child by chance happened to wet my knee. Not to mention the turmoil among the ship's crew when I was swimming and shouted for help, and wanted to be pulled on board, and once aboard wobbled because of the rolling sea and signalled "seasick"!

The adults, too, reacted with politely amused surprise at the guests' open playfulness and not without uneasiness when we occasionally permitted ourselves a hug, or tossed a child up in the air or whisked one round, or made any other bodily contact. Closeness or touching is at any rate something very neutral in China, this is my strong impression. People have — despite or because of the crowds of people — a small, untouchable, empty space around them, which also marks a boundary for feelings and reactions. You see it also in gymnastics, in acrobatics and dance. Touching is functional, never sensual. This restrictiveness applied even in the pre-school. The adults' attitude to role-play is very restrained. You observe and support, make a suggestion here and an improvement there, but never anything personal as a stimulus or prompt to development.

Do not let this make you think the staff are uninvolved. They prepare toys, dressing-up clothes, costumes and props for dance and theatre, and they plan and organize excursions and study visits so that the children really get enough time to work over their impressions. Creative play is not entertainment either, but an important part of the children's upbringing. In this the children are concretely to acquire love of work, respect for the elderly, politeness and hygiene, at the same time as they apply knowledge and concepts to do with types, quantity, figures and letters, order and organization, responsibility and co-operation.

Is there a *right way* to play, and is it more important than *that* you play, I ask myself? And is it intentional that the grown-ups keep outside?

In discussions with staff and teacher trainers — many and lengthy — the very professional attitude was confirmed that pre-school staff should behave like grown-ups and not "like children", but that at times they intervene in play for pedagogical reasons. Examples they gave were of children playing animals, and an elephant or tiger parent hitting its child, or a sales person or a client behaving impolitely or in an "uncivilized" way. But such adjustments are unusual because they are seldom needed, and in all cases they are made from an adult level.

I tried to describe a way of working pedagogically through drama which we at least aim at in our pre-school teacher training, and which involves active participation and through role-play re-creating situations which give children the opportunity to express and work over experiences and feelings, such as conflicts or jealousy, fear, disappointment or prejudices. This aroused the interest of our Chinese colleagues, but no pronounced enthusiasm. "Our children do not have such problems," they might state, and I must admit too that they really did not seem to.

Another and fully comprehensible argument against adult interference in play was the practical one, that a pre-school teacher and a nursery helper can hardly devote undivided attention to a little group of children in a class of 30–40 children. Furthermore, the system of age-streamed classes provides for significantly less dynamism in the roles. The children generally play at

Pictures of the children who have succeeded best in living up to the four beautifying ideals during the week are attached to the cherry tree. The children themselves decide who these are.

The visit is over. Zai jian! Bye, bye!

the same level, and no conflicts worth mentioning arise between the individual and the group.

If all the children's role-plays are pushed off "on rails", meaning that the children become accustomed in their play to acting according to a given pattern, you do, of course, get these strange gaps when it comes to spontaneous reactions. To me it is a disconcerting thought that the children never get the opportunity to become attuned to feelings and develop the capacity for encounters with other people's different behaviour, which to my mind are so important for being able to develop tolerance and understanding and in the long term a preparedness for encountering your fellow human-beings in all the controversies which life itself arranges. Here the staff arrange "life" as the world of work in miniature and the scenery literally follows the ideals of the syllabus; for instance, "not being frightened by health checks and all kinds of prophylactic vaccinations".

The distinct absence of feelings in role-play situations explains something of the calm and the concentration on imitating — hence also something of the observer's initial enchantment. This resembles grown-up people's delight in all sorts of miniatures, dolls' houses as well as model railways; and it perpetuates the myth of a "happy childhood when innocence and tranquility followed closely in our steps". There are many feelings which do not fit into this picture and which as a result have to be made extinct or suppressed.

But — there is also in the Chinese pre-school an accepted register of feelings, or rather a keyboard of emotional states which one is allowed to play, on condition that harmony is maintained. The most important ones are joy, charity and pride, with a clear hint of their opposites, egoism, shyness and thoughtlessness. But not even these easily visible and easily-controlled motive forces seem to play any part in creative play, but are reserved for the verbally presented models, poems, stories and songs. The syllabus prescribes different moods for these too: happily, in a lively way, solemnly, or forcefully.

The fact that children are seldom or never encouraged to use their creative imagination or fantasy may also provide an indication of the limits of creative play. A child who discovers the potential of creating a make-believe setting, situation or role and by so doing makes herself independent of external aids such as toys, scenery or role costumes — this child creates for herself or in company with friends an *internal* space in which the frustrating laws of the surrounding world can be directed, changed and even repealed. In this internal space many childish revolutions and counter-revolutions take place, to which adults only have a narrow channel through sensitive and involved participation in the make-believe game. I do not wish to claim that Swedish pre-school staff are especially keen or talented in this area, but in China I met little or no response to such thoughts.

Perhaps a creative imagination and the internal space belong to the "individual traits" which are related in the syllabus to differences of environment, education and genetic factors, and which teachers are encouraged to suppress indefatigably, as they can leave lasting traces for the rest of their lives. But there is evidence against such a conclusion in the same syllabus in quite unambiguous words. The children should be allowed to "see a lot, listen a lot, think a lot, speak and do a lot" so that their intellect, talent and character are in lively development and under their own momentum.

Perhaps dynamic drama work is for the present simply an under-developed resource in pre-school pedagogy which is in fact still being built up and which is clearly feeling its way both in training and in the field. This is, by the way, also the case in the Swedish pre-school where one all too rarely sees the staff active and pedagogically involved in children's drama. But the assessment system, the chart with flags, flowers or other symbols which show the children's progress — does not this influence children's play so that they feel they are being watched and cringingly try to earn points?

Oh, no, replies a teacher almost with indignation. We really do not strive for people who have been drilled like that. In any case the children take part in the joint evaluation and they often know each other better than the staff do. Each and every one has a vote and uses it. Besides, no "flags" are given for the creative play!

But the self-criticism was not absent from our discussions. On many occasions they commented on their shortcomings in satisfying the children's needs for experimenting freely with materials such as sand, water and clay. And our hosts all considered that the children should be given greater freedom to pursue their own activities, but that they were now just at the start of a development which, among other things, required extensive studies of Western pedagogy, too, and although this was by no means unfamiliar to them, it was not yet possible to make immediate use of it.

Everywhere they were genuinely interested in our views and advice, but, as one principal put it: "We are in China, we understand that you see everything from your point of view and you react to, for instance, our discipline. But it also builds upon what we have learned from the West. Your freedom, we discuss it and must evaluate it from our point of view. Discipline suits our country and our cultural tradition. We have a long history of civilization and we wish to retain it. After everything that the gang of four destroyed and the ten-year trauma of the cultural revolution, we are having difficulty in getting back to our civilization, but it is necessary."

Roads to adult culture

When Chinese children are thus brought up in their pre-school years with the many models of adult culture, there are naturally striking results. The children behave as conscious bearers of a culture, and take the compulsory performances for foreign guests as something natural.

They sit there, well prepared, dressed up and made-up, but calmly occupied with their normal activities, which they interrupt without difficulty when the guests they are expecting arrive. They present their various numbers with accuracy, and they help each other if needed with changing and props. A children's orchestra take their seats with the same dignified gravity as any philharmonic. They sit in the way specified, with their instruments, and "get set" in the playing position at a sign from the conductor, who may well be one of the children. Solos are performed without nervousness and with calm confidence in their own capacities. One also admires the teachers' skill in arranging the pieces of music and dances so that from the children's basic repertoire of movements, tunes and rhythms, many artistic and entertaining variations are extracted.

When the children start school, they are consequently in possession of a lot of knowledge and skills, and they can undoubtedly continue to develop a particular talent, even within a demanding selective system.

Thus we found, for instance, at the Music Academy in Peking several *streaming skills?* pupils in their first years of school who were accorded distinctly serious music teaching after thorough entrance exams. At the Children's Palaces they have — as well as entertainment like roller-skating, ball games, swimming, etc. — artistic activities like theatre, dance, sculpting, calligraphy, painting and music also. Nothing is completely open to all, but selective in consultation with the school and teachers. Quite academic, too, in my view, with an emphasis on study and technique and less than sensitive to the children's or young people's intentions.

Here, for example, one could see a group of pupils learning to sculpt, working on a portrait of a friend. Admittedly one could well distinguish individual variation, but the same polished naturalism was a feature of the work of everyone. Even small differences in the way clay was applied were removed in the final phase. The same dry, classical style was developed in painting, with a still life in which lemons, a pewter vase and grey velvet were carefully shaded out at every easel.

Perhaps the young students in pre-school teacher training had more freedom after all. At any rate the young girls worked with great joy and enthusiasm at creating their own choreography and costumes for a dance production which was part of their training. But this was for their own development, it was emphasized. For the work in the pre-school they learn particular dances and songs in the same way, as these will in their turn be passed on in teaching the children.

Which is more important, I ask, to copy or to create?

I immediately get the question back, what do we think? I try to summarize the philosophy underlying work in Swedish pre-schools: that children must be allowed to experience and experiment with means of expression and materials, and progress through developmental phases in their creative process before they can profit from technical knowledge.

Our hosts represent the opposite view: first study and copy, then acquire skill and after that — if the talent is there — develop a distinctive style.

At an art exhibition in a Children's Palace there were, however, many genuinely personal but hardly childish ways of expression. There was a friendly mix of different styles, including naïve painting, expressionism and even some almost surrealistic dream paintings, alongside variations on traditional Chinese painting, both subtle paintings of flowers and landscapes and masterly studies of animals or space realized with a few strokes of the brush.

Alongside the learning of creative cultural activities in the spirit of the good examples, there is also an education or rather an accustoming to participate with interest in the culture of the society and the adult world. According to the syllabus, children are to learn to appreciate arts and culture, which is an ambitious goal, if one takes into account the limited provision of theatre productions, concerts, exhibitions, films and other cultural activities directly aimed at children. Both in China and in Sweden this is a question of priorities, and one should bear in mind China's developing country economy when one makes comparisons. Just as here in Sweden, children in some regions of China have to wait until well into their schooling before they can experience live theatre, music or an opera performance put on specially for them. Given the scarcity in the cultural provision, pre-school staff more consciously exploit and appreciate what there is.

To associate naturally and without solemnity with history's art treasures, and to give the children great freedom to experience monuments, museums and temples close up. To point out with pride that both radio and television provide special programmes for pre-school children, and to show the same careful appreciation of the day nursery's own children's books as the ones one may be fortunate enough to borrow from a library. You have to have experienced a Chinese pre-school's special atmosphere of peaceful concentration, undisturbed by rubbish on the radio, cassettes and comics, to understand the joy over a book, a song, a story or a dance. And the special arrangements made on holidays like International Children's Day, with theatre, programmes of entertainment, exhibitions and even flights, must mean for Chinese children a unique celebration, not least because their Mummies can also have a half-day off work.

To the inevitably rather summary pictures of some specific features of the pre-school's cultural upbringing that one can draw after three weeks, one should add the universal, strong impression one gets of Chinese society's positive attitude to children, and the agreement between the messages children meet inside and outside the pre-school. What one learns to strive for matches the attitudes and value judgements in adult people's ways of treating children.

What this means for the development of a child's character we can only imagine with difficulty, we who in our work in the pre-school often feel that we are thwarted by the society around us, with its contradictory demands of toughness and kindness, that you should look after yourself and assert yourself and at the same time — from very early on — cope with the grown-ups' problems and conflicts, ranging from equality in the family to unemployment, environmental pollution, alcohol and drugs and violence.

With all her discipline, her friendly but strong authority, the "mother country" China wants to give her children a harmonious childhood and puts a great deal into efforts to give of her best. Whether — and how — the children, when freeing themselves from this motherly embrace, will be able to avoid conflicts and resist "the temptations from the West", which are still fairly thinly trickling in in the form of Coca-Cola and disco romance — that is another and still unknown story.

Are the Chinese models any good for us?

It is impossible to travel around China without making comparisons every day and wondering what one can learn. But comparisons easily become unjust, because one cannot keep in mind the whole time the political, cultural and traditional differences which inescapably make for different conditions for cultural work in pre-school, too. Just as Chinese administrators study Western education from their own starting-point, we need to relate ideas from other countries in a more thorough way — and less opportunistically — to our own society, our cultural traditions, one is tempted to say — if we have any!

Just look at us seven well-educated Swedes, for example, in our embarrassment when we were expected to be able to offer something in exchange to Chinese children in the way of song and dance! To be able to sift out from our memory, unprepared, an authentic Swedish dance game which we both mastered and would vouch for — that was at any rate no natural expression of a living, shared cultural tradition. You must forgive us if some Chinese children have got a rather crude notion of "*musikanterna från Skaraborg*".

To revert to my sketch of problems of the cultural climate of the Swedish pre-school, there is, of course, no Chinese people's medicine as a panacea. Still I think that we need to take up the concept of *cultural education* in our pre-school debates and learn from Chinese models, too, on essential points. We must ask ourselves how our training of pre-school staff can provide a better foundation of knowing and confidence when it comes to confronting commercialism, and not allow the fear of uniformity to restrain us from establishing some basic pattern for cultural work in the pre-school.

How can the pre-school give the children a sense of shared cultural belonging which makes use of valuable differences of traditions and background? How can we fight injustices in access to children's culture which costs money?

In Swedish pre-schools there is a wealth of commitment, imagination, and not least loving relationships between children and adults — how can we exploit it so as to give the children in addition the foundation of joy in work, sense of order and self-discipline which makes it possible to exploit freedom and creativity?

Questions like these are not new, but need to be asked again when discussing goals and guidelines. The confusion about goals which I hinted at initially would certainly not disappear but would possibly be clarified if we could agree on some essential cultural values that the pre-school takes responsibility for.

Three charities, four efforts, five graces. . . . Shall we make a list?

5 Sun, gymnastics, herbs and vaccines

On child health care in China

Lars H. Gustafsson

You must remember that China is a developing country, says Doctor Paul L. Fan in an interview later in this chapter. During our journey I repeat these words often. We are in a developing country, I think to myself, it is important not to forget this.

Why is it so easy to forget that China is a developing country? What kind of picture of China did I actually have before I came here? Did I have any picture at all, other than the political stereotype, whatever that may be? It fades away so quickly when you travel around here, people impose themselves, low key but real. All these people!

I have travelled in a fair number of countries, including several developing countries; impressions from these trips flicker before my eyes at times now, too, not least when we go out into the countryside. But China has something completely of its own that I have never met before, a kind of peace, naturalness and dignity. It feels healthy, but it also makes one often feel like the primitive, rough-mannered European that one in fact is, a slightly pretentious upstart without roots.

We travel through one of the world's most developed countries culturally, morally, humanly. Is that why the concept of a developing country becomes so meaningless? Is that why we forget so easily that China is still from an economic point of view a developing country, one of the poorest countries of all in the world, with an economy which in many respects is typical of a developing country?

169

But mostly China serves as a mirror during this journey, and in it we see our own country, our image of children in Sweden. This, then, is a chapter on Swedish child health care in a Chinese light, and I have chosen to write it in a free, slightly rhapsodic form, with three interviews forming the centre-piece of my reflections.

People are in any case what is most important, I often think during the trip, I must write about the people and not so much about the systems. China has become a stick for beating others with in debates on political thought and we forget about the people. There are a lot of them, maybe one thousand million. But right now I am thinking of them more as individuals. It is a lasting impression of mine from China, as from some other countries I have been in, that one can sit down with some people, gradually get close to them in an everyday conversation, and suddenly discover that despite everything it is the similarities and not the differences that take one by surprise.

Home call in Peking

I am often in this area, all the mothers know me! says Dr Liao, on our way with an interpreter to a home call in the west of Peking. Dr Liao is a woman aged roughly 45. She has a soft but warm voice, and happy, alert eyes. She is a child health paediatrician, the closest equivalent of which in Sweden is a nurse at a children's welfare centre. She is attached to one of Peking's children's clinics, but is responsible for a neighbourhood with nearly 1,000 children. She visits the neighbourhood health centres three days a week and also makes her home calls then.

We have a lot of faith in home calls, she says. We do not think that parents should have to come to the health centre with their children before the children are three months old. I usually make three home calls to every family in the early months, but sometimes it turns out to be more.

The family

Dr Liao exchanges a few words with a mother on the street, and then we arrive at No. 22, Shi Banfang. Here live Hao Ping-Sheng and Chi Chong-ying with their daughter, who today is one month and six days old. It is a small house on the inner side of a traditionally shaped courtyard. The house has two rooms and an extra bedroom, where Hao's father usually sleeps.

Hao welcomes us and asks us to sit down. Tea is served by an elderly woman.

She is our neighbour and our friend, explains Hao. She helps us with our daughter for a few hours each day, so that Chi can rest. Chi is still so tired.

Hao is an opera singer. He works at one of the larger Peking opera houses. They are at present rehearsing a performance which has not yet had its première. That is why his hours of work are slightly more flexible at the moment, and today he has taken time off in order to be present at the doctor's home call.

Chi works at a photography shop, where among other things she colours black-and-white photographs. At the moment she is on maternity leave, and she thinks that she will have her leave extended beyond the obligatory 56 days.

Wearying in the beginning

It is beginning to get a bit better now, says Chi to Dr Liao. But she still screams.

Dr Liao has started examining the girl on the parents' beds. She weighs her with a steelyard, listens to her heart, feels her stomach and hips.

— It was wearying in the beginning, says Chi, turning towards me. The delivery lasted almost a whole week and I bled so much. I was absolutely dead afterwards and I have not really recovered yet. And the girl weighed only two point seven.

— But now she weighs three kilos and eighty grams, not bad, don't you think? says Dr Liao. What do you feed her with?

— She is only breastfed, answers Chi — it works better now. In the beginning it was laboriously slow, she was always on the point of falling asleep when eating. It may be because I did not feel good myself.

— You can have this brochure from me today, says Dr Liao. It is about breastfeeding and some other things too. Here you can see precisely how much the weight should go up.

We know that already, Hao puts in and and shows us a reference book on child care that he has bought at a bookshop. Dr Liao nods approvingly and explains to me that such books are still expensive and may be difficult to get hold of.

Screams in the evenings

— It is so odd, says Chi, she is quiet and good in the daytime, but every evening between ten o'clock and midnight she screams. It makes no difference what we do, even if we pick her up and carry her round she goes on screaming.

— In the beginning we did not understand what it was all about, but then we noticed that it was the same every day, that this was how she was quite simply. I thought she was hungry, that she did not get enough food. But feeding her did not help either.

— We took her to the children's hospital one evening when we were really worried, says Hao, and at least they made it clear to us that she was eating enough. "It is the same with all parents who have just had a child," the doctor told us, "they always think the child gets too little food."

— So now I feed her every three hours during the day, says Chi, but never more often than every fourth or fifth hour at night. Before I was at it all the time.

— And we also try to take turns carrying her, says Hao, it is too hard on Chi otherwise.

Dr Liao tells them something about babies' colic, and I mention that I have seen children with colic in the evenings both at home and in other parts of the world.

— That is good to hear! says Hao. Because when it happens to you, you really think you are the only one in the whole world with it!

Vomiting

She also vomits, says Chi. Immediately after she has eaten, a little spurt always comes up again. And at times it seems to be so much that I get quite worried. What is the reason for it?

— It is because babies' stomachs are different from slightly larger children's, explains Dr Liao. She sketches on a piece of paper and describes how the upper orifice of the stomach functions, in exactly the same way as we usually do at my own children's welfare centre many hundreds of miles away.

Is it Dr Liao you ask for advice, when you get worried about something? I wonder. Or are there others to ask?

— My father is actually a doctor, says Hao, but to be quite honest, he does not know so much about children. So we prefer to turn to Dr Liao. We like her very much, she is so fond of children and she feels so responsible for all the children here.

— That is not so surprising, laughs Dr Liao, as I am here so often, I know everyone here. By the way: this is the last home call I'm making here, next time you are welcome to come to the health centre. I am there Mondays, Wednesdays and Fridays. Come whenever you want, but before not too long. I want in any case to see her before she is three months.

Being a father

I ask Hao about how he looks on being a father. I point out that he shares with Chi the work of carrying the girl when she screams, and I wonder whether this is the usual thing in China.

— Yes, nowadays I would say almost everybody is like me, says Hao. But this has not always been so. In the old days the fathers never took any responsibility for the care of the tiny children. My father, for example — I cannot remember that he actually ever cared about me. But now it is different, now we try to share equally.

— But do you really do it? I wonder, and tell him something about the situation in Sweden and how far there may be between theory and practice at times.

— Of course! Hao interrupts me and gets excited. Certainly it can be difficult. It is easy to feel inferior as a man. For example, I often feel that I am being criticized by Chi. I think that I am doing things as well as I can, but it is still not good enough for her!

— But certainly a lot has happened, says Dr Liao, just in the time I have been able to observe. The fathers take a much larger share of responsibility now. Both parents have jobs, usually, and you have to help each other if you are going to manage.

— On your point about looking after children, says Hao, I must ask you something. The other day I went out with her for a walk in the sun. But she squeezed up her eyes, she never once opened them. It was perhaps a mistake to take her out?

Chi, the neighbour and the interpreter burst out laughing, but Dr Liao says that it was a good thing to go out with the girl, that he should go on doing it, but perhaps shade her face against the sun. To me she says that she always has to back up the parents so that they dare to take their children out, earlier they were kept indoors much too much.

The children's welfare centre

While I sit gathering together my notes and recollections of the trip to China, it is mid-summer in Sweden. I have just come home from a morning at the Svartbäcken children's welfare centre in Uppsala. I sat there on the floor with a group of parents and their two-month-old children. Tanned and with bare feet, we talked about colic, vomiting, and about how much one dares to have children out in the sun. I sketched and described how the stomach functions in new-born babes — and suddenly I was back in my thoughts on the home call in Peking. The recognition strikes me again. Not merely that we talk about the same worries, but also the way we talk about them. The television news has reported on the census in China in a bantering and ignorant way, the editorials are about the nuclear arms threat and the economic world order. But at the world's children's welfare centres, a constant, low-key but intensive exchange of experience about vomiting and colic is taking place.

The children's welfare centre is my second home, my home place of work. I have had a doctor's consultation time at the centre at least once and often several times a week for 15 years now. Colic, breastfeeding fatigue, rashes, crooked feet, sleeping trouble, cohabitation problems — but also anxiety, relief, pride, aspirations and feelings of purpose . . . everything begins to become part of me. If I feel lost when I am travelling abroad, I merely need to find the nearest children's welfare centre, and I immediately feel at home!

From milk drops to divorces

It is usually said that the first children's welfare centres in Sweden were the aid stations which the association "Milk Drop" established in a few towns at the start of our century. Milk Drop was a voluntary organization which worked to improve conditions for children at risk, primarily slum children of the towns. The aid stations handed out milk, other types of food, clothes — and at times children were medically examined, too.

During the First World War there was widespread famine among children, particularly in the cities. The country was cut off, and in the countryside the crops had failed for several years. Malnutrition was common, and in its wake swept the epidemics: polio, diphtheria, tuberculosis and Spanish flu. Milk Drop's aid stations then came to fulfil an important function for the children most at risk — just as did the stations set up by the Swedish Save the Children, which had just been founded.

But it was not until the 1930s that society became seriously committed to an expansion of children's health care, and it was not until the end of the 1940s that our present system, with children's welfare centres covering the entire country, was complete.

It was natural that child health care had in the first place to work with the major health problems of children at that time, namely infectious and deficiency diseases. They persistently exhorted mothers to breastfeed, gave advice on supplementary food, distributed vitamin A and D drops, and vaccinated against a range of serious diseases.

The picture changed gradually. We brought the infectious diseases under control, infant mortality sank to the lowest in the world, deficiency diseases became rare. Eating too much and eating wrongly became greater problems than malnutrition.

As infections and deficiency diseases became less common, new problems came to the surface. Among these were accidents involving children, child abuse and other psychological and social problems in the family, motor difficulties, vision and hearing problems, speech retardation. It is easy to get the impression that these problems have become more prevalent, but that is, of course, not the case. Considerably more children died in accidents 30 years ago than now, children were abused quite definitely more often then than now, both physically and psychologically. What has happened is that we now have the opportunity to involve ourselves in what was earlier overshadowed by children being threatened by hunger and death from serious infections.

With time the organization of child health care has been brought in line with the panorama of problems we now work with. Psychologists, speech therapists, physiotherapists and dieticians have become natural members of our working teams. The nurse has turned into more of an educationalist, and the doctor's role, too, has changed. Ideas of parent education are becoming established, and have in many cases led to changed forms of work. At my centre, just as at many other places, all consultations are now for groups. This means that all parents belong to a group. You no longer come to a consultation alone, but together with the others in your group.

Health for all by the year 2000

In the autumn of 1979, a large international conference was held in the skating town Alma Ata in the Soviet Republic Kazakhstan. It was organized by WHO and UNICEF, and the theme was Primary Health Care, i.e. preventive health care outside hospitals. It was an important conference, which had been prepared over many years. There was agreement that much too great a proportion of countries' total budgets had been devoted to defence efforts and far too little to health and medical care. There was also agreement among the delegates that hospitals and specialist care had been given priority in an unfortunate way in relation to preventive care. They declared that maternal and child health care was the core of preventive care, and finally the goal was set: health for all by the year 2000!

GOAL

At the conference, a number of models for how preventive care could be developed over the next 20 years were discussed. Among the Western countries it was Holland and Canada who led the way, while the Swedish model stayed completely in the background. It was regarded as much too pretentious, and with much too high a degree of specialization to be applicable. Instead, attention came to focus on some progressive developing countries, Cuba, Mozambique, North Korea. But above all it was the Chinese model which ran like an implicit red thread through almost all the discussions. Everyone knew that China had progressed further than most countries in extending good health care to all. But there was uncertainty about the statistics, and the available descriptions of Chinese health care were contradictory. It was known that it functioned, but not really how.

The Alma Ata conference was important. The goal of health for all by the year 2000 has been criticized. Many believe that it is unrealistic and therefore almost a bit ridiculous. But even so, the conference has triggered intensive discussions in many countries of the future orientation of health care. There are clear problems in doing this. There are obstacles of many kinds: political (we must give priority to other areas!), economic (we cannot afford it!), educational (we do not have qualified staff!), professional (we want to work as we have always done!).

In China they have taken the Alma Ata conference and the intensive discussion which ensued with dignified calm. They think that they have been working according to the guidelines of the Alma Ata document for many years, and that the conference did not provide many new impulses. Or, as one of the paediatricians I spoke to expressed it:

— Oh, yes, of course all that is good enough. But we know how we want to go about it. We must have our own conditions as a starting point.

Let a hundred flowers flower!

For a foreign visitor, encountering Chinese children's health care is initially quite confusing. We visit children's hospitals, small hospitals, health centres, and everywhere we are told how child health care is organized at their place. We are in a thoroughly organized socialist country, and I am expecting to find a pattern, a plan of organization worked out centrally. Some time goes before I realize that I am on the wrong track. The goals and principles have been worked out centrally, but the organization differs according to local conditions.

Thus the children's hospitals at some places take an active and involved responsibility for directing child health care in their catchment area. This applies, for instance, in Chengdu, where the consultant in charge of the children's clinic, Dr Paul L. Fan, has a strong personal commitment to health care problems (see interview on p. 184). At other places child health care seems more to lead its own life, certainly in collaboration with the hospital but with a more independent profile.

Children are examined as a rule in the home until they are three months old, and after that either at health centres or at special child welfare centres on hospital premises. Here there are also often special clinics for children at risk, for instance for children suffering from malnutrition or with retarded development. Children attached to a pre-school are examined by special health care staff.

aspects of child health care.

In the towns, children's hosptials have more influence on child health care, and the children are invariably examined by special child health paediatricians (see below). The further out in the countryside you get, the less the influence of the hospitals and the more health care is looked after by barefoot doctors. This also means that the quality of child health care drops with the distance from the big cities, and as 80% of the population live in the country, this is serious. All the paediatricians I spoke to testified to this:

— Our coverage is good now, they say, we do see practically all children. This is a fantastic advance. But we have worries about the quality.

The barefoot doctors

The barefoot doctor is a key person in Chinese health care and the concept has been known for a long time throughout the world. The barefoot doctor system was expanded during the cultural revolution, but originates long before that.

The idea is simple. Within the smallest administrative unit, covering roughly 2,000 people (in the towns a neighbourhood, in the country a production brigade), there is to be a health station with staff who are sufficiently competent both to make an initial, fairly qualified diagnosis of illness and to direct health care work in the area. It is best if these people have roots in the area and know the people who live there. So a barefoot doctor training has been offered to one or two of the area's inhabitants.

The problem has been that this training has varied in quality so much, as has the initial level of knowledge. During our journey we meet barefoot doctors who appear to be very well educated and competent health care workers. But we also meet those who can scarcely bear comparison with a Swedish hospital orderly, at least as regards training. The Chinese have been in a hurry, particularly during the cultural revolution. They are now trying to remedy the mistakes with further training.

The child health workers

In China the concept "doctor" is used in a way which does not conform to international practice, and this has created a good deal of confusion. The barefoot doctors are an example of this. They are virtually comparable to what WHO now calls primary health care workers. In China it has not been mainly the training but rather the independent status which has been underlined by the title "doctor".

Another example of this is child health workers. Their training roughly corresponds to that of a Swedish child nurse. They are often attached to a children's clinic, where they are given further training and supervision by specialist paediatricians. But they are independently responsible for child health care and carry out all their functions on their own. They differ from a Swedish child welfare centre nurse mainly in that they examine, evaluate and treat the children themselves but can naturally ask for help in a diagnosis from a specialist paediatrician when in doubt. Many people feel, and to some extent I am one of them, that Swedish child health care would benefit from being organized in just this way.

There is another point which is interesting to compare from a Swedish point of view. Child health workers are exclusively concerned with children, and time after time they emphasize in China how important this is. They point out often that the barefoot doctors with their broad orientation cannot possibly look after the special interests of children adequately. That is why child health workers are needed.

again, emphasis for the importance of childhood!

In Sweden the National Board for Health and Social Affairs, in the official report on Maternal and Child Health Care, has come down in favour of specially trained children's nurses disappearing from open care. Their functions should be taken over by district nurses. When I tell some health care workers this, they shake their heads. They cannot understand it. "We want to give children top priority," they say, "they need special resources, don't they?"

I meet several child health workers and accompany them while they work. I am impressed by their knowledge and perhaps even more by their capacity to create a warm and trusting bond with children and parents.

The panorama of problems

Children's health problems in China are the same as those one meets in many other developing countries today. Basically they are malnutrition, wrong diet and other deficiency diseases, plus infectious diseases of various kinds. It is difficult or impossible to get hold of reliable statistics, but there is no doubt that there are considerable local variations. The problems are least in the towns and greatest in remote border areas. Dr Fan returns to this in the interview on p. 184.

Today's health problems in China resemble a good deal those we had in Sweden in the 1920s and 1930s. It is therefore natural that the direction children's health care has taken resembles that of Swedish child health care earlier. Efforts are thus mainly concentrated on physical health checks for children, breastfeeding publicity, advice on diet, vitamins and vaccinations. These must be the right priorities and seem thus completely natural.

The small sting of disappointment one can feel as a Swedish child health worker is therefore not due to finding shortcomings in the system. Rather that one soon realizes that the questions that one brought with one from home are actually much too specifically Western for there to be any meaningful answers in the Chinese mirror. Even so, I make brave attempts to steer at least more informal discussions over to topics like children's accidents, caries, child abuse, and psychological problems among children.

Children's accidents

"All crime in China is public! says one of our hosts, as we sit chatting during a fast, almost breakneck bus journey through the outskirts of Xi'an.

I have again steered the conversation to children's accidents, and ask what happens when a child is run over in the traffic.

— If a child is run over . . . then there are always 20 witnesses. Everyone rushes up and waits until the police come to investigate. The interrogation is done on the spot, and is decisive for how the court will find later. Anyone who runs over a child always gets a tougher sentence than someone who runs down an adult — you always have greater obligations towards a child than towards grown-ups! Then it also depends on the outcome of the accident — if the child dies, the sentence is more severe.

— If you run over a child, you must always reckon with a tough sentence, often several years in prison. If the driver has behaved in a manner which was clearly dangerous for all concerned, and it is assessed that he alone is responsible for the accident, he even runs the risk of the death penalty. Admittedly the risk is not great, but it is there. We have to look after our children.

Children thus have a special legal status in China. That is the case in Sweden, too, but this virtually means the opposite. For a long time it was less risky from the point of view of the driver to run over a child than a grown-up. It was only after Stina Sandel's tenacious struggle in the 1960s that this distortion in the judgements of the courts was to some degree rectified.

The particular protection accorded to children under Chinese law — what does it imply for attitudes to children in society in general? Or is the legislation just a result of a positive view of children which is already there? What lies behind the difference between Sweden and China on this point? This question is central, and I shall revert to it later in this chapter.

Let me for the present merely state that it is felt in everyday life. This became quite evident during the continuation of our journey, when I followed the bus-drivers' way of driving extra carefully: certainly they have to speed up, when criss-crossing between bicycles and carts, but as soon as there is a child near them, they reduce speed and the horn is used, although they are required now by law to avoid unnecessary honking. I also observed that very few little children are out in traffic on their own. They are carried by their parents, have their hands held, or they are taken by bicycle — in different ways in different parts of China. In Chengdu they stand up on the rear wheel baggage holder tied to their parents' back with a strap! It looks dangerous, but there they claim that this is the safest way. The Chinese, of all people ought to know what it is possible and impossible to do on a bicycle, and I never see any narrow escapes.

All the paediatricians I speak to reject the idea that children's accidents are a real problem. I have heard this in all the developing countries I have been in, and Swedish paediatricians probably said the same at the beginning of this century, although we know that four times as many Swedish children died in accidents then as do now. The reason is natural enough: other diseases dominate the picture.

I am used to studying children's environments with my accident glasses on, and during the trip I note a number of risks which should in all reason give rise to accidents: badly stored chemical products, dangerous electrical equipment, open fires and hot stoves, increasingly hectic traffic in the cities with a rise in the amount of motorized transport.

But at the same time I encounter a way of tending and caring for children such as I have not met anywhere else, a kind of natural, collective sharing of the responsibility for all the children in one's vicinity.

So my impressions are contradictory and make me unsure. Are the accidents perhaps as few as they say? Or are Chinese paediatricians in 10 years' time going to take part in our worried discussions about how we could protect children better? The answer is soon going to reveal itself, as they are in the process of rapidly bringing infectious and deficiency diseases under control.

Caries

I am pretty certain that I have never in my life met so many children in such a short time as during the journey to China! They make an almost overwhelming impression: healthy, mostly well-fed, well-disciplined, but happy, fearless and inquisitive children.

For somebody with a medical training, who can never quite slip off his child-welfare-centre-doctor's identity, some other observations mix with this. For example, I see dental caries everywhere. Caries — this universal sickness, which is more a sign of the beginnings of welfare and incorrect diet than of real welfare.

I work in Uppsala. Here there is good dental health care, a high natural fluoride content in the water, and aware parents who are more worried about risks from the side-effects of fluoride than about caries. But at the end of 1960s I was the district medical officer in Härjedalen, and encountered there as high a frequency of dental caries as I do in China now.

Again I am reminded of how quickly the development takes place. What we today regard as self-evident was unusual a mere 20 years ago. The journey through China also becomes a journey through our own health care history.

I take up the problem of caries with a number of health workers. They are aware of it, but give it low priority for the moment. The consumption of sweets is high. Many children gather around the stands in the street where they make artistic sticks of melted sugar.

I mention the Swedish system of having sweets on Saturdays. They have never heard about that in China, but they immediately become enthusiastic about it. Several point out that it is an idea which is fully in line with Chinese people's health work, which is based on brief but extremely clear messages. The seventh day — sweets day!

Child abuse

Child abuse is one of those highly topical child health care problems which we, like many earlier visitors, are interested in seeing in the mirror of Chinese reality. Our reasons are many and obvious.

There is increasing evidence that child abuse is related to the amount of violence in society. If the level of violence is high and if corporal punishment is a common instrument of child upbringing, the number of cases of child abuse is greater (see, e.g. Dagmar Lagerberg's book *Du skall icke slå* (Thou shalt not hit, 1982).

It has been established that child abuse practically never occurs in cultures which do not permit corporal punishment. This is true for, among others, Eskimo societies which have not yet been disrupted by our Nordic or American civilization, it is also true of certain Indian tribes and equally of the inhabitants of the Polynesian islands — when these do not figure as immigrants in New Zealand, because there they adjust quickly to British upbringing and instances of child abuse become numerous.

China has often been mentioned in this connection, not because they claim in China that child abuse does not occur. This is claimed in many countries, among others in countries which are close to ours and where we have cause to believe that abuse is very probably more frequent than with us.

Rather because so many visitors to China have returned to the West filled by the warmth and the absence of violence they feel they have experienced, both in the relationship between child and adult and between children amongst themselves. They have wondered to what extent this is an ancient cultural pattern and to what extent it is connected with events after the revolution of 1949.

Our Western reflections on these issues are well known in China, and you can see that they are used to discussing them. The picture which emerges from our numerous talks about children and violence is also fairly unambiguous.

Child abuse was common before, they assure us. Many grown-ups tell how they were beaten as children. Other aspects of upbringing were also in many senses hostile to children — one can cite the binding of girls' feet as an example. It was therefore natural that as part of the revolution, they set to work on these problems, which many had reacted against even earlier. The binding of girls' feet was prohibited, as was all corporal punishment.

There has thus prevailed a clearly expressed prohibition of corporal punishment in China for more than 20 years. This has gradually begun to produce results and progressively changed people's views on children and methods of upbringing. They admit candidly that all the problems have not yet been solved. Many parents forget themselves at times, particularly the ones with children of school age. It is also hinted that the older generation sometimes cannot manage to live up to the rules in force today. But social control is strict, and no one believes it possible that any child could be abused in any more systematic way without neighbours immediately stepping in and stopping it all.

This picture does not sound mysterious to me, rather completely natural, in the light of our knowledge today of child abuse. Like earlier visitors, we see only isolated examples of raised voice or more hard-handed reprimanding of children. We, too, end up being captivated by all the warmth we see in the interaction between child and adult, and equally by the constructive play when children are together, which has practically no elements of violence.

The Chinese picture in the mirror is positive and encouraging. Our own corporal punishment law has only three years behind it. I have discussed it in many parents' groups and know that it is well known. During the 15 years that I have worked at the children's welfare centre it is evident that a change of attitude has taken place among Swedish parents. Ten years ago it was usual for people to defend their right to inflict corporal punishment on children. This was considered more or less necessary in certain situations. This kind of attitude is growing more and more uncommon. Many admit that they have forgotten themselves on some occasion. But they regret it and do

not believe in corporal punishment as a method of upbringing. This is a large
step forward on the Chinese road!

A talk to Dr Paul L. Fan, Chengdu

It is still wrong diet, deficiency diseases and infections which are the
great health problems among children in China, says Dr Paul L. Fan,
consultant paediatrician and Director of the Sichuan Provincial People's
Hospital, Chengdu.

We are sitting in the reception room of the administration block, Dr
Fan, I and the interpreter. They have laid tea for many more, but the others
in the group are on an alternative programme. That suits me well today, it
means that our talk gradually becomes unconstrained and personal. Dr Fan
sits leaning back in his armchair, his hands folded on his knees. He is wearing
the usual uniform-like cotton suit and the Chinese peaked cap. He is about
60. To begin with he is discreet in the way he talks, becoming gradually more
enthusiastic and intense. Sometimes he gets impatient when the interpreter
translates, and he begins then to speak to me directly in English.

Large differences

You are asking me how things are in China, he says. But I can only tell
you how things are here in Chengdu, and scarcely even that. And that is the
way it is everywhere, you can get a few examples of what it is like during this
kind of trip, but you do not know how things are in China. China is a
continent, and things are different everywhere.

This is one of our great problems, that the national statistics we have are
so incomplete. They build a good deal on guesses and estimates, and there
are many sources of error. We do not even know how many of us there are!
That is why this summer's census is so important, it provides the basis for all
statistics, in the health field as well.

I shall give you an example of differences. In 1979 a study was made
here in the province of Sichuan to find out how widespread it is for children
to have the wrong diet. It turned out that the proportion of children with a
slightly wrong diet was 70% in rural areas but less than 3% in the towns! And
even that is not the whole truth. During the first months of life children are in
fact better off in the country, because the mothers there breastfeed their
children more than in towns. But when breastmilk is no longer sufficient
after six months, the situation becomes completely reversed.

Dr Paul L. Fan, consultant paediatrician in Chengdu.

Out in the country, and perhaps above all in border districts, we still see a number of cases of polio, tetanus and tuberculosis. Rickets and iron deficiency are common illnesses. But in the towns too there are great differences, particularly between children who attend a day nursery and the ones who are at home. I know that one can perhaps question the pedagogical content of day nurseries, especially in relation to the smallest children. But from the point of view of health, there is no doubt that the day nursery has great advantages. There, as you know, they go to great lengths to give children a correctly balanced diet.

Getting priorities right

When there is a shortage of resources, it is important to get your priorities right, says Dr Fan. As I see it, there are two areas we must give high priority to today: partly health care in the country, partly health care for children under the age of three.

At my clinic we have decided to take responsibility for child health care in a people's council more than one hundred kilometres from here. We are treating it as an experimental area where we look at what can be done by simple means to raise the quality of health care. One problem is the barefoot doctors. In the days of the cultural revolution a health care organization was built up in which the barefoot doctors were key people. But what they did not take the trouble to do was to give them the necessary training. We are

now trying to provide further education for the barefoot doctors. It is a
major task, which is going to take a long time.

Then we have established a children's welfare centre here at the hospital. This I really had to fight for. But I felt that we needed to have a children's
welfare centre of our own, to try out new methods and for the training of
doctors and nurses from the whole province. Would you like to see it?

The children's welfare centre

We go off across the courtyard to the children's welfare centre. It is
soon clear that this is what Dr Fan has set his heart on, and he glows as he
shows off their activities. It is the best equipped health unit I saw during our
trip. On the walls hung demonstration charts of various kinds, mainly those
showing gymnastics programmes for babies.

I have great faith in gymnastics exercises and other physical training to
improve health and prevent infections, says Dr Fan. Here in Chengdu we
often talk of the significance of "the three baths": sun baths, fresh air baths
and cold baths. It is important, particularly during the six cold months of the
year, that the children are out in the sun as much as possible, and have cold
baths or showers. I am, by the way, one of those who believe in babies
swimming, I would very much like to start that here, but we have so few
pools.

It is fairly quiet at the children's welfare centre during our visit, but
there are some parents there with their children. When I pause to look at
what is happening, I note that some kind of testing of the children is taking
place.

These children are here for intelligence testing, explains Dr Fan. Just
now we are testing the intelligence of all the children in certain age groups.
We are trying out a couple of different tests, the American Denver and
Gesell tests but adapted to Chinese conditions.

Psychological problems

Then we are back in the reception room again, lean back in our
armchairs, and are served more tea.

Why are you testing the children? I ask. Do you see many psychological
problems among your children?

That is not why we are testing, replies Dr Fan. I will explain later. Psychological problems? I understand why you ask, I have done some reading about the psychological problems you see among your children in Sweden and in the rest of the Western world. And I could answer: No, we do not see any such problems here in China. But then I would not speak the truth, of course we do. But still, I cannot imagine that we have as many problems as you. It is still unusual for us to meet parents who have such great problems with their children that they discuss them with us. They are solved at home, or with the help of neighbours and good friends.

But there is one exception, an important exception. I refer to the teenagers. There is among young people today a good deal of restlessness, aggression and a kind of unhappiness, perhaps not as in your part of the world but serious enough for us. Some of it may be due to the cultural revolution, to all the feelings which were aroused without anyone really taking responsibility for what happened. But whatever it is due to, it is a genuine problem, and we have to do something about it soon if it is not to get out of control.

The single child campaign

But why are you testing the children? I ask again.

We want to standardize a test for Chinese conditions, we have no good tests and need them. Just like you. It is as simple as that. But to some extent it is also connected with the single-child campaign.

As you know, we are trying to get parents to have just one child. Virtually all parents understand why, and give it their full support. In the towns, that is. In the country it is much more difficult. But even in the towns, parents may run into a problem. Take, for instance, parents who have a child who later turns out to be damaged or develops a serious illness. It is very difficult for them to accept that they will not be able to have another child.

Now there is a regulation stating that I, as consultant in charge of a children's clinic, have the right to issue a certificate to the parents giving them the right, with the full support of society, to have an additional child. I do this in consultation with the parents in cases where there is something seriously wrong with the first child. And then it is important to discover and isolate such handicaps as early as possible, while the parents are still young and have the strength and will needed.

You have to see things as they are: China is still in many respects a developing country. This is reflected in, for example, attitudes to handi-

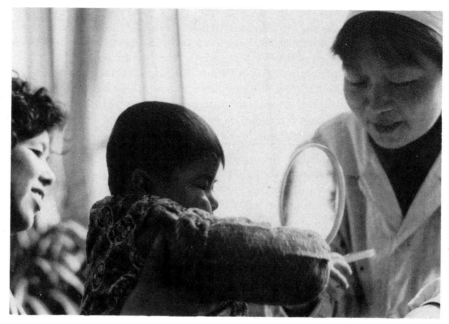

The children are tested at the chldren's welfare centre.

capped children. They are often abandoned by their parents, they may be
left at a railway station or in the foyer of a hospital. It has always been like
that. If there were no regulation on the right to an additional child, the risk
would increase of parents who for some reason were displeased with their
child simply getting rid of it, in order to get the right to have a new child. This
would be indefensible from the point of view of the society.

So the single-child campaign confronts you as a paediatrician with a
range of new ethical problems?

Dr Fan thinks over the question for a long time. Then he says:

Yes, that is clear. It is not uninteresting. But on the other hand I think
one has to look at it like this: one cannot separate one's own private ethics
and one's medical ethics too much from the ethics of the society. I think like
this: my philosophy of society tells me that the single-child campaign is
necessary. I have thought it over and over, but I have no better alternative.
Have you? I would not go along with any sterilization campaigns as in India,
I think that is far worse. The situation is serious, my friend, we cannot wait
and wonder any longer, we have to take responsibility for future generations
too. So I have accepted the single child campaign.

Psycho-Social problems

There is a word which more and more often sticks in my throat when I try to speak it. It is the word "psycho-social". Everything is becoming so psycho-social in Sweden. It is psycho-social problems which dominate nowadays in children's health care work, and in order to tackle them we have adopted a psycho-social way of working. Great!

I often have occasion to think about our psycho-social reality during the trip. The day before our home call, I am sitting chatting to Dr Liao in Peking.

No, she says, it is rare to meet any psychological problems among our families.

When I then, after the home call, point out that she in fact talked with the family about psychological issues, problems with sleep and the role of the father, she looks at me with wide open eyes and says:

Do you call that psychological problems? I call that everyday worries! That's what I talk about to all the families.

I have in my possession an essay written at the end of the 1930s by the Swedish paediatrician, Arvid Wallgren. It deals with sleep problems and loss of appetite, and, firmly anchored in people's everyday lives, it is one of the best things written on the topic. Nurses worked with everyday psychological problems long before the term a "psycho-social" way of working was invented.

You do not have to follow child health care work in the field in China for very long to see that it resembles very much our own. They work as much on everyday psychological worries as we do, and they have an attitude towards parents which promotes trust and co-operation.

At the same time it is clear that they do not get involved in people's personal problems in depth, or in other kinds of social problems. These are not defined as child health care work, but rather they are felt to be questions for relatives, neighbours, and possibly for the neighbourhood mediating committee (see p. 203).

Many paediatricians in responsible positions are interested in discussing how psychologists can participate in child health care. But it soon becomes clear that they are mainly interested in their testing ability. They want to be able to test children in order to identify different kinds of deviations early on.

The children's welfare centre — authority or discussion partner?

During the trip to China I had with me a short text written by Professor Jundell of the Karolinska hospital and published in 1911. It deals with the feeding of babies, and was certainly a modern and useful text for the time. At the same time it provides a good picture of how paediatricians of that period looked upon their role.

Jundell regards mothers (fathers are not mentioned) as well-meaning but ignorant, at times rather stupid, and always at the mercy of superstition and folk-beliefs. It is not least maternal grandmothers and quacks that he considers dangerous enemies of children.

The paediatrician and the nurse represent informed knowledge and competence, and the prime task of the children's welfare centre is to wage war on superstition and ignorance. Advice is therefore categorical and authoritarian, and anyone who does not follow the advice given is considered irresponsible.

We can today see the reverse side of the self-ascribed authority which the professional health care staff cultivated earlier. It is easy to understand how it arose — it may have saved children's lives — but today it is uncomfortable and an obstacle. It has contributed to many parents feeling increasingly incompetent. They scarcely dare to change from one brand of nappy to another without first asking the children's welfare centre whether they may!

In the child health world we often talk about this. We regard it as one of our prime tasks today to rehabilitate parents, to get them to recover faith in their own ability. This is no easy task, and the road has been thoroughly mined. Again it is we professionals who manipulate, albeit in a new way. But are we conscious of whose interests we are really serving?

I revert to this later. Here I shall merely state that the child health care I experienced in China reminds me in this respect of what we used to have in Sweden. They regard it as fairly obvious that health care has to take upon itself this mantle of authority. There is knowledge, and this has to be spread! It is the health care staff who know how things are, and they have to instruct the people. Health centres are also used as direct channels for messages from above. The single-child campaign would be impossible without the very active participation of child health care. At the health centres there are large notice-boards with lists of those who have joined the campaign — and those who have not. I am not being critical — this may be an historical necessity. Nor am I certain that the way we have chosen to continue in Sweden is the right one.

Health care in the pre-school

We are in China to look at the pre-school, and in the course of our journey we visit a large number of pre-school institutions of various kinds. I am the doctor in the group, and when visiting the pre-schools I go my own way. I seek out the health care staff, and ask to be allowed to follow them in their normal work, so I get plenty of opportunity to ask questions. They do not speak English, but the whole thing is made possible through one of our hosts volunteering. She is herself interested in health care in the pre-school, particularly in the work done to improve diet.

The children look healthy everywhere! We all notice this and discuss it at times. We are used to visiting Swedish pre-schools, used to being with children with runny noses. Here we scarcely see a single child with a cold. And yet virtually all are here! We count the number of children again and again. In groups of 35 children, all are present often, all apparently healthy. Occasionally, one or two children are absent, seldom more.

It is due to the health training, say all whom we ask about it.

The doctor at the day nursery

The pre-schools are large by Swedish standards, often with 300–400 children. At each pre-school there is a paediatrician, usually employed full time. Alongside her (all the paediatricians I meet are women) she has a nurse. The nurses function very much as assistants to the paediatrician and almost correspond to Swedish nursing auxiliaries.

The paediatrician and the nurse are to be found at a small health centre on the pre-school's premises. Often they have one or two spartanly furnished rooms. Attached to these there is a sick bay with eight–ten beds. The entrance to this is often at the rear of a house, with a little garden, separate from the rest of the pre-school.

Early in the morning all the children at the pre-school are examined. In some pre-schools the doctor and nurse go round the different groups and do the checks. They ask the staff if they have noticed any signs of illness among the children. The older children can speak up for themselves. Then all the children have their throats looked at, with the help of a torch. At one pre-school this is combined with giving the throat a disinfectant spray. I do not succeed in finding out what it contains — it is just being tried out, they explain.

At other pre-schools the daily checks of the children have been delegated to the pre-school teachers. There they have been trained by the doctor, who goes round with the nurse seeing that everything is done properly.

When all the children have been examined and the morning work has got going in the pre-school, a representative from each class attends a brief meeting at the health centre. They discuss the health situation and fix times for the children who are to come to the centre for a more thorough check-up later in the day. The doctor sometimes issues instructions. For example, she asks someone to take a particular child's temperature after the afternoon nap and report back to the nurse. She also advises on which elements should be included in the gymnastics programme of the day.

The purpose of the morning checks is to trace children with the beginnings of an infection quickly. Then they are taken out of the group and put in the sick-bay.

The paediatrician is generally attached to a children's hospital nearby. She is usually there for a few hours a week to take part in the rounds, conferences and further education. She then usually also makes a point of visiting any children from the pre-school who may be in hospital for investigation.

It is important to emphasize that this system, with paediatricians and nurses permanently attached to pre-schools, is typical for the larger pre-schools in the towns. In rural areas, conditions are different. We visit among others a small day nursery in a people's council where health care is looked after by the paediatrician who works at the production brigade's hospital, i.e. a system more like ours.

The sick-bay

Longing to get back? Oh no, it is so nice to be here. I want to stay here for a long time!

This is a five-year-old girl speaking, and the words come spontaneously and from the heart. I am sitting on a rock in the garden of one of the sick-bays I have found at a large pre-school in Chengdu, chatting with the two children who are staying here just at the moment. One boy and one girl, both five. They come from two different pre-school groups. There is a child nurse with them. She always works here in the sick-bay. If no children have been admitted, she helps the nurse with some of the other jobs.

打予防针

小针头，亮晶晶，
针头里面药水清，
我忙卷袖伸手臂，
阿姨给我来打针，
预防针，作用大，
增强体质抗疾病。

On a large slate blackboard in the textiles factory's day nursery there is this illustration of the principle in the syllabus: "not being frightened by health checks and all kinds of prophylactic vaccinations".

Both the children in the sick-bay have had respiratory infections with a temperature. Their temperature is now normal and they will remain a further couple of days in the sick-bay before they are re-united with their friends. That is why I ask whether they are longing to get back.

They think it is nice to be able to be on their own, says the child nurse.

This is not difficult to understand. The sick-bay's garden is like an oasis in the large pre-school. The child nurse plays with the children in a manner which I have not yet seen grown-ups do during our trip. She jokes with them, puts them on her knee, and tells stories. She provides them with individual contact which they must be extremely unused to in the large groups, she gives them time and warmth. Falling ill cannot be very threatening at this pre-school.

It is unusual for the sick-bays to have their own staff. The usual thing is for one of the assistants in the class to go along with "her" children to the sick-bay and stay there until they have recovered. A couple of the paediatricians I speak to are strong advocates of this system. They think that the children need their ordinary caretakers to an even greater extent when they fall ill.

Sick-bays are especially common at the pre-schools which function more or less as weekly nurseries, but I also encounter them at other day nurseries. The staff spend the night there when there are sick children, and it is felt that this is preferable to transporting sick children back and forth between home and pre-school. Occasionally a sick child can stay temporarily with someone such as a paternal grandmother. On the other hand, it is unusual for parents to be able to take time off work to look after sick children.

The treatment of children with infections varies among the different pre-schools, depending on the training and orientation of the paediatrician. Some of them have more faith in Western medicine, others in Chinese medicine. Often elements of each are combined in the treatment. The two children I go to see in Chengdu have both been given tetracycline, a kind of broad-spectrum antibiotic which we are reluctant to use with small children in Sweden, because of the risk of side-effects, but which is widely used internationally. They have also been given a generally-boosting Chinese herbal medicine. This is prepared by the health staff themselves in a space next to the pre-school's kitchen, and in such large quantities that all the children in both classes that the sick children come from can also be given the medicine for a few days for purposes of prevention.

Food is important

When I turn up unannounced to visit pre-school health centres, I often find the nurse deeply immersed in the study of tables. When I ask what she is doing, she explains that they are to do with diet.

New guidelines for the nutritional value of pre-school food have been worked out centrally, and now they are trying to implement this. Several of the nurses sigh:

It is so difficult. We are not used to reading these kind of tables. And even when we have understood everything, it is not so easy to apply. We must, of course, take into consideration the food which the children and the families are used to eating. And the kitchen staff do not understand why they should need to change a way of preparing food which has worked well for all these years.

At most of the larger pre-shools they have established working parties consisting of the doctor, the nurse, the caterer and one of the teachers. They meet every week. They discuss diet in general, make an overall food plan for the coming two–three weeks, and decide in detail on the diet for the coming week. They do their figures and check that everything is in accordance with the tables. Then the week's menu is put up on a large notice-board.

There is no doubt that diet in the pre-school is regarded as an important road to improved child health. Several paediatricians and health politicians point out, as does Dr Fan, the advantages of an expanded pre-school precisely from a health point of view, perhaps mainly because of the guarantee it provides of all children getting a properly balanced basic diet.

When I look through one week's diet, it is evident that the nutrition calculations are well up to the standards of WHO. What we possibly react against is that it is still common to have sweet biscuits and cakes as snacks. But dental care is not yet a high priority concern in China.

Health training

Of course it is important that we can quickly find the children who are ill and give them the right treatment. But it is the preventive measures which are most important of all. That is why we are here!

So says a paediatrician whom I talk to at a pre-school in Xi'an, a statement which is then repeated, in various forms, by almost everyone I meet during our trip. They are thinking of vaccinations. But most of all of diet and health training.

Health training — what could that be? I am very interested in the question, not least since I observed on an earlier visit to the Soviet Union the emphasis they placed there on being outdoors, baths and physical training. This, too, is something we are far from unfamiliar with in Swedish child medicine of an earlier time. In paediatric books from the beginning of the century a lot of advice is given on "toughening" treatment of various kinds: sunshine, being outdoors and cold rub-downs, preferably combined with the gymnastics system of Ling, sporting activities to strengthen the body, and ideally plenty of trips out in the country.

Since then, advice of this kind has, if not come into discredit, at least been pushed into the background in our country. It has been considered "unscientific" compared to more narrowly aimed and specifically medical measures such as a progressively expanded vaccination programme. There is no research showing that a health training programme of the kind conducted in the Soviet Union or China has any positive effect, they say. The truth is probably rather that there is no research at all worth mentioning in this field. For various reasons, researchers have chosen to take up other questions.

This is a shame. Infections are still a large problem in our pre-schools, though perhaps not in the sense that in the long term they threaten children's lives and health as they did in the past. But the high frequency of respiratory infections, and the absence from school they cause, is a problem for children, parents and staff. And, not least, they constitute a threat to the educational ambitions of the pre-school.

In China they consider it natural and quite obvious that health training is effective and they smile with almost kindly forbearance if one expresses reservations.

We know what things were like earlier, before we started with health training, say many of the older staff. There were plenty of infections then. We fully understand your situation.

The gymnastics programmes have been tried out thoroughly. They are published in centrally-produced documents, but you can see local variations. For instance, in Sichuan province they have worked out a number of programmes of their own, which they have just reported on to the paediatric research institute in Peking.

What is perhaps strangest for us is the programme used with the smallest children, i.e. children below the age of two. Every day these children are laid one by one on something resembling a table for medical checks. Then a passive programme of movements is worked through: a child nurse systematically goes through the various groups of muscles and carries out passive movements: she stretches their arms above their heads, folds them over their chests, stretches them out straight, bends them behind the neck, stretches them down towards the hips, etc. Then it is the turn of the head and then the legs. The whole programme takes roughly ten minutes.

The passive gymnastics programme for the smallest children has two aims: on the one hand to stimulate development, on the other as part of measures to prevent infection. We ask whether it would not be better to have the children on the floor and to stimulate them in various ways to move actively. And the reply is:

That does not provide the same comprehensive training. Children easily "forget" to use certain muscles, they choose the simplest movements, which are not always the ones which give the best training. In addition you must remember that the floors are cold in winter, you cannot have any children on them then.

No, of course — how forgetful we are! Our floors, too, were cold once. Where did we put our children in the winter?

As soon as the children start walking, they begin introducing progressively more active training elements. At one pre-school we see children aged one-and-a-half creeping through hoops and being lifted ten centimetres from the ground holding on to a pole. They do somersaults and walk along benches keeping their balance.

Every day at the pre-school begins with half an hour's gymnastics programme, as soon as breakfast and the health check is over. The educational content is described elsewhere in the book — as a doctor I notice how systematic the programme is. Certainly nothing is left to chance; it must provide a broad and comprehensive training of movements.

The children are out as much as possible, they often have lessons outdoors. Outdoor activities are always organized, the teachers are always there. They themselves may go into the shade of a tree, but they make sure that the children get a proper dose of sun every day if possible.

At some places there are other elements in the health training. In Peking and Xi'an we see how the children are taught to massage certain areas around the nose, in front of the ears and on the neck, to prevent infections. In Chengdu we never see this, maybe because the leading paediatrician there, Dr Fan, is doubtful about the value of it all.

Sweden is behind

Various features of health care in the pre-school are of course debatable. But what strikes me above all is how *present* it is. The presence every day of the paediatrician and the nurse, morning check-ups, health training, discussions about diet — everything must contribute to making both the children and the staff health-conscious in a way which leaves Sweden lagging far behind.

Once Sweden had a system of special day nursery doctors. This had big disadvantages: it functioned well in some places, in others it did not function at all. It also led to the division of responsibility between the children's welfare centre and the pre-school becoming unclear — some children were forgotten. In many places there was also poor communication between the health care system and parents.

So the system was changed. Since 1980 the "landsting" (regional health authority) has had responsibility for health care in the pre-school. This means in practice that it is the child welfare centre which has to look after health care in the pre-schools in their catchment area. The idea is that pre-school children, too, should come to the children's welfare centre with their parents. In addition, the centre nurse and doctor should visit every day nursery group once a term. The nurse should also visit the part-time groups.

I know there is a good deal of local variation. But seen in the Chinese mirror, it is tempting to state categorically: our system does not function, it is poor! Many centre doctors never go to pre-schools, they do not really understand what they should be doing there, if they are not supposed to have their stethoscopes with them. Nor do the nurses always see the purpose of it, either. Many have complained that they have met scepticism and some uncertainty on the part of pre-school staff. They refrain from going there. This leads in its turn to their knowledge of the pre-school never becoming very great. This is noticed by the pre-school staff, whose scepticism increases, and the vicious circle is complete.

Our system has now been in operation for three years. It is time to reconsider it fundamentally. I think it is good that children's welfare centres have the responsibility for health care in the pre-school, but a new content needs to be put into it. Here we can learn from China. Educating people to increased health-consciousness should be a central element of pre-school pedagogy, and here medical staff have much to give. But then we would have to get into the pre-school in a completely different way from hitherto, otherwise we should not be there. In the long term, I think that children's welfare centres should be moved out of health care centres and into the pre-school's premises!

Handicapped children

At our pre-school we have only one child with special difficulties. The other 359 children are normal children.

We are sitting in the teachers' meeting room at the pre-school of the university in Xi'an. All morning we have been going round the 40 classes, and all of us have seen him.

He is a five-year-old boy. He wears glasses, but one sees immediately that they are unable to compensate for his seriously reduced vision. He has serious co-ordination problems, and at first I think that they are due to his poor sight. But after being with him for half an hour, it is obvious that he also has other handicaps, in particular cerebral paresis.

He is sitting at his place in the large group — 35 children. When I am there they are in the process of folding paper. The other children are patient and supremely competent in following the complicated instructions that the teacher gives. But the boy cannot keep up at all, he folds his paper haphazardly, everything goes wrong. Initially they pretend not to notice it, but after a while one of the nursery helpers comes forward, squats down, says a few words to him and then folds his paper so that it is right. Then she goes back to her place right at the back of the classroom.

We enjoy having him so much, he has made such progress, says his teacher afterwards. When he came here a couple of years ago, he could barely walk. He must have mostly lain in bed. And talking, he could not do that at all, we were even unsure whether he could hear. But now he talks and moves really well, as you can see. His sight is extremely poor, but he has been given a pair of special glasses which do at least help a little.

We ask whether he is given any special individual training.

No, not as such. We think it is best for him to be with the group as one of them, that is what we always do. All the children should belong, none should be put outside the group, that only leads to their getting a kind of special position which is not good for them. But certainly he clearly needs extra help. We try to give him this in the simplest and most natural way right in the classroom. And we have talked about it openly in the class, about his difficulties. So all the children know about it, and it is nice to see how they do everything possible to help him.

How common is it for you to have children with handicaps of this kind in the classes?

At our pre-school we may have had two or three in recent years.

If you cannot cope with them here, what happens then? we ask, but they do not understand the question. It is obvious that you cope with the children in your charge, what do we really mean? When we insist that there must be children with such serious handicaps that they cannot have any kind of a meaningful existence in an ordinary pre-school, they concede that this is correct. But such children never come to the pre-school in the first place. They are in special institutions.

But at this pre-school with its 360 children there must surely be more than one child needing special support and stimulation?[1]

Translators Note
1. The source of this concept is the pre-school bill of 1973, number 136, in which the government suggests that certain children should be accorded priority in the pre-school. The bill considers it "a matter of urgency that education authorities take steps to seek out those immigrant children who are in need of special support and stimulation in their development, and where possibe to provide them with a pre-school place before they reach the age of six." The pre-school law itself (of 1976) makes provision for "children who for physical, psychological, social, linguistic or other reasons are in need of special support in their development". The concept has often been used as a cover term for any potential problem children.

Needing special support and stimulation? That is surely what every child needs!

Home for handicapped children in Shanghai

Ever since the discussion in Xi'an we have stressed that we want to see a home for handicapped children, so in Shanghai a visit to the Children's Welfare Institute is arranged. This makes one of the strongest impressions of anything on our trip.

The home is a vast institution in the middle of the town. We walk through ward after ward. I have never seen so many handicapped children at the same time. Here there are 590 children aged up to 16. 450 of these are foundlings — they have been abandoned by their parents because of their handicap, left at a police station, in a hospital foyer or on the doorstep of the home. Nowadays they try to trace the parents but there are generally few chances of finding them.

You must understand that this is an ancient Chinese custom. A deformed child means misfortune for the whole family, so they abandon it. It is no longer permitted to abandon children, and it is not as common as it was earlier. But it is so deep-rooted, it is difficult to get people to think differently. Here at the home we think it is frightful. The children, of course, need their parents, even if they are here.

The children have been placed in different wards according to age and the degree of handicap. Here there are retarded children, some seriously, some mildly. Some are easy to identify medically: children with Down's syndrome and other chromosome deviations, albinism, hydrocephalus, microcephali, in other cases the diagnosis is unclear, for the home's doctors, too. There are also autistic children and children with motor handicaps.

In several wards the majority of the children are permanently bedridden. But the principal was on a study tour of, among other places, Sweden a couple of years ago, and now they are trying to make the children mobile as far as possible.

I learned a great deal in Sweden, your care of the handicapped is the best I have seen. But we do not have anything like the same resources. For example, we have no physiotherapists and no specially trained teachers. We have to try to manage anyway.

In the babies' ward I find a couple of children who look typical cases of premature birth.

Yes, that is right, they were born prematurely, and that was enough for the parents to abandon them. Premature birth meant misfortune in ancient Chinese popular belief, and such children used never to be allowed to live. This has changed, but there are still parents who do not dare to keep a prematurely born child.

I also find several children with a hare lip and no other sign of handicap, a five-year-old girl with a strawberry mark on her cheek, two children with head burns, children who in all other respects are normal. It is impossible for us to understand how they can have been abandoned, unless one takes into consideration the magical significance of this form of visible handicap.

There are also wards for deaf and blind children. They are empty during our visit — the children are away at their special schools during the week but live at the home at the weekend. These children, too, are usually orphans.

Then there are also some children who do not seem handicapped at all. They are children with difficulties at home, children who have been taken into care because they have been without parents or other relatives who could look after them.

But such children are very rare in China. We have only a handful here, although we cover the whole of Shanghai with its 11 million inhabitants.

Remember you are in a developing country, Lars! I say to myself while we walk around. Even so, for me as a professional the experience is difficult to take. What in the end makes it optimistic is the openness and the strength of the staff's living commitment. Here there is a will to change and develop which lifts the whole institution out of resignation and gloom.

Integration — rejection

The images from the university's pre-school in Xi'an and the home for handicapped children in Shanghai can function as two reverse pictures — one is the image of integration, the other the image of rejection.

But the concept "integration" has many meanings. In Sweden we try to apply a kind of integration through special treatment. Through giving individual support to different children (auxiliary teaching, physiotherapy, speech training, perception training, etc.) we try to get them to function along with other children in a group. The idea is simple: different children need to be treated differently in order to get the same opportunities.

In China integration has a different meaning. It is more a question of accepting deviations, of seeing these as normal variations. The boy in Xi'an was an exception, he was considered a handicapped child. Even so, he was given only a minimum of individual help, they trusted in the healing powers of the group. And that is the basic principle: children are seen as members of a group. By giving the group the best possible care and teaching, each individual, too, can profit maximally: the group itself has an extra potential which is ruined if particular children are extracted and given individual training.

Fundamentally, it is a question of how we look on children and what we want for them, whether we want to give priority to the individual or the group, the collective. This question is discussed at many other points in the book — we revert to it constantly during our trip. But I would like to make a personal comment here:

I have become more and more sceptical about the subtle diagnostic work that we devote our efforts to in Swedish child health care and the pre-school, charting minimal motor, linguistic, intellectual and psychological "deviations" — everything under the cover of giving an ever-increasing proportion of the children what we call "special support and stimulation". I have a strong feeling that we are involved in a process in which we become less and less tolerant, where our notion of what should be called "normal" becomes progressively narrower. I see great risks in it:

More and more parents become more and more deviation-conscious. They become progressively more inclined to consider their children as burdened with problems and deviance, instead of seeing them as the perhaps slightly odd but basically wonderful and healthy individuals they in fact are. The same is true of health care and pre-school staff, and the risk is that we will transmit jointly our worried, charting look to the children themselves: "Which problem do you have then, my little friend?"

Needing special support and stimulation? That is surely what every child needs!

My impression is that in China they have wider limits of tolerance than in Sweden, that they build more on what unites children than what separates them. In that sense they have pushed integration further. But they have also pushed rejection further.

When children fall outside a given limit, they are abandoned. By the parents, but to some extent also by society. Funds for the care of the handicapped are limited, and no real attempt is made to integrate the service into society in the way we are familiar with.

Compared with other developing countries, this situation is by no means unique. It has its causes both in ancient notions with a magical content — and in a tight economy, in which there are harsh decisions on priorities. They have probably little to do with the political system or the single-child campaign. Insinuations of this kind which have appeared in the Western press must be regarded as both malicious and ignorant. Besides, we should be careful not to be too self-righteous. It is not so long ago that we used to leave our handicapped children out in the forest. And this summer there has been a sad debate in the press, with a politician suggesting an increased screening of foetuses in order to reduce the cost to society of handicapped children.

The mediating committee

We try to solve problems without involving the authorities. Things work out more smoothly like that!

Suddenly they are sitting in front of us, two mediators from a neighbourhood in Shanghai. During our journey we have tried to get an idea of the kinds of psychological and social problem which occur in families with children, and what society does to help them. This has interested me, as I have been able to see as a paediatrician in Sweden how psycho-social problems have become a more and more important aspect of the children's welfare centres' work. So I have asked questions at every health centre we visited and with every paediatrician I talked to. Often eyebrows were raised high:

We see very little of that type of problem in China.

But at a couple of places they added:

In any case, that is not really an issue for the health authorities, it must be more a task for the mediating committees.

We have been informed that there is a mediating committee in every neighbourhood and every production brigade, and we have asked several times to meet some mediators. When a meeting is arranged in the middle of a pre-school visit, it comes about so unexpectedly and hastily that we do not even manage to note down the mediators' names. They are two women of about 50, cheerful, open and so outspoken that the interpreter looks momentarily a bit hesitant.

We ask them to describe a case which is topical right now. They confer for a moment.

Conflict between families

We can tell you about a conflict between two families. It is a case that we have worked on a lot recently and we are still not through with it.

There are two families who live in the same street. One of the families lives at number 10. In it there is a boy who is just over 20. The other family lives at number 8, and they have a girl of the same age. The boy and the girl like each other very much and have done so for several years. Now they want to marry and start a family. But the boy's parents are absolutely opposed to this. They do not like the girl's family, and they want their boy to marry a completely different girl. But he refuses to, he does not like her at all.

It has been like this for two years, with constant quarrels between the families. So one day the boy's sister, who is a few years younger, lost control of herself. She went over to the girl's parents and made a tremendous scene, which ended in a real fight. Somehow it just so happened that the girl's mother broke her arm, or had it broken, and just how it happened is not completely clear. She needed help from a doctor at all events. And then she turned to us for help.

We have done a lot of work with these families, we have been there many times. We have tried to explain to the boy's parents what the law is. They have simply no right to prevent the young people from marrying each other. They have retained an old way of thinking which is not valid today.

We have at any rate got the boy's sister to apologize for her venture. And she has also paid the doctor's bill. And now the plan is probably for the young people to marry. But we cannot really say that the families are in agreement. We shall certainly have to go there again. We hope that time will do its work gradually.

Is there not a police investigation after an assault of this kind? we wonder. And that is when the mediators reply, extremely unambiguously:

No, no, we try to keep the authorities out of the picture, things work out more smoothly like that. But certainly, the woman who has been assaulted is free to report it to the police, and then there is an investigation and a court case in the usual way. But of course nobody wins anything by doing that, it is better if matters can be settled amicably.

The mediators

We are not regarded as a threat, say the mediators. We are obviously just ordinary people. We have both worked at a factory. Now that we have retired, we can take on this enjoyable but fairly demanding task. We have lived in this area all our lives, and we know everyone here.

We form part of a mediating committee, which has five members. The chairperson is a man, who gets a fee from the neighbourhood. Then there are four of us women who work as mediators. We do not get paid anything — naturally we have our pensions. We mostly work alone, but at times, as in the case we have just described, we are two together on it, and this is actually better.

Every other week the whole committee meets. There we discuss difficult cases. Then we also have further education. We invite lawyers, teachers, doctors and others to come and tell us about their experience. We have been on study visits to courts of law of various kinds. At our latest meeting we went through the most recent numbers of a legal journal in which some topical cases were discussed in depth. This kind of thing is very useful.

Otherwise we try to be out in the neighbourhood as much as possible. We often pay home calls, at times for no specific reason. Most important of all is, of course, the preventive work. Everybody knows us, they have jointly chosen us as mediators because they trust us, and we always feel welcome.

The local newspapers are another important source of information. We read them thoroughly every day. There are often reports of things happening which we can then follow up.

And we also co-operate with the health centre. They sometimes ask us to help with families who have run into difficulties of various kinds.

Are there no rules about confidentiality? I wonder. They do not understand the question at first, then they smile almost indulgently:

Of course, but they do not apply to us. We are just there to help!

Assault

The case you described was one of assault. Do you see instances of assault within the family, wives or children being assaulted?

We have not seen a single case of a battered wife during the years we have been active here. It is a little more difficult to provide reliable information about child abuse. We have not personally been in contact with any cases, but we know that there are instances of much too hardhanded reprimands, even if they are rare. It was somewhat chaotic here in the final years

The neighbourhood's mediating committee.

of the cultural revolution. Many older children and young people felt towards the end that they could do precisely what they wanted. Now that parents want them to study again, there may be conflicts and then occasional parents may forget themselves. But it is scarcely our concern, it has never been as serious as that.

Pre-marital relations

Young people should not initiate sexual relations too early. This is the official line, and we back it up. It is better for them to use the time for educating themselves, the time for starting a family will come soon enough. Pre-marital relations are not permited.

We are occasionally contacted when a young, unmarried girl gets pregnant. We talk through the situation thoroughly with her, and generally suggest an abortion. Sometimes it has ended with her keeping the child and getting married to the child's father.

Divorces

Divorces are uncommon, but they do occur, and then we are often brought in to mediate and see if any constructive alternative to divorce can be found. There are cases of this succeeding, but sometimes there is no turning back and then nothing remains for us to do but to recommend divorce to the court.

We can give an example. There was a woman who in her youth had some kind of periodical states of confusion during which she could not take care of herself. When she later got married, she did not tell her future husband about this. It went well for eight years, but then she had a trying attack of this kind of confusion again. The husband asked for a divorce. We recommended this. We considered, just as the husband did, that the woman should have spoken about all this before they got married. Then he would have had a chance to make a genuine choice. He never had that chance in this case. So they had to give him a divorce now that he demanded it and insisted.

What happens to the child in such a case?

In this particular case the father was naturally the only one who could look after the child. In other cases we try to get the parents to decide for themselves who should have custody. If they cannot agree, the court has to decide. They often ask us to say what we think.

If the woman in a family has a relationship with another man — is this grounds for divorce?

We have never met a case of that kind — that must be very unusual! Yes, we would think it is probably grounds for divorce, if the husband absolutely demands it. But we would try to reconcile them and find a new platform to build on further first.

On the other hand we have had some cases where the husband has been unfaithful. In a case we are working on now, the husband has been unfaithful with another woman. Now he wants to get divorced in order to move in with the other woman. But his wife does not want that. There the divorce is delayed. And our task is now in the first place to have a serious talk with the other woman. She must realize what her responsibilities are, and she should renounce her claims on the man who is already married. That at any rate is our first stance.

Housing

If the people in a neighbourhood are displeased with what the authorities are doing — for example in relation to housing — are you asked to help then?

That happens, and we pass such complaints on sometimes. But actually this is mainly a task for the neighbourhood committee. In our own neighbourhood we recently had this kind of a case, where we were slightly involved. The drains for the houses in a few streets were inadequate for all the residents, they got blocked and sometimes there was an awful stench there. But there was no money to do anything about it all. Then the neighbourhood committee appealed to the district authority, which then had to go further right up to the city authorities. It was a laborious procedure, it took a long time, but now finally the drains have been put in order.

Professionals and lay-people

As a Swedish child health care worker, I have often in recent years pondered over the limits of my professional responsibility. Where does my responsibility as a care worker end and where does my responsibility as a fellow human being begin?

In China there is an exciting dialectic between relying on professional people and relying on lay-people, a refraction which sheds new light on our debate in Sweden. But it takes time before the pattern starts becoming clearer.

In *health care* you meet a distinctly professional attitude. It does not quite fit my expectations. I have read about barefoot doctors and Chinese folk medicine and expect to find a strong lay element in the care of the healthy and the sick. I do not find this. The barefoot doctors' lack of professional competence is seen as a great problem. And folk medicine is practised with the same professional responsibility as Western medicine, often in combination with this.

In fact the responsibility of the professional has at times been pushed further in China than in Sweden. An example of this is the health care in the pre-school. That medically trained staff should check all pre-school children every morning — how would we react to a suggestion like that? We should certainly regard it as unreasonable and superfluous. But why?

Once more it may be wise to think back in time. In the regulations for day nursery doctors in force in Sweden in the 1930s and 1940s there was a set of rigorous stipulations for limiting infections in the pre-school. One was that no child could return to the group after absence due to illness without being checked by a doctor first. Today we leave all such assessments to parents and pre-school staff.

One of the causes is a different view of children and infections. We usually point out that the transmission of contagion is at its peak the day before a child falls ill and that it is not therefore meaningful to isolate a child once it has fallen ill. But the fact is that we also seem to be prepared to accept a greater number of infections in the pre-school than they are in China — and than we used to in Sweden. We have a tendency to think in terms of the health risks for the individual child and of the parents' difficulties in taking time off work rather than of the educational needs of the pre-school group. Are we right in doing so?

Another cause is probably a growing faith in the medical competence of parents and pre-school staff. We think that the medical assessment to be made is no more complicated than what any reasonably well-educated parent or nursery helper should be able to manage. As professionals we should only use our efforts on those questions where our knowledge is really needed. This sounds right.

But the question is whether we are in the course of withdrawing too far. A Chinese pattern of thought carried over to Swedish conditions would perhaps look like this:

It is debatable how extensive the child health care service should be. But if we are going to conduct this at children's welfare centres and pre-schools, it has to be of the best quality. That the pre-school's health care is mostly a facade is bad. And that child nurses are no longer considered necessary in open care is deeply worrying. It is possible and probable that earlier on we stretched our professional responsibility too far. But that is a separate problem, and cannot be solved by lowering the competence of professionals.

Within Chinese *social care* a quite different line is followed from the one in health care. The mediating committee in Shanghai provides a good example. Here they consciously stress organized volunteer work, building on experience of life, knowing the people and being trusted by them. But this is not enough — further education is necessary for the mediators to be able to perform their work with sufficient competence.

There used to be mediators in Sweden, too, even if they were limited to the task of mediating in marital disputes and did not have the back-up from society and the general public which the Chinese mediating committees seem to have. The Swedish mediating institution is a thing of the past and has been replaced by trained officials employed at family counselling offices and family-law departments.

A personal memory springs to mind — I recall the child care committee I was a member of at the end of the 1960s. It was in a small, thinly-populated council before many of these were amalgamated. The committee was politically appointed, but party membership had not been given much consideration. It was more important that the different villages in the council were represented on the committee. Work in the committee built entirely on the members knowing people. There were no social workers but the members of the committee themselves largely carried out the tasks of a social nature. They were responsible for their village and talked sense into people.

One of the justifications offered for amalgamating councils was, as is well known, a wish to provide people living in thinly-populated areas with access to a more competent social service. There were probably also good reasons for this. But did we choose the right road?

Level of development or philosophy of man?

In child health care in China you meet a professional attitude which in some respects goes further than our own. In social care they consciously stress the work of lay-people. I have shown that a similar pattern can be seen in our own country 30 to 40 years ago. I have drawn several such parallels in this chapter. I have done this not so much to understand China but more to understand our own development. That is really what I am writing about.

A comparison between China's present and our own history can be fruitful. But it can become deeply dangerous also for us, if we do not simultaneously see the profound cultural differences there are between the old oriental culture and our own new west-European civilization. It is a question of the philosophy of man, human origins, purposes and responsibility. It is therefore also a question of what kind of children we want.

It is thus much too facile to claim that our problems of yesterday are what we meet in China today and that our present-day scourges are therefore going to be those of China tomorrow. China's solutions can never be ours, nor *vice versa*. But our own image can be given a clearer profile in the Chinese mirror.

Parental education — a Swedish model

A topical Swedish pearl to try to capture a mirror image of is parental education. I am myself involved in a parental education project at my children's welfare centre and I have invested a considerable amount of energy and enthusiasm to get our model with group consultations to function. It has actually gone well and we think we can justifiably be proud of the activities we run.

It is therefore natural for me, on every visit to a health centre or children's welfare centre during the journey, to ask whether they have any parents' groups. And look — I get a bite! Several places people nod in recognition and continue:

Certainly, we sometimes gather the parents together to give them information on some important matter. For instance, we have spoken about diet. And the single-child campaign.

But, I suggest, with the Swedish manifesto resounding at the back of my head, that sounds to me more like unilateral information from your side. Do you not let the parents meet in groups to exchange experience with each other? So as to strengthen them in their role as parents?

Their role as parents? Meet? At the centre? Of course, parents meet and talk about how it is to have children. But that is what they do at home. Why should they come here?

I feel so stupid! I try to tell them about Swedish disorientation, about the distance between the generations, about parents' feelings of incompetence and failure, about people moving and thin social networks. And they listen politely.

You must, of course, solve your problems, says a paediatrician. But I still do not understand what the children's welfare centre has to do with all that. That is obviously not health care, it is really something that people must take responsibility for themselves. Do you not have any mediating committees?

No, we have no mediating committees and not much solidarity with our fellow humans either, I think to myself silently. But we do have parental education — always something!

Again — I am one of those who are strongly in favour of parental education, I have worked hard with it myself, and I still believe it is needed, that it is necessary. And yet — what is it we are up to? What disturbs me most is that it is *us*, society's paid professional workers, with health care as a speciality, who have got it into our heads that we should create self-esteem, confidence and security in our parents. Who — apart from the Swedish National Board of Health and Social Affairs — has given us this mandate?

Sometimes I have a horrid feeling — a feeling that we are in the process of depriving people of something fundamentally important. I have trouble in putting my finger absolutely squarely on the sore spot. It has something to do with human dignity and inner self-respect. Only, I have had such trouble in giving expression to this feeling in the past — it is so easy to be accused of being reactionary and hostile to knowledge and of advocating social disarmament. Nothing could be more alien to me. That is why it is so liberating to meet, in a progressive socialist country which one can really not accuse of guarding the individual's rights at the cost of the community, such a faith in people's capacities and such a feeling for their dignity.

Here it is not a question of development. I cannot imagine that the Swedish model of parental education will be relevant in China even 30 years from now. On the other hand I am fairly certain that Swedish parents long before that will have shaken off our well-meaning manipulating!

The golden middle way — does it exist?

One night I dream about my children's welfare centre back home. I dream that it has moved to a pre-school in Uppsala, where it is part of a joint construction with an open pre-school. The centre is managed by a children's health care committee. There are about ten members of the committee, mostly parents from the area. They draw up guidelines for the activities and each has specific tasks. Two function as child environment ombudsmen — they guard the external environment of the children in the area and they know everything about the risk of accidents. Two are pre-school ombudsmen — they go round together with the nurses at the pre-school and see that the health training and health education function as they should. Two are responsible for the children's welfare centre's premises. The latest thing that has been done is that money has been saved up for a loom and an electric coffee-machine and these are now in the waiting-room. There is also a duplicating machine which an additional two members are responsible for — these are the editors of the children's magazine of the area. And then there are two who are responsible for courses, various courses being planned according to the parents' wishes.

The committee has explained to me that I have done a good job, but that the time has come for re-thinking. I am welcome at the children's welfare centre, but not as often as earlier. Once a month is enough. They are going to rely on a nurse instead.

In a cold sweat, I wake in my hotel room in Hangchow. What sort of nonsense is this? I think. I thought we had agreed that you cannot transfer China to Sweden. Not even my own centre!

How are children doing in Sweden — and in China?

The debate in Sweden about how our children are doing is full of contradictions and to some extent a muddled one. There is today a tendency to paint Swedish children's reality in gloomy colours. People talk of Aniara-children[1] as confused children, "a whole generation of children being lost".

A succession of research reports has provided for such a negative picture. During the 1970s came a whole series of investigations about children who were in a bad way, in which problem after problem was uncovered. For instance, today there is a great deal of talk about sexually exploited children and about children of mentally retarded parents.

Other often-cited reports have shown that 5% of all children having the four-year-old standard check show such psychological symptoms that measures need to be taken; that elements of violence have increased in children's games; that misuse of intoxicants has become more common at lower ages; that the incidence of child and youth crime is greater; that the number of cases of anorexia and suicide has increased, even in pre-puberty, and that Swedish children do not feel loved by their parents.

I have myself participated in writing research reports on this theme, so I know that a great deal can be criticized in many of the studies done, and perhaps particularly in the ways they have been presented. I know that some of the results have been exploited in an uncritical and misleading way in public debates and in the mass media, without the researchers themselves actually getting a hearing. Some truths are good value for a certain time, during which nuances and modifications are simply not welcome.

What is often lacking is a historical perspective. In such a perspective it comes out fairly clearly that the position of children in most respects has never been as good as it is today. Children were in a much worse way earlier, physically, psychologically and socially. What has happened is that the perspective has changed. Despite all the talk to the contrary, society has become more and more child-oriented, and the conditions which children lived under 20–30 years ago and which were regarded as normal then would never be accepted today.

Translators Note
1. Aniara (1956), a science fiction epic by Harry Martinson, describes a spaceship with 6,000 people on board, who have left the planet Earth after it has become virtually uninhabitable as a result of irreparable radiation damage. Aniara goes off course and flies into endless space. This is the diagnosis of humankind's (= Aniara's children's) situation in the age of the atomic bomb since starting, with technical-logical virtuosity but without moral aims, to meddle with the secrets of creation.

At my children's welfare centre, vast numbers of children pass before me. The centre is situated in an old urban area with a very heterogeneous population. I see all the children from the area, and what strikes me is how many healthy, secure, wonderful kids we have! And how many ambitious, involved parents, who are willing to do a great deal so that their children will do well.

But I also work a good deal with children who are in a bad way, often along with people from the social services, and I therefore also know how miserable some children's lives really can be, so miserable that it is often difficult to describe things in a way which those who have not had close contact with such children can comprehend.

At grass roots level, too, way below the winds of fashionable debate, the picture is thus variegated and difficult to interpret. My picture looks like this:

I believe that most Swedish children are better off and are doing better than children did earlier. But at the same time there is a small group of children who are really in a bad way. What disturbs me most is that the gap between the many who are doing well and the few who are not is, so far as I can see, widening. The causes are obviously many and connected, among other things, with the economic-political development of society and also with a social policy which has in part failed.

During the trip to China I often had the opportunity to imagine the many contradictory pictures of Sweden, to see whether the new lighting contributes anything new to them. The picture of the Swedish debate on upbringing also comes to mind, a picture which is virtually a caricature.

It is bizarre that we can conduct such a foolish ephemeral debate on upbringing as we in fact do! It is strange that we always believe that at precisely this moment we have finally hit upon what is right, that we always have a tendency to regard our own time as having usefully sobered up after the errors committed a decade earlier. It is all the vogue to speak about the lost 1960s today, about a *laissez faire* mentality and pedagogy, and think that we are better now. Norms, rules, daring to be a parent, setting limits . . . the fashionable messages of the day make me want to throw up, not because they are wrong, not because they are put forward, but because they are put forward and marketed as the ultimate truth. Again!

The Chinese picture

It is useful to have pictures and reverse pictures from Sweden with one on the journey. Because in China, too, we meet pictures which are contradictory and difficult to interpret. The picture we choose to present will depend on the goals we have, on whose interests we want to serve.

I can, if I want, present a malicious picture. Then I should stress the health problems still needing solution in the rural areas, I could talk about the tendency to want to separate children and parents through "interning" little children at weekly nurseries, I could describe the health training as "gymnastic drill", I could describe the shortcomings in the care of the handicapped as a manifestation of "élitist thinking" and link this to the political system without mentioning anything of the historical reality, I could deplore the single-child campaign and see it as a manifestation of the totalitarian state's control over people's private lives. And so on, and so on. I do not intend to present such a picture. Others have already done so. Besides it is not fair.

I can also present a picture which would fit into current Swedish debates and perhaps give rise to an interview in one of our national newspapers or at least in a provincial one. Then I should have to focus on all that business about norms, I think. I should write about all those children who look so free and secure, despite such strict discipline, about unanimity in the society's value judgements, about parents and teachers daring to teach clear ethical rules which hold everywhere. I will leave this picture, too, to others who can describe it better. It is at least truer than the first, even if mightily adjusted to Sweden.

Let me instead stick to my medical onions. My main impression from China is of a uniquely successful child health care when compared to equivalent countries. There is no doubt that they have come far in the fight against the traditional threats to children's life and health: infant mortality, malnutrition and infectious diseases. The child health care I saw in action functioned well, and what surprised me was more the similarities with our own care rather than the differences. I was specially impressed by health care in the pre-school, where we have much to learn.

What made the deepest impression on me was how seriously children are taken, both in everyday contact between adults and children and in the more overall societal planning. Children are really considered the administrators of the future, and the Chinese are prepared to invest a great deal in order to give them sufficiently good tools — and a country worth administering. I think this is what makes the journey through China such a restful pause in one's existence, despite the intensive programme — not once do I need to speak up to defend children's rights. That is being done by everyone around us already!

6 Children of the towns and villages . . .

Orvar Löfgren

Meeting of cultures

Happy and uninhibited kids dancing and singing in colourful costumes. The same pre-school children sitting silently in neat rows in a classroom on tiny green chairs, their hands decently behind their backs. The well-disciplined crowd dissolved in shouting, noisy games during the break — at a tempo and noise level which seem more familiar from Swedish day nurseries.

Many have pondered over how these things can be combined. Why do these well-drilled kids not appear more cowed, how does one learn to combine submission with fearlessness?

Benefiting from the knowledge of other study delegations' fates and adventures, you arrive in China on your guard. You assume that the programme has been neatly organized and that model institutions will follow each other on parade. If the ordinary tourist experiences one dance performance at a day nursery, we are probably going to experience a score. What can one actually learn about China and the conditions in which Chinese children grow up?

We travelled there to learn something about China's children and about China, but also to try to get our own Swedish conceptions of children and children's institutions into perspective: through being confronted with a quite different cultural pattern. The cultural shock did not fail to materialize, either. We were given a good shaking-up, bewildered by contradictions and by discovering that so many of our own concepts and ways of thinking did not fit. We often asked questions which our hosts could not see the purpose of and sometimes got answers which we could not understand.

216

Part of the Chinese culture shock is due to time and place being blended in a surprising way. Not only is one travelling on a foreign continent, one also has the feeling of travelling in time. Old and new are constantly juxtaposed. There we were sitting in our tidy excursion bus with well-trained guides watching the 1800s and 1900s parade past in the traffic. Honking lorries, Russian models of the 1950s, old women with latrine carts, hordes of cyclists, peasants carrying, pulling or dragging their burdens on their way into town, highly-polished official cars sweeping past teams of mules. In the market throng, stands where you could buy dried monkey's paws for use against rheumatism jostled with the sale of film star magazines and plaster statuettes of the same make as in Western shopping arcades. Outside the hotel, old women stood at dawn worthily doing Tai-chi gymnastics, while university students jogged past along the boulevard.

As my daily concern is to study the transformation of Swedish peasant society into the "folk home"[1] of the 1900s, this mixture of a traditional peasant society and a thoroughly rationalized country of the future was fascinating. Time after time I had a feeling that what we saw now had happened before. The parallels to the developing country Sweden's rapid transformation were many, despite the great cultural differences. But what is specifically Chinese in China's development, what can we recognize from the construction of our own folk home? Such comparisons can easily be misleading. The similarities can be superficial, the differences ostensible. But in the best of cases the comparisons can help us to stand back from our own fairly provincial debate on the conditions in which children grow up.

For a three-week-tripper there is the constant problem of getting a grip on *what* it is that one sees: what is ideology and what is reality, or rather what kind of reality does one meet on trips round the city, on home calls, at day nurseries or journeys out to people's councils? One suspiciously looks for cracks in the facade.

The official image of society contains in itself future visions and priorities, and says a lot about practical and political problems. I have chosen in particular to focus on the ideological image, not only because of the limitations of a short journey but also the fact that, if you want to understand why the pre-school looks as it does, you have to get an idea of the goals which

Translators Note
1. A Swedish dictionary definition of a "folk home" is "a well organized society which takes good care of its citizens". This is the Welfare State dreamed of by Swedish Social Democrats in the 1930s. The folk home was a society of material security, with social benefits and social services for everybody. Reforms should be attained by harmonious co-operation across all sections of society. The folk home ideology is associated with such great Social Democrat leaders as Per Albin Hansson and Ernst Wigforss.

permeate everything, from the arrangement of games and teacher training to views of the child and the role of the family in the society. China is an ideological country in the sense that the ideology is clear and open: they know what they want and they say this clearly.

The gulf between the manifestos and everyday realities is usually deep, but the ideology itself is not so much an attempt to conceal reality as to *charm* it. For a Swede who is used to seeing moral messages more discreetly wrapped up, this explicitness can be troublesome or provocative. With the ubiquitous pointers, the contours of a utopia and a land of the future are drawn. They tell how China should develop and how the Chinese should be. The strong ideological colouring can make the boundaries between utopia and reality fluid even for the Chinese — at least for the Chinese who look at the world around them from a desk in Peking.

But if one wants to understand why today's discussion of family policy, children and the pre-schools looks as it does, one needs a historical perspective, because in China history is really lived in the present. Today's situation must always be related to the fantastic challenge which building up the country after the Second World War involved.

A retrospective glance of this kind also provides a reminder that China is still a peasant society and that the majority of Chinese children grow up in rural environments which are completely different from city life in Peking, Shanghai and Kanton. So my discussion of family policy and the conditions in which children grow up does not begin at the day nursery in the towns but among peasants in the villages. How has China's transformation appeared to them?

History seen from the villages

When Mao Zedong on 1st October 1949 proclaimed the birth of the Chinese People's Republic, he took over the leadership of a peasant society, looted and torn apart by war. The history of China in the 20th century has been bloody. The old empire had slowly disintegrated in the 19th century while the colonial powers ruthlessly exploited the internal contradictions in the country and acquired decisive control of both the economy and politics. The hundred years prior to 1949 are above all the time of many humiliations, when the old, proud, great-power China was converted to the site of countless invasions, battles between power-hungry generals, desperate peasants' revolts.

The strong nationalism which today permeates Chinese daily life is nourished both by pride in a civilization stretching back many thousands of years and by memories of this recent humiliation. In the older generations' consciousness, the difficult years during the Japanese occupation from 1937 to 1945 stand out especially clearly. Then both the communists and the nationalists fought against the occupying power. After the end of the Second World War, the fighting continued between the old nationalist Guomindang government and the Communist Party, fighting which had gone on since the 1920s. The nationalist government had gradually lost more and more of its popular support, while corruption and the power of the generals had spread.

The People's Republic was thus born out of chaos, repression, war and poverty, out of a society with enormous class differences and a vast cultural gap between the traditional upper class and the poor peasants.

The 30-year history of socialist China is not only about trying to build a new society, but also about tough political disputes over how the development should be phased. Views of family policy, of the role of school and the pre-school in the society have therefore changed along with political fluctuations.

It was the poor peasants who provided a broad basis for the revolution, and after the victory in 1949 their hunger for land was satisfied by a reform programme which turned the class structure of the villages upside down. Rural people were divided into five categories: landlords, large farmers, "middle farmers", small farmers, plus tenant farmers and farm labourers. The landlords and large farmers were deprived of their land, and as class enemies they now ended up right at the bottom of the social ladder — they were even stripped of the right to vote and other civic privileges. The economic differences between different groups of peasants were still considerable, however, not least between rich and poor agricultural regions. In the middle of the 1950s the state therefore tightened its grip on agriculture through a collectivization programme, which was, even so, considerably less drastic than the Russian one. To a large extent the new collective units were built up around existing villages, which were often dominated by a single family clan.

But these reforms did not solve the problem of the differences between rich and poor villages, between lean and fat districts. In 1957 they started preparations for creating considerably larger collectives, the people's councils. Under the slogan "The Great Leap Forward" they planned a mass mobilization, one of the most important aspects of which was to create a new spirit among the peasants. Now they were not only to produce collectively but also to live and think collectively.

Ambitious plans were drawn up. Families should eat together in dining-halls, children should be looked after at day nurseries, old people at homes for the aged. They even planned to build new collective living quarters in order to further emphasize that the old, traditional primary unit — the peasant family — was to be replaced by a new and larger community.

Enthusiastic reports came from the newly-established model councils. The new socialist person could be portrayed thus in 1958:

"In Chaoying council the bells ring and the whistles are blown at dawn. Within a quarter of an hour the peasants are ready for work. At the word of command of the platoon and company leaders, the columns march with banners flying out to the fields. One can now no longer see peasants in little groups of two or three strolling out to the fields. Now marching songs and stepping out in time can be heard. The slack life style which has characterized the peasants for centuries has now gone for ever. What a fantastic change! To adapt to collective work and collective life, the people's councils have set in motion a development in which whole villages are merged and the population moved from one place of residence to another. The peasants load up their luggage on their backs and travel in groups to new flats near their places of work. What a splendid change! Traditionally peasants have valued their houses, inherited from their fore-fathers, higher than anything else. But now private property, farms, and even some of the livestock have become the property of the people's council, all the links which used to tie the peasants to their property have been severed, and they feel freer and lighter in heart than before. The peasants say: 'It does not matter where we go. We are always at home in our Chaoying home.' There is nothing of their old home that they long for. The people's commune is their home."

"Now there are dining halls and day nurseries in the villages. All the houses are locked, as the whole population marches out to the fields or the workshops. The old custom of preparing food or bringing up children in separate households cannot be maintained. The pattern of the individual family, which has existed for thousands of years, has been completely smashed." (Domes, 1980: 33)

But the reality was otherwise. The party leadership had grossly under-estimated the tenacity of the traditional peasant culture. Resistance increased out in the villages.

All over the country thousands of day nurseries had been hastily impro- vised, but the experiments with collective child-minding did not work out well. Here is a glimpse of one people's council:

> "In the beginning the day nurseries to which all the council's children were sent were just a piece of land on which a dozen children played under the eye of a grown-up. It was very difficult to take care of the children. It only needed the 'auntie' to turn her back for a boy to disappear or another child to cry and want to go home. Some mothers said: 'We would rather have our children at home' and stopped sending their children. . . . The children sat on the bare ground. . . . A millstone had to serve as a round- about. After eating badly cooked or cold meals the children got diarrhoea. On one single day there were twenty cases of diarrhoea in the nursery. When the children fell ill, the parents' productive capacity fell; the mothers began to curse the day nursery." (Domes, 1980: 36)

But it was not only a question of parents taking their children out of the new, improvised day nurseries. Old people ran away from old people's homes, and people began secretly preparing their meals at home. They refused to march in military formations, skimped their work and did not look after shared equipment. In some parts of the country the opposition grew into open resistance, and things were not improved when some army units which were sent out to crush the uprising made common cause with the peasants. The situation began to become critical and the party leadership was forced to retreat. "The Great Leap Forward" ended in a rapid stride backwards, or rather: the Russian development model was confronted with the Chinese realities. Collective barracks were forbidden. The peasants were guaranteed the right to private ownership of their houses, their gardens and their small livestock. Every commune could decide for itself whether to have central kitchens, old people's homes and collective child-minding, and in most cases the family resumed its old tasks. The day nursery, in the form in which it had been introduced out in the villages, had not met with a favourable response among the parents.

The people's communes were converted from being spearheads of the new collectives into administrative units. Instead it was the smaller units, the production brigades and particularly the production teams (15–25 house- holds), who themselves organized the joint work and the joint ownership. At the same time more room was made for private cultivation and craft products which could be sold on the free market.

The next large campaign, the cultural revolution of the 1960s, passed by everyday life in the villages with fewer traces. It was mainly directed against the intellectuals of the towns and involved an attempt to check the growth of a new élite of civil servants and highly educated people, but it also had the goal of bridging the gap between manual and intellectual labour, between rural and urban. The hundreds of thousands of students and officials who were sent out "to get to know the peasants" experienced an often shocking reminder of how different life was in rural areas, as regards children's upbringing, sex role patterns and family life.

After the cultural revolution and the fall of "the gang of four", this gulf between town and country has if anything continued to widen, but China is still today primarily a peasant society and every attempt at changing the society must take the conditions of the peasants as a starting-point if it is to have a chance of succeeding. Time after time the ideological campaigns have turned out to be too poorly rooted in everyday realities out in the villages.

Seen from the villages, the political struggle often amounts to a struggle about ducks — the eternal tug-of-war about how much space the peasants should be allowed to organize their own economy. The small private sector has a key importance for the individual household: it is based not only on personal gardens where the cultivation of vegetables is intensive, but also on the ducks swimming in the irrigation ditches, the chickens running around in the courtyard, and the pigs rooting around down the village street. It is based on the bamboo which grows around the house and can be woven into mats, baskets and much else. There is great creative imagination in handicraft work, and here child labour is important.

In the mornings you see rows of carts on their way into town with the production collective's goods, but also an even flow of peasants on their way to the free market. Their burdens are small, a piglet on the bicycle's baggage-holder, a basket full of eggs, a bundle of vegetables. But business is brisk on the free market square. Here everything from ducks and onions to home-made sun-hats, bamboo chairs, fireworks and decorations is sold. Here there are also craftspeople offering their goods and services, shoe-makers, tailors, watch-menders and smiths. It is this private sector which is now expanding and it is around its conditions of existence that there is a constant struggle.

To the peasants the great ideological conflicts in Peking may often seem very remote. They listen distractedly or patiently to the political rhetoric, whereas every regulation on the right of privately owned pigs to find food on common land, on ducks' access to irrigation channels or rules for the free market are carefully attended to.

As we have seen, the peasants are not defenceless, either. They protest through passive resistance, through pretence, through turning a deaf ear, through ingeniously circumventing new regulations.

Seen from Peking, this broad popular mass may seem to act as a permanent brake on a sensible development, like a conservative force full of irrational wishes, anachronisms and feudal traditions. The masses do not understand what is good for them and at any rate have no higher political consciousness.

"All good things are five"

The political wind of change after the defeat of the cultural revolution can be detected from the poster boards along the avenues in Peking. Chairman Mao is nowadays only there in one single copy, at the entrance to "the Forbidden City", the old imperial palace. All the other portraits of him, of Marx, Lenin and other leaders have gone. During our trip we see a yellowed picture of Mao very occasionally out in rural areas.

The poster boards, when not advertising Chinese goods — often with both Chinese and English texts — cover the current campigns for the single-child system or a better traffic code. The new political line can perhaps be sensed more clearly in the actual form of presentation than in the text. Exhortations to show consideration to others in traffic or not to spit on the street do not figure in a framework of everyday contexts. In clear colours, a land of the future is painted on the large surfaces instead. The text stands out against a background of motorways straight as an arrow, tower blocks, well-kept lawns, shining cars and occasional pedestrians in neat Western dress.

This land of the future is presented in many guises during our journey. The key words in today's ideological message are DEVELOPMENT, FUTURE, CIVILIZATION, TECHNOLOGY and SCIENCE. The direction of the new political line for marching to the land of the future is clearly drawn.

For Westerners the element of slogans in the official Chinese message can sometimes make one feel uncomfortable. They are often built up around the principle "all good things are five", "bad things are three" or "the gang of four". . . . This distillation of politics into rhymes and memorable maxims has not merely a long tradition in China, it is also a necessary form of political communication in a peasant society of one thousand million inhabitants who are not allowed to hover in uncertainty about what the current political line is.

Major political changes require new campaigns when old slogans and memory prompts are replaced or reloaded with new content. Such changes even involve restructuring official knowledge. The old heroes can turn into the new villains, the *petit bourgeois* vices of yesterday can become progressive virtues. This kind of campaign work is given greater weight by contrasting the new good times with the old bad ones, with the years before the liberation of 1949, with the anarchy of the cultural revolution and the confusion under the gang of four and their rampaging. The justification for the present policy is that it represents a higher stage of development and constitutes a natural phase in the progression towards the true and good society. This is why a science such as archaeology is such a consciously political science and why a museum exhibition can contain political dynamite.

The shifts in the campaigns have their own black and white logic, their own ritual forms, but this does not prevent the slogans from saying a great deal about the official line and current political contradictions and problems. If you want to understand what goals are being set now for work in factories, schools and day nurseries, it is important to study the pattern formed by the slogans.

During the cultural revolution, schoolchildren had to learn "to love five things": Chairman Mao, the communist party, the socialist mother country, productive labour, and the nice section of the people — workers, peasants and soldiers. In 1982 the good things are still five, but now the children learn to love the mother country, the people, labour, public property, and science. Underlying this shift is the whole struggle from the years of the cultural revolution, battles about whether ideology should precede the economy, about who the real class enemies are, about how Chinese society should develop, and what the important priorities are.

The victorious faction is now putting a rapid economic and technical development before ideological orthodoxy. The leaders, the party and the basic contradictions in socialism are being played down in favour of a modernization campaign which is not without ideology but rather based on other value judgements.

But what does the new ideology consist of, what is the new policy and how is it anchored in everyday life and the world of children? Today's two main campaigns deal with modernization and civilization: to increase economic expansion fast, and to make people become rational and cultivated citizens — to become "modern". The four modernizations therefore deal with the necessity of investing in agriculture, industry, defence and science, while the civilization campaign deals with how ordinary people should order their lives and change their mentalities. We meet this campaign in the neighbourhood committee's selection of good families, in the day nursery teachers' points system for children, in competitions between different sections at factories and offices.

For a Swede, the list of slogans has an unmistakable ring of the making of the Welfare State in the 1930s. First come "the five emphases" which highlight the importance of discipline, morality, hygiene, external etiquette and internal refinement; then there are the four examples of beautifying work which one should apply to oneself and to the immediate environment: *beautifying one's own consciousness* (cultivating a sound ideological consciousness, a moral character and integrity, and defending the leadership of the party and the socialist system), *beautifying the language* (to use and spread polished language), *beautifying one's own behaviour* (doing useful things for the welfare of the people, working hard, being concerned with the welfare of others and collective interests, observing good discipline), *beautifying the environment* (stressing personal hygiene, and good order in one's home and public places).

The good and the evil

It is no accident that these slogans lead one's thoughts to campaigns for the moral rearmament of the people at earlier stages in our own history. The civilization campaign is not just a question of fighting disease, ill health and of promoting the good of the society, it is also a question of fighting the old peasant society, traditional ways of thinking and life-styles. Behind the wish to develop rapidly a modern industrial society, based on science, rationality and common sense, there is also the élite's impatience with the people, an impatience which we know from Sweden both at the turn of the century and between the wars — even if in different circumstances and with different forms.

Behind the slogans there is a vision of the world, a conception of both the country of the future and the good life, which we met time after time, in senior party officials, in day nursery teachers and barefoot doctors. It is a vision of the world consisting of a merging of socialist utopia, Chinese traditions of thought and Western doctrines of development. In schematic form this mode of thinking can be illustrated by contrasting the good life and the bad life.

The good life	*The bad life*
Harmony and unanimity	Conflict, division and confusion (the chaos of the cultural revolution)
Socialist ideals	Feudal conceptions and extreme leftism
Healthy traditions and good history	Traditional superstition and feudal relics
Morality, civilization, hygiene	Immorality, dirt, disorder
Science and rationality	Superstition and unreason
Collectivism and altruism	Individualism and selfishness
Self-control and good behaviour	Absence of good manners and culture, rusticity
Secure families, secure children, a secure society	A normless society, divorces and extra-marital love
Respect for authority and knowledge	
Planning and being economical	Ignorance, backwardness, stagnation
Good technology	
All development involves progress	

We meet this vision of the world, for example, in the diplomas for successful family planning. They are decorated with an edging on which the symbols of the land of the future are drawn: rockets, power stations, factories and retorts.

We also see it in the new pre-school syllabus. This emphasizes not only education for cultivated conduct and good morality but also the learning of a scientific outlook. Obviously the staff should organize the children's daily lives in a scientific manner, as regards everything from training in sleeping in a correct position to logical thinking.

You do not have to be in China for long to see to what an extent the visions of the good society reflect the thinking and cultural patterns of the small but important group of well-educated townspeople — those whom we mainly meet on our trip, as interpreters and guides, in committees of welcome, behind reception desks. Here it is not only a question of political consciousness but also an expanding cultural gap, which in varying forms exists in all societies in development — our own history is no exception.

This gulf may appear more paradoxical in a society with socialist ideals — there are more double messages. Everyone should serve the people, but the people must also serve the state. The toiling masses are the basis and motive force of society but also an obstacle to development. "Proletarian" can be both a title of honour and a word of abuse.

The massive scale of the society underlines the gaps, too. The world of Peking lies far from daily life in the villages. When our hosts are reluctant at times to see us moving out among ordinary people unrestrainedly this does not need to be an attempt to censor. We soon notice that they were slightly concerned about the reception we might get in residential areas, in village streets and market-places, not because people would be hostile but because they might behave in a much too uncivilized, rustic and blunt way. It was peasantness they were ashamed of, so they did not hold back from sometimes telling off inquisitively staring peasants or intrusive children by referring to the civilization campaign. "It is uncivilized to stare like that at our guests," hissed one of the local guides once to people flocking around the group.

This kind of example can be used as an ironic comment on the gulf between socialist ideology and the conduct of the élite, but that is too cheap a point. We ought rather to find out how a cultural gap is created — even in a country like China — and what consequences this has for practical politics. To travel in China, to experience the essentially different worlds of the villages and of the government offices, is to learn something about the conditions under which alienation and sometimes an unconscious incipient contempt for the people can arise. Here there are obvious parallels to the Swedish folk home construction of the 1900s, but also to some elements in the new moralism of the 1980s. For the well-educated and intellectual, other people's culture can so easily be uncultivated.

Two worlds?

The images of the good life and the bad life led my thoughts unintentionally to the great Swedish manifesto of the 1930s, "Accept", the battle-cry of the Stockholm exhibition of 1931, the book in which the Swedish land of the future is painted in bold colours. In words and pictures there is a presentation of two cultures, A-society and B-society. In B-society peasant culture still prevails, it is characterized by cultural stagnation, poverty, under-develoment. A-society is the land of the future, which seethes with industrial and technical development:

> "Thanks to horse-power, A-Europe has become the Europe of the machines, the banks, popular education, and science; without it, B-Europe has remained the Europe of agriculture, religious orthodoxy and illiteracy."

In the book Present-Sweden and Olden-Sweden are juxtaposed: two worlds which live side by side, but with quite different life-styles and types of people. Olden-Sweden has to be transformed from a B- to an A-society; this is the message in "Accept", which is put forward with an endless faith in development and enthusiasm for opportunities to plan away misery and poverty, both material and spiritual. This optimism grates in our ears today, but in the Sweden of the 1930s there was a dream of the future against the background of the developing country situation that the majority of the people had grown up in.

The China of 1982 is not the Sweden of 1931, but I still recognize important features in the vision of decision-makers, planners and educators and their impatience with B-society and B-culture's resilience and extent. At any rate I experience strongly the conflicting impacts of the two worlds during our journey.

Even before travelling, we knew that it was presumably A-China which we would mostly meet, that the day nurseries, people's councils, factories and homes we would be taken to would be examples of the best, the desirable. This did not mean that our hosts tried to prevent us from seeing less well-polished sides of society such as a home for handicapped and mentally retarded children. We were given freedom to make our own improvised visits and thereby have the chance to experience the contrasts between model institutions and "ordinary" children's institutions. Our hosts' desire for constructive criticism was not just empty words, either. We sat discussing our good and bad impressions informally during many evenings. This openness gave us the opportunity to get a more realistic picture of the great difficulties they were confronted by and the fluctuating possibilities for implementing reforms in practice.

In addition, the model institutions were important to see because they constituted laboratories for the future. This was where they had the resources and the well-educated staff making it possible to implement new educational ideologies. But without the glimpses from the B-society we would have got a very biased picture of the conditions in which children grow up.

The contrasts between A- and B-society were great and instructive. One day I am sitting in the living room of a model family, with a diploma for its good way of life; and a standard of living which even for model families would have been unthinkable ten years ago. Here there is a television set, armchairs, here the bed-spreads and wall decorations, often in Western style, shine with sparkling colours.

The next day I wander with the interpreter along the docks of the city and visit boat people, who live on board the old junks which form both home and place of work.

An old woman waves us on board one of them, invites us into the cabin, pours tea in chipped glasses. She scarcely belongs to a model family. Light and wind come into the cabin from the open sides of the boat. Some chickens stalk around on the foredeck and a kitten plays under the kitchen table. The firewood is in a basket by the iron stove, food hangs from the ceiling in a string bag. Her husband returns from the market with a piece of pork and some vegetables. He is ill and can no longer work.

They have brought up nine children on board and made a living by digging up sand along the river banks and then sailing it to construction sites. Now most of the children have grown up and left home, an 11-year-old daughter lies ill in a corner and watches us. They have had a hard life, says the woman, but things are a little better now. She goes off to a wooden box and fetches the family's identity papers and pension book. They belong to the "mobile people" and live on the fringe of the town society which is otherwise so thoroughly organized. Officially they come under the harbour authorites, but they do not belong to any social collective. They are part of a floating society which the modernization and civilization campaigns do not reach so easily. Culturally speaking there seems to be a great distance to the people in rented accommodation on the other side of the quay.

Everyday life in the villages is far away from life in Peking. Even if we travel by bus and see the occasional lorry, the main impression is still one of people walking and pulling, dragging and carrying.

The effect of contrast would also be strong in day nursery visits. We visited many model day nurseries, but a glimpse of one is enough for present purposes:

We are met at the gate by expectant children and a large sign with flowers saying "Welcome". Nice atmosphere, spacious and light rooms. Here there is no excess of pedagogical aids, but proper things and a staff both well-educated and enthusiastic. We wander from class to class in the day nursery and end up as usual with a cup of tea asking questions. You do not have to speculate whether this is a model day nursery. The walls are decorated with diplomas and in the visitors' book there are plenty of greetings from earlier delegations. We ask the usual questions about what categories of parents send their children here and are given the usual answer "office workers, teachers, army people . . . and workers". There may be an occasional worker's child, but this is a day nursery for the children of higher officials. That is why it is also a weekly nursery, where the children stay from Monday to Saturday. The parents travel a lot and work hard in the service of the state: the élite can see their children less than others. That the children are not any old kids is also clear from wandering through the dormitories and peeping in the cupboards: here there is a standard of clothing which is considerably out of the ordinary. The standard is also generally high otherwise, the teaching, playing facilities, the dance performance, child health care.

The official ideology still prohibits any clear and direct marking of the social differences in day nursery standards. These have to do not only with the social status of the parents but also with the economic viability of the institutions or the local unit which finances them. We visited other well-equipped model day nurseries at factories which were prospering and could afford to invest properly in child care.

In contrast to this well-organized environment is a visit to a completely ordinary people's council. With a driver and a guide I go off one day in search of a fishing village. We make our way to a people's council which is reported to have a fishing brigade within its borders.

Along muddy paths we try to find our way to the beach and the fishing village. The leader of the brigade is there laying bricks on the administration building itself, dries the mortar off his hands and greets us tentatively. It is only when the guide has shown him what she has in the way of official papers, stamped and headed, that he invites us in. The village has its own day nursery, they have to, since both men and women are out fishing for shorter and longer periods of time. But here the institution is a necessary evil, a storage place organized with their own limited resources. It consists of

In the fishing village the day nursery consists of one room with an earth floor packed down hard.

a room with an earth floor packed down hard in one of the long low houses in the village street, where some elderly women are in charge of a flock of children. The furnishings are restricted to some benches with mats for the children to sleep on. My sudden appearance frightens the children — it is the first time that a pale and burly fellow with a camera at the ready stands there at this day nursery.

The situation makes me recall an earlier description from the end of the 1960s in which a day nursery teacher compares conditions in her simple village day nursery with an urban pre-school:

"The children cried the whole time. When we had finally gathered them in one place, they got bored, but if they were let loose, they went off on their own and all one's time was spent in hunting them again. There was only one room for the children and not many toys or books. This village day nursery was really something completely different from the day nurseries in the town. Sometimes we could try to teach them a song. There were children from three to six together. There was no difference between different classes as in the town. The children had mainly to be kept together when their parents were at work. For the peasants the goal of life is just to grow more food. Unlike in the town, there is no time-tabling of activities. Things just happen . . . ." (Parish & Whyte, 1978: 223)

The difference is great between country and city, although it is possible in more prosperous and industrialized people's communes in rural areas to find day nurseries which definitely live up to the urban standards.

But most children in China do not go to a day nursery at all. They live in a rural world which in both economic and cultural terms is remote from towns and model councils. The contrast really only came home to us one day when we drove across the plains in central China. Satiated with the official programme, we asked the driver to pause in the middle of the landscape so that we could wander on foot into the nearest village:

We stride in the clay along the irrigation ditches and fields, where every square metre is under cultivation. It is fantastically green and luxuriant. The rape is one metre high, the rice has just been planted, everything grows so that you can hear it. Every piece of land is as well kept as an allotment. Here all the planting, thinning and tending of the earth is done by hand, and everywhere in the landscape we see people working. The farm buildings are bunched together, caulked with clay and with thatched roofs as on the farms in Skåne. At the corners of the cottages thick clumps of bamboo sway. People flock to watch this heap of tourists spreading out between the houses.

Some of us are waved into a courtyard by an old woman surrounded by children and grandchildren. One family lives on each of the three sides of the courtyard, she says, while the barefoot and toothless village people huddle around us. She fetches the best bamboo chair in the house and wants to offer tea. In the half darkness her husband lies. He is ill with a strange sickness, she says. He will not even eat eggs, and the doctors say nothing more can be done. It must be cancer, says the interpreter we have with us.

There are swarms of giggling kids of all sizes. Here there is neither a day nursery nor a single-child system. Several of the very young women are pregnant, one of them is carrying a one-year-old in her arms. We feel the warmth of their reception, are invited inside, and once again it is as though we are being helped by a time machine. A moment later we are sitting in the bus on the way from the peasant culture towards Chengdu and our Western hotel.

So we have been reminded anew of the gulf between A- and B-society, a gap which in China is primarily a contrast between urban and rural. Such glimpses of another life were also a reminder of the gap between utopian ideals and everyday reality. A society dominated by hundreds of millions of peasants cannot be changed at the drop of a hat. During the 30-year history of the People's Republic, this peasant society's resilience has time after time made itself felt: the confrontation is between how people ought to be and how people really are.

In order to understand the tension between what is desired and what is possible in Chinese politics and societal change, you have to appreciate how the past has created the present. The people are not always as malleable as the decisions-makers would like. The road to the land of the future is bordered by proud, abandoned plans and tough compromises. At times one may be gripped by the feeling that the ideological campaigns come and go while the people's everyday culture remains. Things are not so simple. Out in the villages, too, there is a mixture of new and old, the peasant family does not remain outside the influence of either the economic reforms or the new social policy.

Rural children and urban children

Today the family is not seen as a feudal relic but rather as one of the necessary foundation stones of the good society. The importance of a harmonious family life is often stressed, as is the importance of subordination to the authority of parents. But conditions for family life are quite different in rural and urban settings, just as there is still great variation between the different country districts in this huge country. Let me make this difference more concrete with two examples.

The four-year-old who hops around wearing rabbit ears at the textile factory's large day nursery is more and more often the family's only child. Both parents work, and have realized what considerable material advantages this type of family planning involves. This has perhaps been a source of hot controversy with the paternal grandmother, who would like nothing more than to look after her grandchildren, but the parents sense the generation gap in the ideology of upbringing, and are afraid that granny will spoil the kid. They are anxious to give their child as good a start as possible, and

Most children in China do not attend a day nursery at all. They live in a village world which both economically and culturally is remote from towns and model councils.

they know that school and book learning are decisive for a future professional career. So they are attracted to the pre-school's training programme, dance, music, early reading and mathematics training.

The day nursery is an important resource in their lives. If they work shifts, it could just as easily be Daddy as Mummy fetching and leaving the child. On work-free days, you can see them proudly strolling in the park with a child dressed up in cheerful, sparkling colours. In this kind of family the father is involved in taking care of the child in a way which would have been unthinkable for grandfather.

The four-year-old who trundles around on the village street is looked after by older siblings, by a paternal grandmother or a female neighbour while the parents are at work outside the village. These conditions for upbringing have in many senses more in common with Swedish peasant life 50 years ago than with the urban day nursery child. From early on the child is incorporated into the children's collective of the village, small groups of children who wander around, build dams in the irrigation canals, squelching in the clay, chase chickens, and follow the various activities of the adult world. They soon learn to look after themselves. As in Peasantsweden, school is often seen as a necessary evil, not because the knowledge one gets there would be useless, but the school's world is different from everyday peasant life. The children get their most important education in work, because here in the village children are an economic rescource. Children can do much: mind the household's pig, tend the water buffalo, feed the hens, weave bamboo, run errands, collect grass from the edges of the dikes, gather firewood, fetch water. They are very useful already as six-to-seven-year-olds.

Nor is upbringing anything that people speculate especially much about or discuss together. The art of turning kids into proper people is not based on exhortation or programmes of upbringing. Children can follow what happens, watch, and imitate as well as they can. The contradictions between the generations are not so great, either. The paternal grandmother still passes on much of the traditional pattern to the grandchildren, all the unwritten rules and self-evident attitudes she grew up with.

What does her inheritance of traditions look like? In the first place, it is based on a conception of family and blood relatives which is radically different from ours. The family is defined mostly as the male line. That is why sons mean something. They continue the family and they are responsible for the parents. The daughters grow up knowing that, like their mothers, they will leave their own family, be married into a new family where they will be considered as being foreign. Age is also important — it decides who should show respect for whom in the family. Younger siblings are subordinate to older ones.

Traditionally the most important family link is the one between the father and the eldest son. He is the person who at some point will take over the farm and power in the family, so their relationship is very tense. For the sons the father represents the strict, taciturn figure demanding absolute obedience. He is a fairly distant being.

The children's freedom is greatest when they are tiny. They are treated more as little, cute things than individual personalities. They are pets to be carried, hugged and joked with. Children who step outside the permitted limits can get a sudden reprimand, a clip on the ear or a slap.

One family lives on each of the three sides of the courtyard of the clay-caulked farm building. There are swarms of kids of all sizes.

It is possible that the village's old paternal grandmothers (maternal grandmothers do not, of course, belong to the family) think that recent decades have meant a radical transformation of these ingrained traditions, but outside observers have noted how much of the traditional family and upbringing pattern still lives on in the villages. After setbacks during "The Great Leap Forward", the party has not made any attempts on the grand scale to re-cast the peasants' family pattern. The family remains important, and at school children are admonished to preserve the traditional respect for their elders. What really means something is still work. (Cf Parish & Whyte, 1978 and Wolf, 1978).

There is also a tough tradition of contempt for women, which the authorities have tried to come to grips with in recent decades. Out in the villages it is still very important to give birth to a son, so that the male family line remains intact. This is so important that when trying to introduce the single-child system in rural areas, a reserve quota of "extra children" has been created for families who have had a daughter and where there is a risk of the family line dying out.

Another reason for the difficulties of the single-child system winning acceptance in rural areas is that children are traditionally not only an important labour resource but also an insurance for old age.

It is difficult to develop a central family and child policy in China. Exaggerating a bit, one can say that it would be as though we in Sweden should have a family policy which could satisfy both the small peasant households of the 1920s and the civil servant families of the 1980s. The functions of the family, the conditions in which children grow up, and parents' ambitions are still essentially different in this huge country. Added to this is also the cultural gap itself, the changing value judgements of *how* children should be brought up and for *what*. (The campaign against the corporal punishment of children has, for instance, been more successful in the towns than in the country.)

China is not just a developing country but a country with a thousand-year-old tradition of such cultural distinctions between élite culture and popular culture. To me, therefore, it was not surprising to recognize the well-educated townspeople's complaints about the peasants' primitive bringing up of their children. I have encountered the same complaints time after time in Swedish debates on upbringing in the inter-war period and at the turn of the century. What the complainers often do not appreciate is that what is wrong with the people out in the villages is not that they lack an ideology of upbringing but that they bring up their children in different ways, with other means and goals.

The Chinese model and the Swedish . . .

The comparisons between Swedish and Chinese folk home construction are discordant in several ways. Admittedly, the educational ideologies and the civilization campaigns are influenced by Western thought, but we should take care not to draw parallels too quickly. The inheritance from an earlier time is not merely present out in peasant villages but also in debates on society and plans for the society. The strong emphasis on morality in pre-school upbringing has a long tradition in Confucian moral philosophy. Morality has always merited capital letters in China.

There is also a risk of our over-emphasizing the importance of the programmatic in day nursery upbringing. Just as in our country, there is even at the day nursery a hidden curriculum which is seldom verbalized or discussed. The hidden curriculum lives like a cultural undercurrent, it constitutes self-evident ways of dealing with children, of speaking to them or touching them, of organizing a meal, furnishing a classroom, arranging a singing game or dealing out materials. This hidden curriculum has the clear stamp of traditional Chinese culture.

In my introduction I spoke of the great paradoxes in Chinese day nursery life, the mixture of discipline and uninhibitedness, self-control and spontaneity. Self-control and non-aggressive behaviour are old Chinese cardinal virtues, like respect for the authority of grown-ups. Growing up in such a densely populated society, in intensive proximity to the whole family and to neighbours, means that conflicts and tensions had always to be kept in check.

Chinese children have constantly had impressed on them the importance of controlling oneself, of not fighting or provoking. A contentious child brings shame on the family and is a threat to concord within the family and the neighbourhood. In addition there is the traditional emphasis on hiding behind a mask, not showing strong feelings, not crying or shouting: on behaving politely.

Small children learn both at home and in the day nursery to subject themselves to adult initiatives as something self-evident. Viewing babies as pets, as passive objects of love and adult interest, is a part of this early and unconscious education. The mere fact of tiny children almost invariably being carried or held by grown-ups or larger siblings has a strongly imprinting effect. Body language is a far more effective medium of learning than explicit exhortations.

The same pattern is also found in the babies' section of the day nursery, which almost always makes a more melancholy impression than the lively pre-school classes. Even babies are physically put through gymnastics by the staff. It is useful for motor development, but part of the bargain is a confirmation of subordination, and this gets hidden in the child's body memory. Anyone who has seen a group of two-year-olds patiently standing in a queue along the wall in order to climb through a ring one by one knows where the basis is laid for future self-control. This tradition of seeing the really small children as objects also contributes to giving the sections for the smallest children more a character of storage places for children.

In the same way there is a tradition going back several thousand years of subordination to the collective. That the good of the family takes priority over the individual is one of the old unwritten rules, in other words the whole concept of the individual, which is so central for us, is difficult to translate to Chinese conditions. The emphasis on the collective in day nursery life is, moreover, to a great extent a question of collectivity directed towards the adult. The gymnastics on the courtyard, the arrangement of the chairs in the classroom, everything stresses communication between the individuals in the group and the leader rather than between the children in the group.

But what about the spontaneity, joy and curiosity? Well, they are probably mostly promoted by security, by the unambiguous message of how children should be, by the adults' love of and interest in children.

One factor which makes being a child a secure state has also to do with the actual organization of the society. In China you are never alone, it is a tremendously more open and public society than ours. Everywhere there are adults who find it natural by virtue of the authority of their age to intervene, admonish or help children. This has not only to do with ideology or a cultural pattern but also with the organization of the actual society, how children function in actual environments.

China is still a conglomeration of small local societies, whether villages or town blocks. Here in these environments there is a tight social network, the scale of things is manageable for children, the adults feel responsible, and everyone agrees on the rules for how people should behave with each other.

That was also once true in our country not so terribly long ago, and is still so in some Swedish environments. But in large scale society, fellowship and control are organized in another way, just as the old communal values are withering away. We live in a more privatized way in a world where there is not *one* set of norms but several. Parents often regard the upbringing of children as a private territory, and other adults are careful not to interfere with the behaviour of other brats, whether in the courtyard, on the underground or outside a shopping centre. There is today a large portion of cultural uncertainty as regards what one can and should do with other people's children.

The uncertainty also applies to one's own child. Upbringing today is something which is constantly being analysed, we are subjected to a flood of good advice and rules or an upbringing package which is marketed in the mass media and public debate. Children stare at us reproachfully from posters and book covers: Are You a Good Parent? One thing is certain — never before in history have there been so many parents with such a guilty conscience, so many parents who do not think they are good mothers and fathers, at the same time as we can state that the majority of parents invest time, energy, knowledge and material things in their children to an extent which would have been impossible earlier. In Peasantsweden children had to learn to look after themselves, to live alongside their parents. In today's society you cannot tramp at your parents' heels down the village street or out in the fields. Contact between children and adults is based to quite a different extent on demands for entertainment. Sitting at home as a single parent in a two-room flat with a three-year-old who is constantly nagging at one to build something with Lego bricks can drive absolutely any grown-up crazy, but above all this kind of structure instills the feeling that one does not manage to make oneself as accessible for children as one should. Upbringing is for us saturated with gnawing "ought to, should, must . . ." (cf Ehn, 1983).

By this I do not wish to claim that parents have a guilty conscience for no reason, but that we should to a greater extent see the cause not in personal but in societal shortcomings. Why do we so often feel that it is such a burden to have children, to look after children, to take care of children in our society?

The medicine to cure the confusion about the right upbringing or parents' guilty conscience is not to try to turn the clock back. The longing for "the good old society" is based more on dreams of how it should have been than how it in fact was.

Some of the differences between China and Sweden are simply due to our dealing with two societies which are situated differently in history and development. It is no accident that there is a lot of talk about morality and hygiene, gymnastics and civilization, the nation and science in China today. These phenomena are familiar in other countries which are in the middle of a process of transforming a peasant society to a unified nation and welfare state — not least our own fifty years ago.

The clear transparency of Chinese society creates security for the children. China is a good country to be a child in, it is only as a teenager or grown-up that the drawbacks of the system appear.

It is as a teenager that one begins to notice the double messages in the ideology of the state. Through the open-door policy which welcomes Western technology and science, more unwelcome guests also slip in, the temptations and dreams of the consumer society. On the one hand, the good land of the future is presented with the help of Western props, on the other hand there are warnings against the bourgeois decadence of Western culture. Beethoven is good but not Abba, romance is allowed but not sexuality. On the wall calendars, Chinese mannequins pose in seductive Western style at the same time as the authorities keep a very watchful eye on the importation of teenage culture. Sometimes one gets the feeling that the leaders — a pretty elderly collection of gentlemen — grossly under-rate the yearning for Western vanity and colour at the same time as they over-rate their capacities to steer this demand in a traditional Chinese way by closing doors and formulating prohibitions.

Teenage problems are talked about more and more often in China, and we could notice a certain helplessness as to how this problem should be tackled. At the Children's Palace in Shanghai we were told that nowadays they have ritualized entry into the adult world by collecting all those who have just turned fourteen to listen to a lecture on "a healthy start in adult life", with old party veterans telling moral stories and standing forth as good examples. What is the good of such exhortations when every day and every hour you see tough teenagers, all dressed up — expatriate Chinese visiting — self-assured types with cassette tape-recorders, cameras and fashionable clothes? Compared with them one can only feel like a yokel rural cousin.

The state and the people

Pictures of China tend to be painted in black or white. The totalitarian slave society is set up against the socialist dream country, almost every societal phenomenon can provide contradictory interpretations. Where some see collective fellowship and solidarity, others see control and standardization. It seems reasonable to make the picture slightly greyer.

Reality is both multiple and fluctuating. People from the neighbourhood committees can function as committed lay people and mediating links upwards in the bureaucracy, just as they can serve as listening-posts and informers for the state.

In the same way it is difficult to assess clearly what effect the ideological campaigns have on Chinese daily life. As early as in the day nursery environment, we could notice how easily they are converted into a catechism, how the message gradually becomes banal and thin when it is put into practice. In the day nurseries where the children were awarded red flags for good behaviour on a board for marks, civilized or cultivated behaviour often becomes synonymous with sitting quietly and nicely in class. The whole campaign tended to be beyond the children's comprehension. In the same way competitions to score points for hygiene at places of work can easily degenerate into formalism. The corridors of the trains were washed down endlessly, but in the toilets it continued to smell nauseatingly. Thus the campaign messages can be gutted and turn into ritual form and incantation.

Another effect of the many exhortations and the repeated messages is that people learn how not to listen to them or learn to assess new decrees and ideological U-turns tactically. You lie low until you know whether the new line really holds. Thus influence often does not hit its target — in China just as in other societies. Politics easily becomes ritual — there is always a Lenin quotation which can be used to support a change of direction in the party.

The most important ideological influence is not contained in these slogans and decrees but in the influence built into the way daily life itself is organized, in the order of things, the silent language between people which is seldom given conscious form or made the subject of analysis. This is as true of life at the day nursery as it is of other situations in society. It is true of upbringing in China as well as in Sweden.

Literature

DOMES, JÜRGEN 1980, *Socialism in the Chinese Countryside. Rural Societal Policies in the People's Republic of China 1949–1979*. London.

EHN, BILLY 1983, *Ska vi leka tiger? Daghemsliv ur kulturell synvinkel*. Lund.

PARISH, WILLIAM & WHYTE, MARTIN KING 1978, *Village and Family in Contemporary China*. Chicago.

WOLF, MARGERY 1978, Child Training and the Chinese Family. In ARTHUR WOLF (ed.), *Studies in Chinese Society*. Stanford.

Appendix

Curriculum for the pre-school
(Trial version)
Developed by the Ministry of Education of the People's Republic of China
October 1981

1. The pedagogical task and age-specific characteristics

Pedagogy in our country aims at fostering a generation of new people of high communist ideals, morality, knowledge and physical strength, who are strongly committed to contributing to their native country and to humanity. Education in the pre-school from ages three to six is part of the work of socialist education. In conformity with the principle guiding education in our country and the overall goal in children's upbringing, the task of pedagogy in the pre-school must be, with due regard to age-specific characteristics, to give the children an education which develops all sides of them: the body, the mind, morality, and an aesthetic sense, an education which makes them grow up in a healthy and lively way and which provides a solid basis for entry into the primary school and for the establishment of a generation of new people.

Between the ages of three and six, children grow relatively slowly as compared with the earlier phase, generally about five centimetres per year, while their body weight increases by about two kilogrammes per year. Throughout childhood the system and the organs of the organism develop constantly.

The ossification process of the skeleton proceeds fairly rapidly, and it is characteristic of the chemical composition of the bone tissue that the proportion of water is large and the proportion of solid matter and inorganic salts is fairly small. It has great elasticity and plasticity, and if subjected to pressure, it is easily bent, deformed or broken. The ligaments of the joints are comparatively loose, the joint cavities are shallow, and to prevent dislocation or damage, bending and stretching must be avoided. The big muscles develop before the smaller ones, which are not yet fully developed. The muscles are relatively soft, lack strength and resistance, and tire easily. The skin is fairly delicate, the outer layer is thin and relatively unable to resist infections, so external damage must be promptly treated.

The heart develops fast, and a five-year-old child's heart weighs four times as much as a newborn child's. The wall of the heart muscle is thinner than a grown-up's, and the heart's capacity comparatively small, the quantity of the blood flow is small and its power limited, so the heart must not be subjected to activities of excessive length or excitement.

The child's immunity is not yet fully developed and because of this, children are easily affected by all kinds of infectious diseases. They must therefore

243

be vaccinated in good time. Thorough attention must be paid to everyday hygiene, disinfecting, etc.

The windpipe is smaller and narrower than with grown-ups, there are many blood and lymphatic vessels in the respiratory lining, which can easily become swollen as a result of infection; the relative growth of the lung alveoli is fairly low and the number of lung alveoli is smaller than with adults, as a result of which respiration difficulties easily arise in connection with respiratory tract infections. Active participation in appropriate outdoor activities can contribute to increasing the capacity of the lungs and promoting the adaptation of the respiratory system to the external world.

The degree of calcification of milk teeth is fairly low. Their organic structure is fragile and they can easily be damaged. If the teeth are unevenly positioned, if oral hygiene is poor and dietary intake inadequate, dental caries will often occur, so dietary intake must be monitored and good habits of oral hygiene must be established.

The digestive capacity is fairly limited. The gastric juice and the enzymes which stimulate the digestion capacity are present in smaller quantities than with adults. The function of the digestive tract is unstable and its adaptive capacities limited, so too much food, extremes of cold or warmth, psychological instability or other problems can all influence the normal functioning of the digestive system.

The concentration of the urine is fairly low and the bladder fairly small, the function of regulating the evacuation of urine has not been sufficiently developed, so urinating is frequent. The habit of urinating in good time and at given times must be established; the urinary tract of girls is short and close to the anus, so it is easily infected. Attention must be paid to good habits of living and the hygiene of the external sexual organs.

The brain develops fairly rapidly. The brain of a three-year-old already weighs three times as much as at birth, roughly 1,000 grams. Thereafter it grows fairly slowly and at the age of six the child's brain weighs approximately 1,250 grams (an adult's brain weighs roughly 1,400 grams). The child's brain functions develop constantly. There is constant refinement of the division of the cerebral cortex into layers, cell division, formation of the myelin sheath in the outer layers of the nerve fibres, and the regulation of the cortex's reactions to external stimuli. The stimuli to and the control of the nervous system, are, however, by no means in balance, so excessively monotonous or extended activities easily lead to tiredness.

Every mental process in childhood is characterized by concrete images and lack of consciousness. The capacity for abstract generalizations and conscious thought has just begun to develop.

The child's perception differentiates gradually. The recognition of things or phenomena which are alive or pictured is easy for the child, whereas there is inadequate familiarity with more complicated matters like space and time. The level of consciousness when observing objects is fairly low and the child can easily be influenced by external stimuli and change the object of its attentions. With correct guidance, the 5–6-year-olds should definitely have developed their determination, persistence and capacity to generalize from their observations.

Children's attention fluctuates a great deal. They find it fairly easy to concentrate their attention on things they are interested in, but not for long stretches of time. After training they begin to be able to systematize and control their attention.

The child's memory is in large measure characterized by unconscious and direct sense impressions. Along with the development of language the child develops conscious control of memory step by step. In addition to mechanical memory, the child already has the capacity for cognitive memory and recalls far better what she or he understands than what is not understood.

The child's imagination still mainly involves reproduction, although creative imagination is on the verge of developing. The thematic content in the imagination of a three-year-old is malleable and often goes to excesses. With training, the content of the imagination of the 5–6-year-old becomes gradually richer, and on the basis of verbal descriptions they are already able to create new images and mirror these in games and drawings.

The thought of the 3-year-old child takes place within the framework of immediate sensations and concrete operations, and thereafter gradually moves over to concrete iconic thought, which becomes the primary form of thought throughout childhood. Because of this the child relies even more on lively and distinct images in order to become acquainted with and understand things. At roughly six years of age the child begins to develop abstract, logical thought, and language combined with familiar knowledge and experience can be used for analysing, synthesizing and creating comparatively abstract concepts out of objects in the world around.

Childhood is the period when language develops rapidly. 3–4-year-old children can manage all the essential sounds of language and, as knowledge and experience gradually become richer, vocabulary increases daily. The vocabulary has many content words (of these the majority are nouns and verbs) and few function words. Sentences mainly consist of main clauses with few subordinate clauses. With appropriate guidance, as the child gradually develops control of the form and grammatical structure of sentences, the 5–6-year-old child becomes much more proficient at using the spoken language coherently. Because of limited knowledge and ex-

perience, inadequate vocabulary and inadequate understanding of the correct meaning of words, the child can, however, not express her or his thoughts exactly, so that in speech many linguistic errors often occur.

Children's feelings are not stable, they are aroused and change easily and can be seen. Their feelings are often dominated by external circumstances and influenced by the feelings of people around them. With correct guidance, children's feelings tend to stabilize and children develop some capacity to control them. Children's feeling for morality, beauty and logic begin to take shape. Children's self-control and their capacity to carry through their wishes and actions are clearly beginning to develop, but are still not completely stable.

Between the ages of three and six the personality generally begins to take shape. In view of variations in the environment, educational conditions and hereditary factors, there are specific differences in children's physical and psychological development, and these are manifested in personality, interests, abilities and other individual features. These can leave traces which will last throughout life, so the teachers must be indefatigable in bringing up the children.

Because children are developing physically and mentally in all ways, 3–6-year-olds begin to need to participate in the practical activities of adults in society, particularly in work and in studies. But as they lack knowledge and experience, and their capacities are limited, they cannot yet take part in adult activities properly. This is the primary contradiction in the psychological development of the child between ages three and six, and play is the best way of overcoming this contradiction; it is the best way of promoting children's psychological and physical development.

Taking as one's point of departure the educational principle of our country, and combining this with the specific features of this age range, in concrete terms the task of an all-round, developing education is to give the children an initial stimulation of their bodies, intellects, morality and sense of beauty as follows:

To guarantee that the children obtain the necessary nutrition, to work hard to ensure hygiene, to establish in the children habits of good hygiene and the capacity to manage things on their own, to develop their basic motor skills, to harness the children's interest in physical activities, to improve the functioning of the organism and to strengthen the children's bodies so as to protect and promote their health.

To teach the children the elementary knowledge and skills required for life in their environment, to stress the development of the children's attentiveness, observational skills, memory, cognition, imagination and linguistic proficiency, to encourage their interest in studying, their will to acquire knowledge and good study habits.

To provide the children with an introductory education in the "five loves" (to love the mother country, to love the people, to love work, to love science, to love and protect public property), foster their feelings of solidarity, friendship, honesty, courage, their capacity to overcome difficulties, politeness, being well disciplined, and other qualities of good character, cultivated behaviour, and a lively and uninhibited nature.

To provide the children with elementary knowledge and skills in music, dancing, art, literature etc, to foster the children's interest in these subjects and to begin the development of their receptivity, their ability to express themselves, creativity etc *vis-à-vis* life around them, nature, and the beautiful in literature and art.

Teaching in the pre-school normally takes place in classes grouped by age. The youngest class consists of 3–4-year-olds, the middle one of 4–5-year-olds, and the eldest class of 5–6-year-olds prior to entry to the primary school.

Taking actual local conditions into consideration is permitted, including teaching two classes together.

2. Pedagogical content and requirements

The pedagogical content and the requirements in the pre-scnool are specified in terms of eight areas: habits of hygienic living, physical activities, ideology and morality, language, general education, mathematics, music, art. While the content and requirements for each area are adapted to each age group (youngest, middle and oldest), teaching in the later classes must continue to consolidate the content and requirements of the first and second classes.

Habits of hygienic living

To provide the children with teaching in and a simple and elementary knowledge of hygienic living, to establish good hygienic habits in the child and the capacity to be independent.

The youngest class

1. Step by step, with the help of an adult, to learn how to wash one's hands and dry them on one's own towel before eating, after using the toilet, and when one's hands are dirty.

2. To go to the dining-room cheerfully, use a small spoon correctly, wipe one's mouth after eating. To establish the habit of drinking water.

3. To go to bed quietly and sleep in an appropriate position. With the help of an adult, to be able to put on and take off clothes, shoes and stockings properly, and store them in the right place.

4. To learn to go to the toilet, to establish the habit of a daily bowel movement.

5. To learn to use a handkerchief correctly, not to snivel or to put fingers or dirty things in one's mouth, step by step to lay a foundation for regular habits of having one's hair cut, washing one's hair, washing one's feet, bathing, and trimming one's nails.
6. Knowledge of how to use the teeth, developing the habit of rinsing one's mouth in the morning and in the evening and after eating.
7. Knowledge of the function of the eyes, not drying one's eyes with one's hands or with dirty handkerchiefs.
8. Knowledge of the function of the nose and ears, not picking one's nose, not digging in one's ears or sticking foreign objects in one's ears or nose.
9. To sit, stand and walk with the body in the right position (natural, comfortable, no excessive restrictions).
10. Not being afraid of health checks and all sorts of prophylactic vaccinations.

The middle class
1. To learn to wash one's hands and face correctly.
2. To go to the dining-room cheerfully, to chew one's food in small pieces and swallow quietly, not to be fussy, not to leave food, to learn to use chopsticks.
3. On one's own and in good order to put on and take off clothes, shoes and stockings properly, to store them properly where indicated, to learn to make one's bed.
4. Step by step to take care of one's toilet needs oneself.
5. To learn to blow one's nose correctly (to cover one nostril and blow gently through the other).
6. Not to throw fruit peelings or scrap paper just anywhere, not to spit, blow one's nose or answer a call of nature wherever.
7. To possess general hygienic knowledge about how to protect one's eyes, to keep a correct body position when

reading and drawing.
8. To possess a general hygienic knowledge about how to protect one's teeth, to learn to brush one's teeth.
9. To possess general knowledge about how to avoid all sorts of roundworms, parasitic diseases and intestinal disorders. Not to eat food which is not clean.

The eldest class
1. To wash one's hands and face correctly and fast, to establish the habit of brushing one's teeth morning and evening.
2. Not to be noisy when going into the dining-room, not to throw rubbish just anywhere, to tidy up and clean up after oneself after eating.
3. To go to bed quietly, to put on and take off clothes, shoes and stockings quickly and properly, to distinguish between right and left, to make one's bed.
4. To keep oneself clean and tidy, when coughing or sneezing to be able to use a handkerchief to cover one's mouth and nose. Girls learn to comb their own hair (short hair).
5. To keep public places clean and tidy, not to climb up onto or over chairs and tables, not to dirty walls.
6. To know how to protect one's sight, not to read, write or draw when the light is too bright or too weak or in sunshine, to remain in the right position when sitting.
7. To possess general knowledge about what happens when milk teeth are replaced by permanent teeth.
8. To know when to put on more or fewer clothes in good time depending on the weather and before and after sport, not to be excessively active before and after eating.

Physical activities
Training of the children's bodies so as to promote their normal development. Increasing their capacity to adapt to the

natural environment and strengthening
their physique. Developing the children's fundamental movements so that
these are performed with suppleness,
harmony and correct body positions.
Fostering a good moral character with
traits of resourcefulness, courage, well-
disciplined behaviour, and a lively and
uninhibited nature.

The youngest class
1. Basic movements
   (a) Walking: walking naturally with a
       straight back.
       i. On a signal, walking in the
          direction indicated.
       ii. Walking one at a time.
   (b) Running: running naturally, with
       elbows in.
       i. Running around the circum-
          ference of an area.
       ii. On a signal, running in the
           direction indicated.
       iii. Within an indicated area, run-
            ning around in different direc-
            tions.
       iv. Alternatively running and
           walking a distance of about
           100 metres.
   (c) Jumping: jumping up naturally
       and making an easy fall.
       i. Hopping on the spot, both feet
          together.
       ii. Jumping down, both feet to-
           gether, from a height of 15–25
           centimetres.
       iii. Making a jump forward, both
            feet together.
   (d) Balancing: the body must not
       wobble to right or left.
       i. Walking between two parallel
          lines 25 centimetres apart.
       ii. Going up and down a slope
           which rises 15–20 centimetres.
   (e) Throwing:
       i. Rolling to each other and re-
          ceiving a large leather ball.
       ii. Practising throwing a large
           leather ball with both hands.
       iii. Learning to pat a leather ball.

   (f) Creeping through and climbing
       over:
       i. Getting past an obstacle
          (elastic thread or a rope) at a
          height of 70 centimetres.
       ii. Creeping forward on all fours.
       iii. Climbing up and down on a
            climbing frame.

2. Basic gymnastics
   (a) Mostly imitation of gymnastics, in
       addition learning one or two pro-
       grammes of movements in the
       standing position, each pro-
       gramme three or four times.
   (b) Learning to follow words of com-
       mand: attention, at ease, fall in,
       unit forward march, run, halt.
   (c) Walking in single file and forming
       a circle.

The middle class
1. Basic movements
   (a) Walking: walking with a straight
       back with arms and legs in time.
       i. On a signal, walking in time.
       ii. On a signal, changing speed of
           walking.
   (b) Running: running in a relaxed way
       with arms and legs in time.
       i. Running in file.
       ii. Within a given area, running
           around in different directions
           and chasing each other.
       iii. Sprinting a distance of 10–20
            metres.
       iv. Alternatively running and
           walking a distance of 100–200
           metres.
   (c) Jumping: with knees bent, push-
       ing off with the front part of the
       soles of the feet and jumping,
       keeping one's balance when
       making an easy fall.
       i. Hopping on the spot to touch
          an object (the object should
          be 15–20 centimetres above
          the fingertips when the child
          stretches).

ii. Making a jump across a straight line, both feet together.

iii. Jumping down, both feet together, from a height of 20–30 centimetres.

iv. A longjump, both feet together, of a distance of not less than 30 centimetres.

v. Running and jumping over two parallel lines not less than 40 centimetres apart.

(d) Balancing: with a straight back, arms and legs in time.

i. On the spot, turning around 1–3 times.

ii. Eyes closed, taking 5–10 steps forward.

iii. Walking between two parallel lines 20–15 centimetres apart.

iv. Walking on a bar, 20–30 centimetres above the ground and 20–15 centimetres wide.

(e) Throwing:

i. Throwing and receiving low and high balls (low balls are below head height, high balls are above head height).

ii. In pairs near one another, throwing and receiving a large ball with both hands.

iii. Patting a ball with the right and the left hand.

iv. Practising throwing objects from the shoulder with outstretched arm (throwing little leather balls and little sandbags weighing 100–150 grams at a target).

(f) Creeping through and climbing over:

i. Getting through a bamboo ring, 60 centimetres in diameter (wicker, plastic tube or equivalent items).

ii. Crawling with hands and feet on the ground and knees bent.

iii. Climbing with hands and feet in time.

2. Basic gymnastics

(a) Mostly exercises in the standing position, in addition learning 1–2 programmes using light equipment according to choice (dumbbells, flower, flag or pole gymnastics etc), each programme 5–6 times.

(b) Learning to follow words of command: attention, at ease, fall in, on the spot march, unit forward march, run.

(c) On a signal, dividing into groups.

The eldest class

1. Basic movements.

(a) Walking: walking energetically and with an even step.

i. On a signal, changing direction when walking.

ii. Walking properly two by two.

(b) Running: running with the trunk leaning forward slightly, both hands loosely clenched, elbows bent, arms to the side, and swinging naturally forwards and backwards, and with the front part of the foot touching the ground.

i. On a signal, changing speed or direction when running.

ii. Sprinting a distance of 20–30 metres.

iii. Alternatively running and walking a distance of 200–300 metres.

(c) Jumping: with knees bent and outstretched arms, arms and legs in time, pushing off forcefully and jumping, keeping one's balance when making an easy fall.

i. Hopping on the spot to touch an object (the object should be 20–35 centimetres above the fingertips when the child stretches).

ii. Jumping down, both feet together, from a height of 30–35 centimetres.

iii. A longjump, both feet together, of a distance of not less than 40 centimetres.

iv. Running and jumping over two parallel lines not less than 50 centimetres apart.

v. Bending and making a high-jump of 30–40 centimetres.

vi. Practising skipping or "rubber-band twist".

(d) Balancing: with a straight back, even steps, arms and legs in time, natural movements.

i. With arms stretched out sideways, standing on one leg for 5–10 seconds.

ii. With arms stretched out sideways and eyes closed, turning around on tiptoe (about 5 times).

iii. Stepping onto an object of limited size (a brick, a plank, cardboard or the like).

iv. Walking on a bar, 30–40 centimetres above the ground and 20–15 centimetres wide, varying movements of the hands and arms (hands at the sides, stretched out sideways, raised in front, raised high, etc).

(e) Throwing:

i. In pairs and 2–4 metres apart, throwing and receiving a large ball.

ii. On the spot patting a ball in different ways, for instance turning around once and keeping patting the ball.

iii. Walking while patting a ball, running while patting a ball.

iv. Throwing from the shoulder with outstretched arm a long distance.

v. Throwing at a target from the shoulder with outstretched arm (the target should be roughly 60 centimetres in diameter at a distance of roughly 3 metres).

(f) Creeping through and climbing over: on the basis of what has been learned in the middle class, harmoniously and energetically creeping through and climbing over obstacles.

2. Basic gymnstics

(a) Mostly exercises in the standing position, in addition learning 1–2 programmes using light equipment according to choice, each programme 6–8 times.

(b) Teaching the children to stand to attention, at ease, fall in, left turn (right turn), on the spot march, halt, walking at ease, walking in file, run, turn left (right).

(c) On a signal, dividing into groups to right and left.

Ideology and morality

To teach the children the first steps of the "five loves" (to love the mother country, to love the people, to love science, to love work, to love and protect public property) and to foster the children's good morality, cultivated behaviour and a lively and open nature.

The youngest class

1. To bring up the children so that they mostly remain in a cheerful and happy mood, so that they do not cry easily and are not shy with strangers.

2. Being able to play in a friendly way with their peers, not grab or monopolize toys, not fight, not tell people off.

3. To love and look after toys, books and necessities, to handle them carefully, not throw them just anywhere, not damage or ruin them. To love and look after trees, flowers and plants, not pick them or break them off just anyhow.

4. To learn to do what one is capable of doing.

5. To learn in one's everyday life to use respectful forms of address and polite

language towards adults (say good morning, how are you, goodbye, thank you, etc).

6. Being able to distinguish clearly between one's own and other people's things, not to take others' things without prior permission.

7. To bring up the children to be fond of their families, love their parents and other members of the family. To like the pre-school and their peers. To respect the teachers and other staff, to respect the older generation and obey it.

The middle class

1. To be able to get on well with one's peers, care about and help each other.

2. To get used to a collective life, respect the rules of the collective, not disturb others.

3. To love and look after the pre-school's toys, necessities, trees, flowers and plants, to put back the things one has used where they belong. To appreciate the food and clothes, and not be fussy.

4. To do things which one is capable of doing oneself, to be willing to serve one's peers and the collective.

5. In everyday life to establish the habit of stressing politeness, to be able to say please, excuse me, please don't be so polite [standard in China, translator's comment], send greetings to someone, say goodbye.

6. Not to help oneself to others' things, but take charge of them and give them to an adult. To be able to admit when one has done wrong, in addition to be willing to put matters right.

7. To love one's home region, love the working people and learn from their good qualities of character.

8. To respect the Chinese flag.

The eldest class

1. To be modest and to give way to others, not to be conceited when one has made progress, to be willing to

learn from the good qualities of one's peers, to rejoice over one's peers doing well.

2. To respect the rules of the collective and the general order.

3. To be able to put toys and books in order, to learn to repair books.

4. Conscientiously and always to do what one is capable of doing oneself, and to serve one's peers and the collective.

5. To be polite and friendly towards other people, to give up one's seat so that guests and members of the older generation can sit.

6. To be able to accept criticism from others if one has oneself done wrong, to know how this can be remedied.

7. To be able to distinguish between what is usually regarded as right or wrong, to know what is good and what is bad, to be proud of the collective.

8. To learn from the good qualities of the veterans of the revolution, the heroes and model figures, and respect and love them.

9. To respect, love and preserve the Chinese flag and the national emblem.

10. To love China's Communist Party, to love the Chinese People's Republic, to love the Chinese Liberation Army.

Language

To teach the children to pronounce clearly and correctly and to speak the standard language. To enrich the children's vocabulary, to develop their cognitive abilities and spoken proficiency. Step by step to develop the children's interest in literary works.

The children of the national minorities learn the language of their own people.

The youngest class

1. To understand and learn how to speak the standard language, to study correct pronunciation. Step by step to

assist the children to pronounce correctly the sounds they find difficult and the sounds which are easy to pronounce wrongly.

2. To enrich one's vocabulary, to learn to use those ordinary words that one can understand, mainly nouns, verbs, personal pronouns and adjectives.

3. To learn to listen when adults and peers are speaking, to be willing to talk to others, to be able to express simply and concisely one's own wishes and requirements.

4. Step by step, to learn to relate in simple sentences the essential content of a picture.

5. To enjoy hearing the teacher tell stories and sing children's songs, step by step to learn to understand the main content of a work. To memorize 8–10 children's songs, with help from the teacher to learn to retell 1–2 simple stories.

The middle class

1. To continue to learn to speak the standard language, to learn to pronounce correctly the sounds they find difficult and the sounds which are easy to pronounce wrongly, in addition to observe the tones.[1]

2. To continue to enrich one's vocabulary, to be able to understand and use even more nouns, verbs, adjectives, numerals, pronouns. To learn to use common adverbs (like *now, still, much,* etc), and linking words (*and, with, together with,* etc), to understand the meaning of words.

3. To be able to listen attentively when others are speaking, and answer ques-

tions uninhibitedly and clearly, and to give expression to one's own thoughts.

4. To learn to relate in complete sentences and fairly coherently the content of a picture, and in so doing to use the new words one has learned.

5. To understand the content of stories and poems, to learn the essential plot of the texts, to be able to recite 8–10 poems and retell 3–4 simple stories. To enjoy books read aloud and to listen to children's programmes on the radio. *?? ¿ no writing*

The eldest class *of characters?*

1. In everyday life to keep to the standard language and pay attention to correct pronunciation and correct tones.

2. To continue to increase one's vocabulary, to grasp even more abstract words, to learn to use adjectives in comparative forms (like *large, larger, largest*); to learn a number of common function words: prepositions (like *on, with, from,* etc); linking words (like *because, so, if,* etc); understand and in addition be able to use a number of synonyms.

3. To listen politely when others are making a speech or talking, to be able to give expression to one's own wishes and to what one has seen or heard in a clear manner.

4. To relate the content of a picture fairly completely and coherently, to speak naturally and uninhibitedly, and step by step to overcome any errors present in the child's speech.

5. To recite 8–10 poems and retell 3–4 stories fairly expressively and to learn to appreciate the narratives of others. To listen to children's programmes on the radio and to relate part of the content of these.

Translator's Note
[1] Tone or the musical accent is an integrated part of the monosyllabic Chinese word. The standard language has 4 tones. The first is high and level, the second rising, the third falling-rising and the fourth falling. The tones mark differences in meaning and it is therefore important for children to learn them correctly.

General education

In order to extend children's horizons, to increase their elementary knowledge of society and nature. To foster their interest in and desire for knowledge about society and nature, so that step by step they enter into a correct relationship to people and to the surroundings. To develop the children's attentiveness, capacity to observe, memory, imagination, cognitive capacity and linguistic proficiency.

The youngest class
1. To know one's own name, sex, age and the names of the most important members of one's family.
2. To get to know the pre-school, the teachers and one's fellow class-mates.
3. To know the names of the toys, cutlery and ordinary objects one is in daily contact with, to know how they are used, and in addition to be able to use them correctly. To know some types of items of clothing, know what they are called, to be familiar with how and in what order they are put on and taken off, and to understand the need to be careful with one's clothes.
4. To know the environment around the pre-school and the citizens' work which is related to the children's lives, to know how their work relates to people and to respect them and their work.
5. To know 2–3 common means of transport, what they are called, their external characteristics and use.
6. To know that "1st June", international children's day, is the national holiday for one's peers.
7. To know the specific features of the four seasons which make the deepest impression on children and people's activities in those seasons.
8. To know 3–4 kinds of common vegetables and fruits and 1–2 kinds of flowers, plants and trees, to know what they are called and what distinctive features they have and what they are mainly used for. With the help of an adult, to grow from large seeds 1–2 plants which are easy to grow.

9. To know 2–3 common kinds of poultry, domestic and wild animals and 1–2 kinds of fish, their names and distinctive external characteristics, their sounds, what they eat, and the uses people make of some animals. With the help of an adult, to rear a small animal, to love and protect little animals.

The middle class
1. To know one's parents' occupations, the addresses of the family and the pre-school.
2. To know some types of factory-made basic household products, their names, characteristics and use, and to know how to use them correctly.
3. To know the places in the surroundings which are involved in the children's daily lives, to know what is done at these places, and to know the tasks which are performed by citizens working there.
4. To know some common means of transport, to compare them as regards clear differences in external characteristics and ways of use. To know some of the rules of the highway code and to follow instructions from the people's police.
5. To know 2–3 kinds of machines which are widespread in everyday life, to know what they are used for, and to know the work performed by those who operate the machines.
6. To know that "1st May", international workers' day, is the national holiday for workers, peasants, teachers, shop assistants, and other working people. To know that "1st October" is the national day, and that Yuandan is New Year's Day.
7. To know the places of natural beauty, famous buildings and sights of historic interest in the home region. To foster children's love of the home region.
8. To know that the red flag with five stars on it is the Chinese flag, to

respect the Chinese flag.

9. To know the names of the four seasons, their distinctive characteristics, and the work of adults and the activities of children during them.

10. To know 2–3 kinds of common vegetables, fruits, flowers, plants and trees and their names, to observe their distinctive differences on the basis of certain external features such as root, stalk/trunk, flower, fruit and other constituents. To plant some easily grown plants, to observe their changes while growing, to know that plants cannot survive without earth, sun, air and water.

11. To know 2–3 species of common domestic animals, poultry, birds, fish, insects and wild animals. To know their names, habits, external characteristics, whether they are useful or harmful, and to observe their distinctive differences.
To learn how to rear small animals, to observe the process of their growth, their habits and special characteristics. To love and protect little animals.

12. In real life and in play to foster children's interest in other natural sciences phenomena, such as that water turns into ice when it is cold, that ice melts and becomes water when it is warm; that a magnet attracts iron; how colours change, etc.

The eldest class

1. To know 3–4 types of factory-made basic household products, to know the names of the materials that they are made of, their characteristics and uses, and to be able to classify them.

2. To know shops and public places which are a part of people's everyday lives. To know and to respect the work performed by the citizens who work there.
To know that "8th March", international working women's day, is

grandmother's, mother's, and aunt's national holiday. To know that "1st August", army day, is the national holiday of the Chinese people's liberation army.

3. To know some means of transport on water, on land and in the air, to observe their similarities and differences, and to classify them.

4. To know some widespread means of production and heavy machinery, to know their names and uses, and to know that it is faster, better and more labour-saving to use machines in manufacturing.

5. Briefly to present some of China's most important national minorities, to differentiate them in terms of their clothing and some ways of life, to know that China is a country of several nations, to foster in the children a respect for the national minority peoples.

6. To know the mother country's capital — Peking. To know that Peking contains Tian'an Men gate (of Heavenly Peace) and courtyard, the monument to the People's Heroes, the memorial hall to Chairman Mao, the Great Hall of the People, etc.

7. To know that the complete name of the mother country is the People's Republic of China, and that one is Chinese. To realize that Taiwan is part of the territory of our country. To know that "1st July" is the founding day of the Chinese communist party.

8. To know the primary school and, as preparation for beginning in the primary school, step by step to learn to understand the conditions for studying in the primary school.

9. Based on temperature, animals' and plants' growth changes and people's activities, to get to know the special characteristics of the four seasons, and know their sequence. To get to know the thermometer, to use Arabic numerals, and on a diagram

to keep simple meteorological records each day (temperature, weather).

10. To know 2–3 kinds each of widespread vegetables, fruits, nuts, trees, flowers and plants and the most important agricultural products locally, to compare their similarities and differences, and classify them. To distinguish between evergreen trees and deciduous trees. To participate in the work in the vegetable garden as much as possible.

To pick and gather different kinds of leaf, seeds and wild plants, to learn a simple way of preserving them.

11. To know several kinds of poultry, domestic animals, birds, insects and wild animals, and on the basis of their external characteristics, habits, their utility and harm, to observe their similarities and differences, and to classify them.

To note the difference between a number of widespread useful and harmful insects locally, to know their external characteristics and habits, to know how people exploit useful insects and birds so as to prevent and treat diseases of plants and to combat plagues of insects. The animals which are useful for people must be protected and the insects which are harmful must be exterminated.

To learn to rear some kinds of small animal, to observe their growth changes and how they relate to people.

12. In everyday life, to observe the wind, rain, snow, thunder, lightning, rainbows and other natural phenomena. To know how wind, rain and snow are useful or harmful for people's lives.

In real life and in play, to foster children's interest in other natural sciences phenomena, such as that a mirror can reflect light; that some objects float on water and some objects sink; that electricity can make an electric bell ring, an electric fan or mill rotate, electric light shine, etc.

Mathematics

To teach the children to understand numbers up to 10, and addition and subtraction. To give them a rough general idea of geometrical figures, time, space, etc. Step by step to develop the children's capacity to think logically and to develop in them correct, flexible and rapid thinking.

The youngest class
1. To know the concepts "one" and "many" and their mutual relations.
2. To compare two groups of objects with each other and to know which group has more or fewer or whether each group has the same number of objects.
3. To learn to count up to 4 in connection with concrete objects, and to be able to state the number of objects counted and, following an example with concrete objects, picking out a given number of corresponding objects.
4. To know the concepts above/below, before/after, large/small, long/short.
5. To know circles, squares and triangles.
6. To know the temporal concepts morning, evening and day.

The middle class
1. To be able to count up to 10 concrete objects and to be able to state their number.
2. To know how cardinal and ordinal numbers up to 10 are formed. To be able to read 1–10 in Arabic numerals.
3. To teach the children how, without being influenced by the size of objects or the way they have been arranged or other special features, to form a correct view of the number of up to 10 concrete objects.
4. To know rectangles and ellipses, to be

able to classify on the basis of the distinct features of shapes.

5. To know the concepts of length, width and height.
6. To know the temporal concepts yesterday, today and tomorrow.

The eldest class

1. To know the constituent components of each number up to 10, and to learn to add and subtract quickly and correctly. To know the signs for plus, minus and equal. To be able to work out practical counting problems.
2. To get an idea of how one counts up and down from a specific number between 1 and 10. To learn to write the Arabic numerals from 1 to 10.
3. To distinguish between odd and even numbers up to 10.
4. With one's own body as a point of reference, to distinguish between right and left, to use measuring by eye and by a natural yardstick as methods for comparing the length, height, width, distance between, and thickness of objects, etc.
5. To know globes, cylinders, squares and rectangles, to be able to classify on the basis of the distinct features of shapes.
6. To learn to divide up a concrete object or shape, etc into 2 and 4 parts, to know that the original concrete object or shape is larger than each part and that each part is smaller than the original concrete object or shape.
7. To be familiar with the clock, to learn full hours and half hours. To learn the calendar and know that a week has seven days, which day it is today, which day it was yesterday and which day it will be tomorrow.

Music

To provide the children with an elementary knowledge of and skill in singing and dancing. Step by step, to develop the children's sense of rhythm and their interest in music and dance. To promote the children's capacity to appreciate, memorize, imagine and perform music. To shape and give substance to the children's character traits and senses.

The youngest class

1. Singing
   (a) To get the children to enjoy singing, know the names of songs and understand the content of songs.
   (b) To learn to sing with the body held correctly.
   (c) To give them ear training, step by step to develop the capacity to articulate clearly and sing the right tune.
   (d) Step by step to learn to sing with a natural voice.
   (e) To sing in unison with the teacher or an accompaniment, gradually to learn to start and finish simultaneously.
   (f) On one's own, to be able to sing a song through.
   (g) To learn 10–12 songs (generally in the range from middle C up to A).

2. Dancing and musical games
   (a) To teach the children to enjoy dancing and musical games.
   (b) To be able to move in time to the music, to develop a sense of rhythm. Movements for imitation: beating a drum, blowing a trumpet, driving a train, the little bird is flying, the little hare is hopping, etc. Basic movements: clapping, nodding, short rapid steps, hopping patting steps, etc.
   (c) To learn to perform 3–4 songs and 4–6 musical games, to take part in performances joyfully and uninhibitedly.

3. Music appreciation
To learn to appreciate 5–6 songs and musical games. To teach the children to enjoy listening to songs and pieces of music.

The middle class
1. Singing
   (a) In accordance with the content of the songs, to learn to sing songs of varying moods (cheerful and lively, solemn and forceful).
   (b) To be able to listen to the lead-in before they sing and during songs, to begin and finish properly, to learn to breathe without interrupting a phrase, and to be able to sing solo for the collective uninhibitedly.
   (c) To learn 10–12 songs (generally in the range from middle C up to B).

2. Dancing and musical games
   (a) To begin properly and to change movements according to changes of music and tempo. Movements for imitation: with the children's everyday lives as a basis, to choose some movements which are easy to imitate and perform, such as a butterfly flying, picking fruit, etc.
   Basic movements: wrist movements, running on toe and heel, stamping, hopping one step at a time, etc.
   (b) To musical accompaniment, to change group formation (one circle, double circles), to learn 3–5 dances and 4–5 musical games, to be able to move expressively to the music.

3. Music appreciation
To learn to appreciate 6–8 songs and pieces of music of varying moods. To establish in the children the habit of and interest in listening to music quietly and attentively.

4. Percussion
To learn to accompany songs and tunes with percussion instruments. To develop the children's sense of rhythm.

The eldest class
1. Singing
   (a) To perform songs correctly and with some expression, in accordance with the content and mood of the songs.
   (b) To learn 10–12 songs (range: an octave from middle C, not higher than D).

2. Dancing and music games
   (a) To musical accompaniment, to move harmoniously and in time to the music.
   Movements for imitation: to imitate movements in the work of adults which the children are familiar with, such as picking tea, catching butterflies, milking, riding, etc.
   Basic movements: running with hopping steps, to go forward and withdraw again, to walk varying the steps.
   (b) To musical accompaniment, to learn to alternate between a few different group formations (a full or narrow circle, diagonal grouping, in file).
   (c) To learn 6–8 dances and 3–4 musical games, in accordance with the content and style of the songs or pieces of music, decoratively and expressively to be able to dance simple dances, to be able to perform the specific character of different roles in accordance with the demands of the musical games and with musical accompaniment.

3. Music appreciation
To learn to appreciate 6–8 songs or pieces of music, with sections of musical pieces as a basis to be able to distinguish between the songs and pieces of music one has already heard.

4. Percussion
To learn to use some types of percussion instrument, and with accompaniment to play in unison turn by turn.

8 Art

Starting from the children's observations of the form, colour, structure, etc of physical phenomena, to teach them to express fully their own feelings and their familiarity with life around them in drawing/painting and handicrafts (clay, paper cutting, toys they produce themselves, and so on). To lay a foundation for the children's interest in art and their appreciation of what is beautiful in nature, in social life and in works of art. To develop the children's observational capacity, imagination and creativity, and to provide training in harmonious and flexible movements of the muscles of the hands, and to provide an initial skill in using tools and materials in art.

The youngest class
1. Drawing/painting
    (a) To become familiar with and step by step to learn to use tools and materials for drawing/painting (e.g. coloured pencils, wax crayons, oil crayons, etc). To learn to sit in the right position when drawing/painting. To maintain a given distance between hand and eye, to hold a pencil naturally.
    (b) To foster the children's interest in colours. To become familiar with and in addition learn to use 3–6 colours: red, green, blue, yellow, black, brown.
    (c) Gradually shifting from playing to using dots, vertical lines, horizontal lines, angled lines, circles, squares and colouring and other methods in order to paint familiar objects, trees, plants, people, animals, etc. To encourage the children to paint freely.

2. Work with clay
    (a) To know the names of the materials and tools used in pottery (clay, modelling wax or dough), to know that these are

intrinsically soft and can be used for modelling.
    (b) To learn to use such methods as to roll out into a strip, roll into a ball, flatten out, bind together, etc in order to shape a few objects simply, and additionally to make models according to one's own wishes.

The middle class
1. Drawing/painting
    (a) To teach the children to use circles, ellipses, squares, rectangles, triangles, trapezoids, and colouring and other methods in order to paint objects they have observed in their everyday lives, simple landscapes, animals (from the side), people (from the front). To be able to paint their basic parts and essential features.
    (b) To learn to add some objects to a simple composition and to express a simple action. To be able to paint freely and according to one's own wishes.
    (c) To be able to choose colours to paint with which resemble those of the real objects, and to gradually learn to distribute the colours evenly.
    (d) To be able to use dots, dashes, little circles, flowers, leaves and other decorative shapes so as to paint simple patterns in clear colours on square and rectangular sheets of paper.

2. Handicrafts
    (a) Work in clay: to learn the technique of kneading, to be able to model the most important features of objects and use some simple aids in order to express a simple action. To be able to model freely and according to one's own wishes.

(b) Paper-cutting:
  i. To learn a few simple folding methods (such as folding a corner, double squares, double corners, etc continuing as long as the paper can be folded) and to fold simple toys fairly neatly.
  ii. To glue ready-made figures or materials from nature one by one in a suitable place.
  iii. To know the names of the materials and tools used for cutting and glueing, and to learn how to use them correctly.

3. Appreciation
To learn to appreciate some artistic objects which are comprehensible to children (paintings/drawings, popular arts and crafts, etc), scenery, celebration decorations, the design of public places, and so on. To start the fostering of children's sense of beauty and their capacity to make aesthetic judgements.

The eldest class

(a) To use all kinds of geometrical figures in order to express basic characteristic features and certain details of objects, in addition to be able to render simply different positions of the body of people and animals (from the sides, from the back, simple movements of the legs and arms).
(b) To be able to paint a simple picture of an illustrative nature based on the content of stories and poems and impressions from one's own daily life. To take the first steps towards learning to organize the whole surface area of a picture appropriately.
(c) In the centre, periphery and corners of a sheet of paper of square, rectangular and rhomboid shape, to use figures and 3–5

kinds of simple pattern with national characteristic features that one has learned, and to paint an ordinary model painting. To be able to decorate paper models of everyday objects with patterns or animals.
(d) On the basis of the content of a sketch, to be able to use all kinds of colour in bright shades.

2. Handicrafts
(a) Work in clay: from a lump of clay, to learn to knead out all parts of an object, additionally to be able to use simple tools and aids for modelling some detailed parts, to learn to model the most important characteristic features and movements of people and animals and to express a simple action.
(b) Paper-cutting:
  i. To consolidate techniques for folding paper learned in the middle class, to learn to use more than two sheets of paper for folding simple linked toys.
  ii. To be able to cut or tear out the external shape of simple objects from a rough sketch or by eye. To be able to use a symmetrical folding method so as to cut or tear out simple figures and window decorations.
  iii. To make toys oneself: to use paper, cloth, needle and thread or materials from nature and non-toxic, unwanted materials to make simple toys.

3. Appreciation
To learn to appreciate paintings and popular arts and crafts which are comprehensible for children. To learn to appreciate the work of oneself and one's class-mates. To foster the children's sense of beauty and their capacity to make aesthetic judgements.

3. *Pedagogical method and factors to consider*

The pre-school's pedagogical task, content and requirements are realized through all sorts of activities, games, physical activity, lessons, observation, work, recreation, everyday life, and so on. Nothing must be neglected to the advantage of other things. One must combat the fallacious tendency to regard classroom teaching as the sole way of fulfilling the requirements of the syllabus, resulting in focussing only on lessons in daily pedagogical work and ignoring play, observation, work and everyday life and other important activities. Making pre-school pedagogy too grown-up and turning the pre-school into a primary school must be resisted.

Play

Children's physical and psychological development is charcterized by a predilection for play and play thus becomes the most fundamental activity in their lives. They are most responsive to teaching in the form of play, so play has an extremely important place in all of the pedagogical work of the pre-school. It is a most effective method for carrying out all sides of the pedagogy of development for the body, the mind, morality and the sense of beauty.

Play in the pre-school can be subdivided into creative play (role-play, building, play involving performing), gymnastic games, cognitive games, musical games, recreational play, etc.

The conditions for all kinds of play have to be created. The necessary equipment for gymnastics and all sorts of toys must be arranged, and objects from nature, unwanted matter and materials which are not poisonous or harmful must be exploited to the full. To create the conditions for play, the measures taken must fit local conditions. The children themselves must be able to take out and put away the toys and materials for all sorts of activities easily.

The teacher's qualities as a leader consist in providing children full scope during play for their enthusiasm, sense of initiative and creativity, and in permitting the children freely and joyfully to choose all kinds of games and activities. This serves the purpose of promoting the development of their intelligence and personality. It must be ensured that the children have enough time for outdoor games and outdoor activities. In the day pre-school, this should be no less than two hours and in boarding pre-schools no less than three hours, which includes one hour of sporting activities outdoors each day.

When planning each day's activities in a pre-school with limited space outdoors, it is imperative to ensure that every class has at least one hour of sporting activities outdoors and that the lessons and other activities are organized outdoors as far as is possible.

Gymnastics

Includes early morning gymnastics and all kinds of sporting activities which are primarily gymnastic games. Local resources must be used and measures taken which fit the local conditions so as to create and develop the material conditions for children's gymnastics games. The teacher must let the children do gymnastics outdoors every day and make sure their bodies are trained. The pre-schools which are in a position to do so can let the children swim, climb mountains, play on ice and in snow.

Lessons

The pre-school organizes lessons in gymnastics, language, general education, mathematics, music, art, etc. Play is the most important kind of lesson in the pre-school. In the youngest and middle classes, in order to promote the children's interest in studying, as many audio-visual methods and games as possible, appropriate to the children's ages, are used. To facilitate entry into the primary school and to prepare for studies there, the element of play in the teaching is, however, reduced in the eldest class, gradually and as the level of psychological development rises.

As the children get older, the length of lessons increases gradually. The youngest class has 6–8 lessons a week, each lesson of 10–15 minutes; the middle class has 10–11 lessons a week, each lesson of 20–25 minutes; the eldest class has 12 lessons a week, each lesson of 25–30 minutes. Towards the completion of the eldest class the lessons can be extended by 5 minutes as appropriate.

Over and above these, there are no examinations or homework in the pre-school. The number of lessons per week for each class can be adjusted locally as appropriate, and adapted to local conditions, but to guarantee enough time for the children for play and outdoor activities, it is inappropriate to exceed the total number of lessons. The number of lessons for each week and each class is planned as below:

Subject	Youngest class		Middle class		Eldest class	
	Autumn	Spring	Autumn	Spring	Autumn	Spring
Gymnastics		1	1	1	1	1
Language	1	1	2	2	2	2
General education	1	1	2	2	2	2
Mathematics		1	1	2	2	2
Music	2	2	2	2	2	2
Art	2	2	2	2	3	3
Total	6	8	10	11	12	12

Training in observing

The pre-school's training in observing is an important way for the children to become acquainted with and acquire direct experience of nature and society. Every activity in the pre-school involves observation. Because of lack of knowledge and experience and specific features of children's psychological development, it is necessary when guiding children in how to observe things to draw on all their senses to the full: watching, listening, smelling, feeling, touching, tasting. The younger the children the more important this is. In order to cultivate children's thirst for knowledge and to establish the habit and desire of observing, the teacher must often guide the children in their daily lives in their observation of objects and phenomena. In this way the basis can be laid for a scientific outlook.

Work

The most important intention behind children working is to foster good morals and habits in the children, so that they love work, and train their capacity to carry out simple manual operations.

Children's work must be adapted to their level of physical and psychological development. What is most important is to serve oneself. In accordance with age, one can increase the content of work so as to serve the collective, to plant things, to rear animals, and so on. One can, if local circumstances permit, establish a small garden.

When guiding the children's work, the teacher must have clear goals and expectations and place emphasis on safety. The fallacious tendencies of not letting children work or using children as labour must be combated. It is strictly forbidden to use work as a punishment.

Recreation

Recreation in the pre-school consists of the cinema, slides, TV, performances, puppet theatre, and other activities. To make the content in children's lives richer, the pre-school must organize the children's recreation activities according to a plan. To protect the children's sight, watching TV should be limited to once or twice a week, about 20 minutes each time, sitting roughly 2 metres from the screen. In all parts of their daily lives the children's life must be organized in a scientific way. Care must be taken to ensure that the children eat and sleep properly and lead lives which are regulated and happy. Stress must be placed on teaching the children to behave in a well brought-up manner and to foster the children's ability to manage things on their own.

There must be an emphasis on the external environment of the pre-school. Trees must be planted in the courtyard in accordance with a plan and the children must be provided with an environment which is clean and tidy, aesthetically appealing and fulfills a pedagogic function.

All the activities of the pre-school usually take place with children of the same age grouped together, but it is also permitted, depending on local conditions, to divide the children into smaller groups according to the number of children in each class, the nature of the activity, equipment and other factors. This is done to benefit all the children in the class and in order to be able to teach them according to their abilities. The teaching of those children who have greater capacities must be expanded in appropriate ways, and the children whose capacities are weaker must be inspired and guided with even greater patience. In the case of children over the age of six, the demands can be increased in appropriate ways, depending on the actual conditions locally.

The teaching materials for each kind of activity can in part be selected from the Ministry of Education's collection of teaching materials, and otherwise be produced or selected as local conditions permit. This is in order to enrich the content of the teaching materials constantly. The teaching materials can be ordered for roughly 40 weeks of the pre-school year.

All the activities of the pre-school must be specifically emphasized and adapted to each other so that they together bring out the all-round development which is the goal of the education. Through all the pedagogical work, attention must be paid to realizing the following requirements:

1. The children's health must be protected and promoted. Their safety must be considered in all activities.
2. The needs of all the children must be attended to and in so doing, the teacher must both set up uniform requirements and teach the children according to their aptitudes.
3. The children must be allowed to see a lot, listen a lot, think a lot, speak a lot and do a lot, so that their intellect, talent and character develop in a lively way and from their own momentum.
4. All the activities must contain teaching in ideology and morality so that the children acquire these imperceptibly.
5. The teachers and other staff must love and respect the children and show this in word and deed.

In order to be able to educate the children well, the pre-school must have close contact and collaboration with the families. Particularly in the more and more common situation of single children, it seems to be the case that contact and collaboration between the parents and the pre-school may be even more important. It must be ensured that the head of the family understands the educational situation and requirements, so that teaching children get at home and the teaching in the pre-school are in agreement and for the benefit of the children while they are growing up. The pre-school must take the initiative in winning support from society and the families for its work, must listen to their views and together bring up a good revolutionary future generation.

(Translated from the Swedish translation of the Chinese original).